VOLUME 133

Laos

Helen Cordell

Compiler

CLIO PRESS

OXFORD, ENGLAND · SANTA BARBARA, CALIFORNIA
DENVER, COLORADO

British Library Cataloguing in Publication Data

Cordell, Helen
Laos. – (World bibliographical series; 133)
I. Title   II. Series
016.9594

ISBN 1-85109-075-4

Clio Press Ltd.,
55 St. Thomas' Street,
Oxford OX1 1JG, England.

ABC-CLIO,
130 Cremona Drive,
Santa Barbara,
CA 93117, USA.

Designed by Bernard Crossland.
Typeset by Columns Design and Production Services, Reading, England.
Printed and bound in Great Britain by
Billing and Sons Ltd., Worcester.

THE WORLD BIBLIOGRAPHICAL SERIES

This series, which is principally designed for the English speaker, will eventually cover every country (and many of the world's principal regions), each in a separate volume comprising annotated entries on works dealing with its history, geography, economy and politics; and with its people, their culture, customs, religion and social organization. Attention will also be paid to current living conditions – housing, education, newspapers, clothing, etc.– that are all too often ignored in standard bibliographies; and to those particular aspects relevant to individual countries. Each volume seeks to achieve, by use of careful selectivity and critical assessment of the literature, an expression of the country and an appreciation of its nature and national aspirations, to guide the reader towards an understanding of its importance. The keynote of the series is to provide, in a uniform format, an interpretation of each country that will express its culture, its place in the world, and the qualities and background that make it unique. The views expressed in individual volumes, however, are not necessarily those of the publisher.

VOLUMES IN THE SERIES

Laos

WORLD BIBLIOGRAPHICAL SERIES

General Editors:
Robert G. Neville (Executive Editor)
John J. Horton

Robert A. Myers   Ian Wallace
Hans H. Wellisch   Ralph Lee Woodward, Jr.

John J. Horton is Deputy Librarian of the University of Bradford and currently Chairman of its Academic Board of Studies in Social Sciences. He has maintained a longstanding interest in the discipline of area studies and its associated bibliographical problems, with special reference to European Studies. In particular he has published in the field of Icelandic and of Yugoslav studies, including the two relevant volumes in the World Bibliographical Series.

Robert A. Myers is Associate Professor of Anthropology in the Division of Social Sciences and Director of Study Abroad Programs at Alfred University, Alfred, New York. He has studied post-colonial island nations of the Caribbean and has spent two years in Nigeria on a Fulbright Lectureship. His interests include international public health, historical anthropology and developing societies. In addition to *Amerindians of the Lesser Antilles: a bibliography* (1981), *A Resource Guide to Dominica, 1493–1986* (1987) and numerous articles, he has compiled the World Bibliographical Series volumes on *Dominica* (1987), *Nigeria* (1989) and *Ghana* (1991).

Ian Wallace is Professor of German at the University of Bath. A graduate of Oxford in French and German, he also studied in Tübingen, Heidelberg and Lausanne before taking teaching posts at universities in the USA, Scotland and England. He specializes in contemporary German affairs, especially literature and culture, on which he has published numerous articles and books. In 1979 he founded the journal *GDR Monitor*, which he continues to edit under its new title *German Monitor*.

Hans H. Wellisch is Professor emeritus at the College of Library and Information Services, University of Maryland. He was President of the American Society of Indexers and was a member of the International Federation for Documentation. He is the author of numerous articles and several books on indexing and abstracting, and has published *The Conversion of Scripts* and *Indexing and Abstracting: an International Bibliography*. He also contributes frequently to *Journal of the American Society for Information Science*, *The Indexer* and other professional journals.

Ralph Lee Woodward, Jr. is Chairman of the Department of History at Tulane University, New Orleans, where he has been Professor of History since 1970. He is the author of *Central America, a Nation Divided*, 2nd ed. (1985), as well as several monographs and more than sixty scholarly articles on modern Latin America. He has also compiled volumes in the World Bibliographical Series on *Belize* (1980), *Nicaragua* (1983), and *El Salvador* (1988). Dr. Woodward edited the Central American section of the *Research Guide to Central America and the Caribbean* (1985) and is currently editor of the Central American history section of the *Handbook of Latin American Studies*.

*To my Mother and the Memory of
my Father*

Contents

Contents

Introduction

Modern Laos is an independent republic in South East Asia, land-locked and bounded by Thailand and Vietnam on either side of its north-south borders, by Myanmar (Burma) and China to the north and Cambodia to the south. It covers an area of 236,804 square kilometres or 91,430 square miles, slightly smaller than the United Kingdom or the state of Michigan. Seventy per cent of its land area consists of mountain ranges, highlands, and plateaux; the Annamite chain runs northeast-southwest through Laos and forms part of the boundary with Vietnam. River valleys cut through the mountain ranges and most are tributaries of the Mekong River in the west, which forms the major part of the western boundary.

The climate of Laos is tropical to semi-tropical depending on the seasons, which are clearly defined by the monsoons. It is between May and September that the heavy rains fall and they diminish during October. From November to January the weather becomes gradually cooler, but thereafter the temperatures begin to rise again to the sometimes oppressive heat of April. This period from November to April also coincides with the dry season. The average temperatures in January, usually the coldest month, are, Luang Prabang 20.5°C (minimum 0.8°C), Vientiane 20.3°C (minimum 3.9°C), and Paksé 23.9°C (minimum 8.2°C); the average temperatures for April, usually the hottest month, are, Luang Prabang 28.1°C (maximum 44.8°C), Vientiane 27.9°C (maximum 39.2°C), and Paksé 29.4°C (maximum 39.4°C). Temperature varies according to the altitude, there is a drop in temperature of approximately 1.7°C for every 1000 feet or 300 metres increase in altitude, temperatures on the upland plateaux and in the mountains being considerably lower than on the plains around Vientiane.

Introduction

Agricultural cultivation is possible on only a fraction of the land area of Laos and apart from the Vientiane plain and the lowlands along the Mekong valley, the cultivated areas are situated in the valleys cut by the rivers, mainly descending to the Mekong, or the plateau regions of Xieng Khouang in the north and Bolovens in the south. Despite deforestation, large areas are still covered by forest, which contains a rich diversity of species and which varies according to the terrain. Laos' timber and mineral resources have not yet been fully surveyed. Moreover, exploration work for gold and petroleum remains in its infancy although there is already evidence available confirming the existence of important reserves of tin.

Laos is a thinly populated country; in 1987 the population was officially stated to be 3,830,000 and the capital city Vientiane only has a population of 120,000. Eighty-five per cent of the population is engaged in agriculture, much of it at subsistence level. The population is composed of a number of ethnic groups, of which sixty-five have been identified officially. The 1985 census has yet to be published but when it is available it will provide the best overview of the nature of the population, its ethnic make-up and its geographical distribution.

The origins of this ethnic pluralism lie in the past. The area was inhabited about 3000 years ago by people, who it is thought, spoke Austroasiatic languages and whose culture is believed to resemble that of the civilizations of Ban Chiang and Dong Son, whose remains have been uncovered in Thailand and Vietnam respectively. The early centuries of the Christian era saw the migration of Tai-speaking peoples from the area of China northeast of Laos into Laos, Burma, and Thailand. In Laos the dominant group of these Tai peoples were the Lao or Lao Lum and today they form almost half of the population. Historically, they have occupied the best agricultural lands and have assumed a dominant relationship with the other groups, which is still largely maintained today. In the past they referred disparagingly to the other groups as *Kha*, literally slave, a term not used now but which may be found in some of the older literature. The government has adopted new terminology to distinguish ethnic groupings: they are classified into four groups, the Lao Lum, the Lao Tai, the Lao Theung and the Lao Soung.

The Lao Lum (sometimes spelt Lao Loum), or lowland Lao, are ethnically related to the Lao Tai and are normally referred to as Lao. They live in the lowland areas, in small villages, where they cultivate irrigated rice fields, although they have practised some additional *swidden*, or slash and burn agriculture in the neighbouring forest areas. They adopted the Buddhist religion and some related elements of Indianized culture. Some would date the adoption of Buddhism by

the Lao Lum to the tenth and eleventh centuries but the
adoption of Buddhism is still believed to have been in the thirt
century, the earliest Buddhist remains found in Laos date fror
seventh and eighth centuries of the Christian Era, a result of the
and Khmer presence in the area. The Lao Lum form about forty
cent of the population and have traditionally ruled the country. M
ethnic Lao also live in the northeast of Thailand, as a result of bor
changes and deportations of population in the nineteenth century

The Lao Tai, also referred to as upland Tai, or tribal Tai, li
higher up the valleys and also cultivate rice. They are frequent
distinguished by the colours of their traditional clothing hence th
names White Tai, Black Tai, and Red Tai. In the past they wer
frequently in conflict with the lowland Lao and with each other. Their
position in the border areas of Laos enabled them to form strategic
alliances with neighbouring powers against the Lao rulers until the
arrival of the French and British in the region introduced the notion
of fixed frontiers.

The Lao Theung group, who live on the lower mountain slopes,
consist of a number of ethnic groups who originally inhabited the
area before the Tai migrations. They are also referred to as the
proto-Indochinese, and speak Mon-Khmer languages, which are also
spoken by similar groups in Thailand and Burma and are related to
the major languages of Mon, spoken in Burma by that ethnic group,
and Khmer, the national language of Cambodia. They usually
practise slash and burn or *swidden* agriculture. The largest groups are
the Khmu (or Kammu) in the north and the Kui and the So in the
south. The Lao Theung were the group most commonly called *Kha*,
meaning slave, a derogatory term no longer used. It signified the
traditional relationship between the Lao Lum and the Lao Theung;
the latter paid tribute to the more powerful Lao Lum in the form of
produce or labour. In exchange the Lao rulers endeavoured to
maintain a stable and peaceful society.

The fourth group is the Lao Soung who live on the higher slopes of
the mountains, they are the descendants of Miao-Yao tribes who
migrated southwards from China to Vietnam, Laos and Thailand
during the nineteenth century, and many of them still remain in
China. The most numerous group among them in Laos are the
Hmong, formerly called Miao or Meo a term now considered
derogatory. They practise shifting cultivation and grow upland rice,
maize and opium as a cash crop. The disruption of the Second
Indochinese war from 1961 to 1973 caused wholesale movement of
many of the mountain dwellers to lowland areas, or refugee camps on
mountain slopes. They are now gradually moving back to their
traditional areas. These ethnic minorities, particularly the Hmong,

were caught up in the war as their traditional homes were in strategic areas targeted for bombing, particularly around the Plain of Jars in Xieng Khouang province.

The Pathet Lao (the group which continued to oppose the French return to Laos and formed an opposition to the Royal Lao Government, established at the time of independence in 1954) led by Prince Souphanouvong, attracted some of the Lao Soung and the Lao Theung because it preached and practised equality. Some of its commanders came from the minorities and it has been stated that the majority of its armed forces were Lao Theung and Lao Tai. Others from the minority groups were attracted to the mercenary armies that the United States funded for its 'secret war', from 1962 onwards, the principal group among these were the Hmong, led by General Vang Pao. Many of these left Laos in 1975 as refugees. The Hmong base their loyalties on family and clan groupings, and strong leaders amongst them attracted their followers to the cause of the Pathet Lao or the Royal Lao Government. Promises of future rewards helped to encourage such followers but despite this, the enormous disruption of the war meant that it would have been impossible for them to have ignored events and to have remained in their traditional villages, those not involved in fighting moved voluntarily or involuntarily into refugee camps. The war also resulted in an increase in demand for opium to finance clandestine operations and at the same time it made the cultivation and collection of this important cash crop difficult.

Just as the ethnic composition of Laos is complex so is the history of the region, for the boundaries which encompassed the area which became Laos fluctuated over the centuries but usually included most of modern Laos. There has been little archaeological research conducted in Laos and much of the country's early history is based on surmise and analogy with the neighbouring areas. There is evidence that the area was inhabited as long ago as 3,000 BC and the culture of those early inhabitants is presumed to resemble that of the civilizations of Ban Chiang, in Thailand and Dong Son in Vietnam.

The most obvious remains of the earlier inhabitants are the circles of standing stones and the huge stone jars still very much in evidence. The menhirs, or standing stones, are found in the province of Houa Phan, the two most important sites being at Sam Kong Phan and Keo Hin Tan. Associated with the standing stones are underground man-made burial pits. It is estimated that these date back to within the first millennium BC. The large stone jars, thought to be funerary jars are found at Ban Ang on the Plain of Jars in Xieng Khouang Province, also referred to as Tran Ninh by the Vietnamese and sometimes in the French literature. The French archaeologist Madeleine Colani described thirteen of the sites. The average size of

the jars is 1.5 metres in height and diameter, with the largest recorded being 3 metres. Associated with the jars are stone discs, some decorated with figures in relief. It has been surmised that their purpose was to summon spirits or to facilitate offerings to the dead. Recent support has been given to Colani's theory that the society of the jars controlled a trade route for salt. These remains in northern Laos appear to represent a distinctive culture of unknown ethnic and archaeological affiliation, although there are some similarities with archaeological evidence in neighbouring Vietnam and Cambodia.

It would seem that the spread of the Tai-speaking peoples into Laos from the northeast started at the beginning of the Christian era. These are the ancestors of the Lao Lum and Lao Tai, who became the dominant groups in the thirteenth century. Before the foundation of the kingdom of Lan Xang (also spelt Lan Chang and Lan Sang), in 1353, which covered most of modern Laos and some of northeast Thailand, the area came under the suzerainty of neighbouring rulers, such as the kingdom of Nan Chao in southwest China and later the Khmer empire of Cambodia. This is another part of the history of Laos which requires further research and archaeological work.

The foundation myth of Laos attributes the ancestry of all Laotians to a common ancestor called Khun Borom. He is said to have divided his kingdom between his seven sons, Lan Xang being the land given to his eldest son, Khun Lo. The myth also explains the existence of neighbouring kingdoms of ethnically related peoples and provides an explanation for the existence of the darker skinned non-Tai inhabitants of the region. Khun Borom is alleged to have handed down precepts for his sons to follow in order to rule and to increase their territories.

The area of Laos over which the Khmer empire of Angkor (the capital of which was situated in the west of modern Cambodia) extended its suzerainty was governed by a number of small rulers, but by 1300 important centres had developed in Luang Prabang, Xieng Khouang, Vientiane, and That Phanom (in modern Thailand). These were Buddhist, Lao principalities, and in 1353 they were united into the kingdom of Lan Xang by Fa Ngum, a member of the Luang Prabang ruling family, who had been brought up in exile at the court of Angkor; he established his capital at Luang Prabang. It was a unity based on the allegiance of the other rulers and it survived for as long as it was considered useful. During periods of strong leadership Lan Xang flourished but it frequently reverted to periods of instability during the three and a half centuries of its existence. Fa Ngum was deposed in favour of his son Un Huan who reigned as Phya Sam Saen Thai, meaning 'the ruler of 300,000 Tai', from 1373 to 1416. His name derived from a census held in 1376 which found the population to consist of 300,000 adult male Lao. A ruler in South East Asia at this time measured his stature by the size of the population which owed allegiance to him and not so much by the area of territory over which he might hold sway.

It was in the next century that the kingdom became an effective state. The Lao Lum population was continuing to migrate southwards along the Mekong River. Between 1442 and 1571 the kings of Luang Prabang began to appoint their sons and relatives as governors of important provinces. At the beginning of the sixteenth century King Visun (reigned 1501-20) defined a distinctive Lao identity, with its own Buddhist culture and symbols, including the Prabang Buddha image.

In 1563, King Setthathirat (reigned 1547-71) moved the capital to Vientiane, at a time when Lao power was at its height. However, in 1570, Vientiane fell to the Burmese and Lan Xang descended into instability. It re-established itself in the seventeenth century under King Surinyavongsa, or Soulignavongsa (1637-94), who ruled over a prosperous and stable state in which literature, the arts, and Buddhism flourished. The Dutch East India Company's representative, Van Wuystoff was one of a number of foreign visitors who recorded what they saw of his kingdom.

A succession dispute at Surinyavongsa's death resulted in the break up of Lan Xang into the Kingdoms of Vientiane, Luang Prabang and Champassak, with Xieng Khouang retaining some autonomy. These kingdoms suffered greatly in the wars waged between Siam (modern Thailand) and Burma (now Myanmar) during the eighteenth century. Siamese military campaigns had reduced all four to vassals by the 1770s and the losses of territory and population to Siam began. The King of Vientiane, King Anuvong, detecting a moment of Siamese weakness, organized a rebellion against Siamese rule in 1827. The results were disastrous for Vientiane and for Laos as a whole. The Siamese wreaked vengeance by destroying the city of Vientiane and removing large numbers of its population to Siam. These removals of population from the Vientiane area and Xieng Khouang continued in the nineteenth century. From 1828 until the establishment of French rule, Vientiane and large areas of central Laos were ruled by Siam and the courts of Luang Prabang and Champassak had to accept Siamese advisers.

Towards the end of the nineteenth century the French began to extend their protectorate over Laos. They saw themselves as the heirs to the Vietnamese territorial claims to parts of Laos and to its tributary claims to Luang Prabang. The Siamese agreed to the establishment of a French vice-consulate in Luang Prabang and when in 1887, the Siamese troops there retreated in the face of attacks from

Chinese marauders, Pavie, the French vice-consul, and his staff, rescued King Oun Kham, of Luang Prabang, who asked for protection from France. During the next six years France extended its presence in Laos, and it sought recognition of its territorial claims from the British, who were occupied with the pacification of upper Burma. In 1893, the French forced the Siamese to agree to their demands to cede all of Laos east of the Mekong River and to pay a large indemnity to France.

The frontiers of Laos as determined by the French, were based on the watersheds of rivers and ignored traditional political groupings, and they proved to be the source of troubles and instability in later years. Luang Prabang was officially governed as a protectorate and the remainder of Laos was ruled directly but in practice, however, they were ruled as one from Vientiane, where the French established their administrative capital in 1900. Hopes of successful economic exploitation of Laos and the use of the Mekong as a trade route soon faded and the French governed Laos as economically as possible with the minimum number of French officials. They used the traditional local village and tribal headmen to govern at the lowest levels, French-educated Lao filled the lower administrative positions, Vietnamese were appointed to the middle levels of administration and French officials were appointed to the highest positions. Luang Prabang retained its king but the heads of the other royal houses of Xieng Khouang and Champassak were reduced to the role of provincial governors.

In extending their rule over Laos the French secured their western frontier in Indochina. They believed initially that the Mekong River offered a route to trade with China. In the early years of their rule they had great hopes for plantation and mining ventures in Laos. The economic benefits derived by the French from Laos were small and as a result after initial euphoria they maintained a small presence in Laos and spent little on public works. Unlike Vietnam, Laos received comparatively little economic benefit from French rule. The French provided the minimum amount of educational facilities in Laos, only enough to provide their needs for clerks. Further and higher education had to be sought elsewhere in Indochina, or in France, and medical care did not extend beyond the cities. France did endeavour to construct an all-weather road network to link Laos with Vietnam, and thus turned their backs on the traditional trade links through northeast Thailand to the outside world. The two products exploited were the tin reserves, mined at Nam Pathene in Khammouane province, and opium. The former resulted in two roads being built through the mountains to the Vietnamese coast. The latter resulted in the development of opium both as a legal and illegal crop in the north of Laos. The legacy of opium has remained with Laos. Throughout the first decades of Laos' independence the cultivation of opium and its trade was encouraged by European criminal elements, and the secret services of France and the United States in order to finance their secret counter-insurgency wars. The socialist government of Laos has discouraged the trade in opium but western journalists report that it continues. Currently internationally-sponsored crop-substitution programmes are under way to eradicate the supply of opium.

There were a number of revolts against French rule, particularly among the minority peoples who resented the imposition of taxes and *corvée*, or forced labour. Difficulties were exacerbated as the French used an ethnic hierarchy to exact these taxes, which reinforced hostilities among the peoples of Laos. The revolts that took place were, however, isolated and the French were able to contain them.

During the Second World War, the Japanese occupied French Indochina, and in September 1940, the Vichy Government granted the Japanese the right to station troops and aircraft there. By the Darlan-Kato Agreement of July 1941, Indochina was fully integrated into the Japanese military system, although the French continued to administer the country. On 9th March 1945, the Japanese, worried by the signs of nascent Gaullism in the French community, deposed the French administration. This was widely known as the *coup de force*. It was a body blow to the French, most of whose soldiers and administrators were arrested within a few hours. The Japanese declared the end of French colonial rule, and King Sisavang Vong, was forced by the Japanese to declare his independence on 8th April 1945. The Viceroy and Prime Minister, Prince Phetsarath, was eager to see an independent Laos and on 1st September he announced that the declaration of independence of April was still in force, before French rule could be re-established. On 15th September, he declared that the kingdoms of Luang Prabang and Champassak were united. He formed a committee called the Lao Issara (Free Lao) who were determined to resist the return to colonial status. The King, however, under pressure from the returning French, stripped Prince Phetsarath of his titles and positions in October 1945. This provoked the Lao Issara to form the Committee of the People and to proclaim a provisional constitution of independent Laos. Faced with the threat of deposition, the King accepted the constitution and was reinstated as a constitutional monarch after agreeing to the installation of a Lao Issara government. He was enthroned King of all Laos in traditional ceremonies in April 1946.

At the same time, the Free French fought to restore French rule and smashed the resistance of the small Lao Issara forces and the

Vietnamese fighting with them. The French reoccupied Vientiane at the end of April 1946 and shortly afterwards the Lao Issara government fled to Bangkok, where Prince Phetsarath set up a government-in-exile. The Lao Issara forces broke into guerilla bands and many escaped to Thailand. A Franco-Laotian convention of 27th August 1946 confirmed the autonomy of Laos and provided for the election of a constitutional assembly. Elections were held in January 1947 and a constitution was officially promulgated in September. Prince Phetsarath refused to have any contact with the French and continued to press for a completely independent Laos; his younger brother Prince Souvanna Phouma wanted independence but was prepared to work with the French; while Prince Souphanouvong, their half-brother, and commander of the Lao Issara forces sought to defeat the French by joining forces with the Vietnamese. The final dissolution of the Lao Issara was brought about by the 1949 Franco-Laotian convention which granted many of their demands. Laos was recognized as independent in 1949, as an Associate State of the French Union, although some powers were reserved. Most of the exiles returned to participate in the new government, but Prince Phetsarath remained in Thailand, only returning to Laos in 1957 shortly before his death. Full independence and sovereignty was achieved with the Franco-Laotian treaty of 1953, Laos remained in the French Union and continued to rely on France for defence aid.

Prince Souphanouvong split from the others in the Lao Issara and withdrew with his supporters, including many of the armed forces into northeast Laos. He set up a Lao state there, the Pathet Lao (literally 'land of the Lao'), and in November 1950, the political arm, the Neo Lao Issara, or Laotian Freedom Movement, was created. Its aims were to restore Laos to true independence and to unite it by removing the divisions and inequalities between the ethnic groups of Laos. They were to be achieved by a programme of armed struggle against the French to force them to leave, developing guerilla forces into a national army, by promoting the rights of tribal peoples, and by the promotion of literacy and appropriate economic development. Western writers have tended to use the term Pathet Lao as convenient shorthand for both military and political branches and this practice has been followed in this introduction, except where there is specific reference to the political party Neo Lao Haksat. The Pathet Lao pursued these aims throughout the post-Second World War period, in the struggle for a truly independent Laos, free from foreign interference. After the French withdrawal, the Americans were substituted for the French. There was undoubtedly Vietnamese help in training and organization but to what extent this was an indigenous nationalist movement and an indigenous army and to what extent a totally alien movement as some of its critics maintain it is difficult to determine. It was this programme, however, which finally brought the Pathet Lao group to power in Laos in 1975. The Vietnamese, meanwhile, had their own aims to pursue, in the prosecution of a war to liberate and unite Vietnam. Laos provided a route, the Ho Chi Minh trail, which enabled North Vietnamese troops and supplies to pass through to Cambodia and South Vietnam, as well as providing a refuge for guerilla units.

The First Geneva Conference of 1954 offered a formula for achieving peace between the rival Royal Lao government and the Pathet Lao. A series of accords on Indochina were signed at the conference; those concerned with Laos were signed on the 21st July 1954. The Royal Lao government, however, refused to allow Pathet Lao representatives at the conference table and so it was the Viet Minh who signed the cease-fire on behalf of the Pathet Lao. This was the first occasion on which the name Pathet Lao achieved international recognition. Laos was left in the hands of the constitutional monarchical government, with the exception of two provinces in the northeast, where pending a political settlement, the Pathet Lao were to concentrate their forces.

The Geneva Conference of 1954 established the International Commission for Supervision and Control in Laos (commonly known as the International Control Commission or ICC). It was composed of representatives from India, Canada, and Poland. Its purpose was to achieve the peaceful integration of the Pathet Lao forces and areas, the two provinces of Houa Phan (also known as Sam Neua) and Phong Saly, into the Kingdom of Laos and to supervise a peaceful political solution to the country's problems. The ICC pursued its work in the face of many difficulties, resources were limited, the members had divergent political views, the interpretation of several clauses in the Geneva Agreement was the source of many difficulties, and supervision was complicated by the difficult terrain in Laos.

The history of Laos between 1954 and 1973 is that of the struggle between the Royal Lao government and the Pathet Lao to find a peaceful and workable solution to the problem of uniting Laos. The factionalism of the politics of Laos was made worse by the exercise of their interests by other countries, ranging from neighbouring Thailand and Vietnam to the major powers of the United States, the Soviet Union, Britain, and France. Prince Souvanna Phouma was the only politician willing to seek a political solution with his half-brother Souphanouvong, leader of the Pathet Lao, but on a number of occasions this was frustrated by pressure from others. The root of the problem was the inability of other nations, particularly the United

States, to accept Souvanna Phouma's political stance of neutralism for Laos as it was considered to be a back door form of socialism. Increasingly money and support, from Thailand and the United States, were given to the right-wing and military factions who refused to work with the political branch of the Pathet Lao, the Neo Lao Haksat.

From 1954 to 1962, between the first and second Geneva Conferences, there were thirteen changes of government in the capital Vientiane. The first task as set by the Geneva Conference was to integrate the Pathet Lao into Laos, both the two provinces of Houa Phan and Phong Saly and their military units. As early as September 1954, the opportunity for negotiations to integrate the Pathet Lao into Laos and the possibility for a peaceful outcome was lost when Souvanna Phouma resigned as Prime Minister after a cabinet crisis. The new Prime Minister, Katay Don Sasorith, was a supporter of the South East Asia Treaty Organization (SEATO), and under his premiership the United States Operation Mission (USOM) was opened on 1st January 1955 in Vientiane, bringing with it US military and civil assistance. No political settlement had been achieved but in December 1955 elections were held in the ten provinces under Royal government control.

In 1956-57 a series of negotiations took place between the Pathet Lao and the Royal Lao government, and these resulted in the Vientiane Agreements. The final agreement, signed on 2nd November 1957, provided for the reunification of the country and the formation of a Government of National Union with Pathet Lao participation and a declared foreign policy of neutrality. Prince Souvanna Phouma formed the Government of National Union in November 1957, Souphanouvong was given the Ministry of Planning. By December the government had resumed full control of the two Pathet Lao provinces. The Pathet Lao had obtained from the Vientiane Agreements the right to form a legal political party, which they did, the Neo Lao Haksat (NLH, sometimes spelled Neo Lao Hak Xat) or Lao Patriotic Front.

Supplementary elections were held on 4th May 1958 for the two provinces of Houa Phan and Phong Saly, where elections for the National Assembly had not been held in 1955. The Neo Lao Haksat contested the elections with a number of other parties and won nine of the twenty-one contested seats, their allies the Santiphap Party (Peace Party), a left-wing neutralist party, won an additional four seats. Prince Souphanouvong gained the largest personal vote. The Lao government took the view that the work of the ICC had been completed by March 1958 since they were carrying out the provisions of the Vientiane Agreements. The International Control Commission was adjourned *sine die* on 19th July 1958.

Introduction

Prince Souvanna Phouma's new government of 1958 was unable to maintain control despite the fact that his party, the Lao Ruam Lao Party (the Laotian Peoples Rally), was thirty-six strong in the National Assembly. A rival right-wing group, the Comité pour la Défense des Interêts Nationaux (CDIN or the Committee for the Defence of National Interests), was formed on the 29th June. The CDIN was a group of younger Lao, composed mainly of educated civil servants and military personnel, whose principal aim was to combat communist influence. The dominant figure in the CDIN was Colonel Phoumi Nosavan. When the United States suspended their aid on the 30th June 1958 because of the abuse of funds, the aid programme, begun in 1953 amounted to almost the entire Lao budget. It proved to be the final pressure and Souvanna Phouma resigned on 22nd July.

A series of right-wing governments followed, backed by the military, and excluding the Neo Lao Haksat from power. In 1959, they sought to integrate the two remaining Pathet Lao battalions into the army, but one escaped to the northeast, rather than accept integration. In July, the NLH leaders were arrested and charged with treason, but they escaped and were able to make their way overland back to the northeast in 1960.

After a series of coups and counter-coups in 1960 and 1961 and the outbreak of serious fighting, the Geneva Conference was reconvened and although an agreement was reached on 21st July 1962, it never proved workable because of the struggles for power between the rightist, neutralist, and leftist factions. It established a tri-partite government of National Union in which all three factions in Laos were given seats. It lasted only ten months, however, and after a series of political assassinations culminating in that of Quinim Pholsena, a neutralist and the foreign minister, the Neo Lao Haksat leaders withdrew from Vientiane. Prince Souvanna Phouma was gradually forced into a closer coalition with the rightists led by Phoumi Nosavan. The fighting between the forces of the Pathet Lao and the Royal Lao government broke out afresh and by 1965 the country was effectively divided between the Royal Lao Government and the Pathet Lao, and remained so until 1973.

In the years which followed this polarization, the US 'secret war' in Laos developed. The build-up began gradually with the recruitment and training of 'Special Forces', guerilla units, of whom the Hmong formed the largest number, whose purpose it was to destroy the Pathet Lao and to contain communism. The other major US activity involved aerial operations based in Laos and northeast Thailand. Bombing missions were flown on a daily basis reaching a peak in 1968-69. The fiction of US non-involvement was maintained both in the region and in the United States. Any reports alleging US intervention received little public attention. The United States military action in Laos initially had the objective of containing communism, but after the direct involvement of US troops in South Vietnam from 1965, US operations in Laos became part of the wider Second Indochinese War. Along the eastern frontier of Laos ran the Ho Chi Minh trail, the supply route for men and arms from North Vietnam to South Vietnam. US military action, particularly bombing missions, was aimed at destroying the trail and the defensive positions along it. Attacks into Laos were also launched from South Vietnam in 1971. Despite the enormous amount of money and resources spent by the United States, the Americans did not succeed in defeating, or even containing, the Pathet Lao except on a temporary basis. The launch of the military might of an industrialized giant against the Laotian peasant and mountain-dweller proved a powerful weapon of propaganda for the Pathet Lao and their supporters. The corruption of Vientiane society by the money that accompanied the United States military build-up, and the deportation of large numbers of the population from the battle zones to safer areas in the Vientiane Plain all helped to weaken the control of the Royal government; little by little it controlled less and less of the country until by the end of 1972 it was estimated that only a third to a quarter of the country was under Royal government control.

The Royal government in Vientiane and the Neo Lao Haksat began peace talks on 17 October 1972 and the Agreement on Restoring Peace and Achieving National Concord was signed on 21st February 1973. It is interesting that this accord was addressed to the International Control Commission. On 22nd February 1973 a ceasefire came into effect, a few days after the Paris Accords on Vietnam were agreed. The cease-fire was respected and by the end of 1973 the Pathet Lao troops had been installed in Vientiane and Luang Prabang. A provisional government of national union was formed on 5th April 1974, established by royal decree. Souvanna Phouma remained Prime Minister, while the Pathet Lao were represented by Phoumi Vongvichit as deputy Prime Minister and minister for foreign affairs, and Souphanouvong was made head of the Joint National Council.

This coalition government stayed in power for about a year and the Neo Lao Haksat stepped up their political activities among students and peasants, but once again external events influenced the history of Laos. The fall of the governments of South Vietnam and Cambodia to the communist forces coincided with military outbreaks against the coalition government in Laos. The successes of the Pathet Lao forces in resisting these caused many of the rightists in the capital to flee to

Thailand. Demonstrations in May, led by students, against the continued United States presence and the activities of the United States Agency for International Development (USAID) were followed by the dismissal of five rightist ministers and a number of generals. New moderate ministers were appointed and a larger number of Pathet Lao officials were taken on in the lower levels of administration. In December 1975, a National Congress of People's Representatives met in Vientiane and accepted the abdication of King Sri Savang Vatthana. The Lao People's Democratic Republic was proclaimed. The coalition government was dismissed and the new government was dominated by the Pathet Lao's other political grouping, the Lao People's Revolutionary Party, founded in 1972, and successor to the People's Party of Laos, the previously semi-secret communist party. Souphanouvong was appointed President, Kaysone Phomvihane became head of the Council of Ministers and Nouhak Phoumsavanh was made minister of finance. Since December 1975 Laos has been ruled as a single-party, socialist state.

The new government launched a programme of socialist political and economic reforms and its foreign relations were firmly linked with Vietnam and the Comecon countries. The old élite were replaced, and many of those who had not already done so left the country. It is estimated that about ten per cent of the population left Laos during this period, including the bulk of the educated population and many of the small capitalists, most of whom were Chinese and Vietnamese.

A new electoral law was promulgated and in April 1988 the National Election committee began to organize local elections. In June of that year there were elections for People's Councils, followed in November by provincial elections. In March 1989, elections were held for the Supreme People's Assembly and a committee was appointed to draft a new constitution. Of the seventy-nine elected deputies, sixty-six were Lao Lum, nine were Lao Theung and four were Lao Soung, five of the elected deputies were women. In November 1989, statutes on judicial procedure were approved. The new constitution was ratified by the Supreme People's Assembly on 14th August 1991 and shortly afterwards Kaysone Phomvihane was elected as President and Khanta Siphandon succeeded him as Premier.

Laos, as a land-locked country, needs to have good relations with her neighbours both for economic and security reasons. Relations with Thailand during this period have varied, initial good relations were damaged by anti-government guerilla operations launched from northeast Thailand. In 1984, there were moves to improve relations which later collapsed when a dispute arose over three border villages, which were occupied by Thailand. In 1987, diplomatic discussions concerning the border began and relations between the two countries improved. Relations with Thailand improved significantly from 1988 onwards. On 6th March 1989, Kaysone Phomvihane signed a decree establishing a Lao-Thai Commission for Economic, Cultural, Scientific, and Technical Co-operation to implement the Joint Communiqué between Laos and Thailand in Vientiane 25th November 1988. Trade across the border and through Thailand to third countries is vital for the economy of Laos and other agreements have dealt with trade and transit through Thailand. The fourteen-year Thai ban on the export of goods classified as 'strategic' to Laos was ended, this ban had covered goods in transit to Laos as well as Thai exports. Three additional crossing points between Thailand and Laos were agreed and implemented in 1989, and it was also announced that Thailand would consider opening more crossing points. Hand in hand with improved official relations has been the surge of interest among Thai companies in investment and trade with Laos. Much of the trade between Thailand and Laos is counter-trade, or barter trade. The inter-dependency of the two economies is demonstrated by the fact that when the border is closed there is a great deal of smuggling between the two countries.

It is only recently that there has been an improvement in relations with the United States. Two subjects have been held by the United States to be vital to improved relations, one is the determination of the whereabouts of United States military personnel designated as 'Missing in Action' (MIAs) and the other is the control of the cultivation and traffic in the opium poppy and its derivatives. Laos has now co-operated with United States officials in joint excavations of crash sites and the search for soldiers and airmen 'Missing in Action', including the successful recovery of human remains at a crash site in Savannakhet Province. In late 1989 an agreement was concluded in which the United States agreed to fund a six-year, US$8.7 million crop-substitution and integrated rural development project in Houa Phan province similar to those in Thailand. It will provide the ethnic minorities of Laos with alternatives to growing opium poppies and includes the construction of thirty-two miles of road, which will help farmers get their crops to market, and three irrigation dams that will increase paddy land. The United States has also agreed to provide humanitarian assistance to war victims in Xieng Khouang province.

The per capita income in Laos at about US$160 is still one of the lowest in the world. The economic legacy of the French colonial period was slight, little had been done to develop the economy apart from the extraction of forest products, the development of tin mining, and the planting of coffee. The economy is very narrowly based and is heavily dependent on subsistence agriculture which renders it very vulnerable to the weather. In 1977-78 and 1987-88 there were periods of extreme drought followed by severe floods; the immediate effect was to cause food shortages and the need to seek external assistance. Drought also affected the ability to generate and sell hydro-electric power. Laos is endowed with natural resources of potential value including timber, hydro-electric power, precious stones and minerals. Tenders have recently been solicited for exploiting the gold deposits in Laos. In addition, traditional products such as stick-lac, cardamom, benzoin, resins, and cotton textiles, as well as handicrafts are exported. The major constraints on Lao economic development are the shortages of capital and skilled personnel, the poor state of the roads, transport and communications, the need for greatly expanded educational and health resources, the problems of the terrain and the small size of the population.

Initially the approach taken to the economy of the Lao People's Democratic Republic was severely socialist, including efforts to collectivize agriculture. This provoked an adverse reaction from the population, particularly as Laos was hit by a series of bad harvests in the second half of the 1970s and again in the mid 1980s. At the Fourth Congress of the Lao People's Revolutionary Party held in December 1986 resolutions were adopted which inaugurated the programme of economic reform that has been introduced since that time. In 1988, measures were taken to liberalize the economy, private trade has begun as has the devolution of state enterprises to semi-private companies. In 1989 legislation to encourage foreign investment and banking was passed. The Third Five-Year Plan, 1991-95, has as its main objective the continuation of the economic reforms. Agriculture continues to be an important area of growth and one-fifth of development expenditure has been allocated to it. Transport and communications have been allocated a quarter of the funding, industry (including agro-forestry) has been allocated about a third and the balance is to be used for education, health, and welfare.

The majority of foreign aid for Laos has been provided by the Council for Mutual Economic Assistance (Comecon), and most of this aid took the form of grants or long-term concessional loans. From 1975 to 1982 about half of this aid was directed towards irrigation projects and most of the remainder was used for infrastructure projects, particularly roads. Similarly the aid provided by the World Bank and the Asian Development Bank has largely been used for irrigation and agricultural projects, much of it for the Nam Ngum dam and the new Xeset dam. The principal Western donors of aid are Sweden, the Netherlands, Australia and Japan.

At the end of 1988 the government issued a code which spelled out the guidelines for foreign investment. It has met with considerable interest both from the business community in Thailand and further afield. There has also been some investment by domestic entrepreneurs, and Laotians returned from abroad. This is usually small-scale but has spread from Vientiane to small towns throughout the country. Small factories have been set up to supply local needs for furniture, plywood, bricks, tiles, agricultural tools, chemicals, sugar, cigarettes, brewing and cement. Some of these have received assistance from Vietnam, while Thailand has supported investment in sawmills, and the textile and garment industry, which takes advantage of the cheaper local labour and the lack of import restrictions against Lao products in industrialized countries. Foreign companies had applied to invest in more than 100 projects and eighty had been approved by February 1990. In 1989 and 1990 more than half of all foreign investment in Laos had come from China. The province of Yunnan in China will build an airfield in Laos' northern Luang Namtha province, and in exchange Laos will purchase Chinese passenger aircraft. Direct flights have already begun between Luang Prabang and Kunming, chief city of Yunnan. Agreements have been signed dealing with investments in tin-mining, geological surveys, the construction of electricity plants, and road-building, all in the northern border provinces. Larger scale foreign investment has been in the field of oil and natural gas exploration. A European consortium called the Compagnie Européenne des Petroles, and the US Enterprise Oil Exploration Ltd. have each been given eight-year exploration licenses with twenty-year exploitation rights in southern Laos. Thai companies have been permitted to mine for gold and rubies about a hundred miles north of Vientiane.

Agriculture, forestry and fishing account for seventy-five per cent of the Gross Domestic Product(GDP) and employ about eighty per cent of the population. Since 1988 the Lao government has encouraged privately-owned family farms to produce surpluses to sell and the availability of consumer goods in rural areas has been increased to encourage this. About a third of the rice is produced by upland *swidden*, that is, slash and burn cultivation which is said to be leading to serious deforestation. In order to provide more food and to prevent deforestation, considerable emphasis has been placed on expanding irrigation, funded in the main by foreign economic aid. However, recent droughts have demonstrated the significant level of dependence on weather conditions. In addition to rice, there has been an increase in cash-crop production, with coffee assuming greater importance in the 1980s and the acreage devoted to its cultivation doubling between 1982 and 1986. In order to improve the diet of the population, there have been projects to improve and develop animal husbandry. Fish in particular forms an important part of the Lao diet and recently an important fishing industry has developed on the Nam Ngum reservoir (fifty miles north of Vientiane), which provides the major source of fish for the urban market of Vientiane. An important contribution to export earnings is made by timber; the government has made efforts to control the rate of logging and to encourage the development of plants for finishing timber in Laos.

The sale of electricity to Thailand provides a major source of export earnings. The Nam Ngum dam was built in 1971, a second phase was completed in 1978, and by 1987 its capacity had been increased to 150,000 kilowatts with five turbines operating. Almost ninety per cent is exported to Thailand under a ten-year agreement. Locally, electricity supplies only five per cent of energy needs but there are plans to increase rural electrification, partly to replace wood as one of the principal fuels in rural areas. In anticipation of increased local demand for electricity, a second major hydro-electric project was begun in 1988 at Xeset in southern Laos, funded by the Asian Development Bank, the World Bank and Sweden.

Substantial deposits of valuable minerals are present in Laos including tin, gypsum, potash, iron, coal, gold, copper, limestone, manganese and lead, but few are commercially exploited. Tin and gypsum have recently been mined with Soviet assistance and exported to the Soviet Union. The lack of an adequate transport and communications infrastructure is a handicap to economic development and much of the international economic aid has been directed to improve it. Japanese and Australian aid has been used to improve river communications and help with port construction and other infrastructure projects. The Australians are providing assistance with building a road-and-rail bridge across the Mekong linking Thailand and Laos, which is due to be completed in 1994. There are plans for a second such bridge in the south which would provide a link from Thailand via Laos to Vietnam, part of the long-envisaged trans-Asian highway. There has been talk of financing a railway in Laos by Thai companies but this seems unlikely in the near future.

The Lao economy still relies heavily on foreign aid and loans for finance, local taxation is not yet adequate to meet all the revenue needs for economic development. In 1988 a restructured banking system was announced; the two national banks, the Banque d'Etat and its subsidiary the Banque du Commerce Exterieur Lao had to change their roles as they lost their monopoly. The Banque d'Etat assumed the role of a central bank and the Banque du Commerce Exterieur Lao became a 'business' bank and used the existing branch about the country, such work has been included where it has been relatively easily found in research libraries, much of the current material on Laos produced by teams of international experts falls into this category.

The bibliography has been arranged under thirty-four main subject headings, entries are arranged in alphabetical order of author's name within these subject groups. Full details of title and author are given for each book, together with publisher, place and date of publication and pagination, where maps or bibliography are included these are indicated. References to articles in journals contain in addition the name of the journal, volume and part number and the pages on which the article is found. It was felt significant for Laos to note within the annotations the presence of significant photographic illustrations. The annotations which accompany each entry attempt to distil something of the content and where relevant the intellectual tendency of the item. The separate author, title and subject indexes offer further means to search the bibliography. The subject index offers access to both broad headings with subdivisions and to detailed entries.

In this bibliography and in the indexes the practice has been followed of referring to Lao, Hmong, Thai, Vietnamese and Chinese authors by their full names in direct order unless because of marriage or the use of Western first names they indicate that they follow Western practice, cross-references are given to other forms of the name in the index. Spellings of personal names have been given as found in published work, thus Prince Souvanna Phouma is conventionally referred to with his name given as two words although it can be given as one word, whereas his half-brother's name Prince Souphanouvong is always given as one word. Honorifics such as Prince, Thao, Phya and Maha have been included in names but are not indexed. In the text the title of Prince is not always used when these figures are exercising a political role. Names of places in Laos have followed customary usage but this has never been exact as it represents Western forms of Lao names, some of which are in the process of changing. Names of the neighbouring countries occur in conventionalized forms, Thailand poses a problem because it was known as Siam before 1939 and so Siam and Siamese are used where these are more historically appropriate.

Acknowledgements

The gestation period of this work has been long and I wish to record my gratitude for the support of those who endured it, in particular my family. My colleagues Ian Brown and Andrew Turton both provided extremely useful help and I would also like to record my gratitude to unknown and unsung library assistants and stack attendants without whom the bibliographer would not survive. I am, however, responsible for any errors, omissions and weaknesses.

Helen Cordell
London
October 1991

The Country and Its People

General

1 Laos: war and revolution.
Edited by Nina S. Adams, Alfred W. McCoy. New York: Harper &
Row, 1970. 482p. maps. bibliog.

An important collection of thirty essays on Laos, originally compiled to rouse opinion
against the US war in Laos, but still valuable for the range of topics covered by the
articles. The essays are grouped under five headings: the land and its people; the
historical development of modern Laos; America in Laos; United States statements on
Laos; and the Pathet Lao. Various aspects of the political history of Laos are
considered for the period 1945 to 1970, and their usefulness lies in their concentration
on specific subjects such as the role of Air America, the role of United States Aid and
the International Voluntary Services, as well as essays which deal with broader themes
such as the Geneva Agreements of 1954 and the policies of various US presidencies
towards Laos.

**2 Kingdom of Laos: the land of the million elephants and of the white
parasol.**
Compiled by René de Berval. Saigon, Vietnam: France-Asie, 1959.
506p. maps. bibliog.

A compilation of articles on Laos which covers various aspects of the country. It was
first published by France-Asie in French as *Présence du royaume lao* in 1956. This
volume is devoted almost entirely to the Lao aspects of Laos, written largely by Lao
scholars, frequently a synthesis of earlier work, presented in a readable form. Some of
the articles serve as a rapid reference source on certain topics. The subjects covered
are geography, history, the Laotian calendar, music, the arts, Buddhism and its
festivals, rites and ceremonies, cookery, traditional medicine, the writing system,
language and literature, proverbs and legends, education, the economy, and
international relations. The quality and length of the contributions is varied, some of
them are referred to in detail in this bibliography where useful.

1

3   **The living Mekong.**
Charles Burleigh.   Sydney; London: Angus & Robertson, 1971. 137p.
maps.

A photographic essay on the people and life along the Mekong River from Laos to
Cambodia. There are brief essays on the geography, history, religion and culture of the
region travelled, as well as details of the actual journey and itinerary.

4   **Life in the Pathet Lao liberated zone.**
Jacques Decornoy.   In: *Laos: war and revolution.*   Edited by Nina S.
Adams, Alfred W. McCoy. New York: Harper & Row, 1970, p. 411-23.

Decornoy, a journalist working for *Le Monde*, where this was first published July 3-8,
1968, describes what he saw of life in the area controlled by the Pathet Lao
government: the damage caused by the bombing raids; the need to cultivate and
manufacture by night, and yet a general level of comfortable plenty for the peasant
farmers; the work on education, schools in the villages where there were none and the
fight against adult illiteracy. A rather fuller version of this account was published as a
pamphlet entitled *Laos: the forgotten war* (Boston, Massachusetts: New England Free
Press, 1969. 23p.), and in this Decornoy adds a perspective from Vientiane and the
other side of divided Laos.

5   **Introduction à la connaissance du Laos.** (An introduction to Laos.)
Henri Deydier.   Saigon, Vietnam: Imprimerie Française d'Outre-Mer,
1952. 140p. map. bibliog.

A useful summary of Lao studies up to 1952 and an introduction to the principal
published sources. It is written in a commendably straightforward way and covers
briefly the topics of religion, religious and secular festivals, Lao language, literature,
music and theatre, as well as a brief survey of the history of Laos.

6   **Laos: keystone of Indochina.**
Arthur J. Dommen.   Boulder, Colorado: Westview Press, 1985. 182p.
maps. bibliog. (Westview Profiles/Nations of Contemporary Asia).

A profile of modern Laos set in its historical context. Useful for its coverage of modern
Laos, the historical review provides a starting point for further reading. Stuart-Fox in
Laos: politics, economics and society (q.v.) provides more specific details on modern
Laos but this is a readable introductory account. Dommen's originality of perspective
is indicated in his subtitle which refers to the geographical position of Laos balanced as
a keystone between her stronger and larger neighbours Thailand, Vietnam and China.
It is her geographical position that has influenced the historical development of Laos
and continues to be an important factor for the present and future.

7   **River road through Laos: reflections of the Mékong.**
James A.Hafner, Joel M.Halpern, Barbara Kerewsky-Halpern.
Amherst, Massachusetts: University of Massachusetts at Amherst, 1983.
76p. maps. bibliog. (Asian Studies Committee Occasional Paper Series,
no. 10).

The Mekong River is the protagonist of this collection of essays, rising in China and
flowing through Laos (where at one point it forms the international boundary with
Thailand), then continuing through Cambodia to reach the South China Sea in

At the end of 1988 the government issued a code which spelled out the guidelines for foreign investment. It has met with considerable interest both from the business community in Thailand and further afield. There has also been some investment by domestic entrepreneurs, and Laotians returned from abroad. This is usually small-scale but has spread from Vientiane to small towns throughout the country. Small factories have been set up to supply local needs for furniture, plywood, bricks, tiles, agricultural tools, chemicals, sugar, cigarettes, brewing and cement. Some of these have received assistance from Vietnam, while Thailand has supported investment in sawmills, and the textile and garment industry, which takes advantage of the cheaper local labour and the lack of import restrictions against Lao products in industrialized countries. Foreign companies had applied to invest in more than 100 projects and eighty had been approved by February 1990. In 1989 and 1990 more than half of all foreign investment in Laos had come from China. The province of Yunnan in China will build an airfield in Laos' northern Luang Namtha province, and in exchange Laos will purchase Chinese passenger aircraft. Direct flights have already begun between Luang Prabang and Kunming, chief city of Yunnan. Agreements have been signed dealing with investments in tin-mining, geological surveys, the construction of electricity plants, and road-building, all in the northern border provinces. Larger scale foreign investment has been in the field of oil and natural gas exploration. A European consortium called the Compagnie Européenne des Petroles, and the US Enterprise Oil Exploration Ltd. have each been given eight-year exploration licenses with twenty-year exploitation rights in southern Laos. Thai companies have been permitted to mine for gold and rubies about a hundred miles north of Vientiane.

Agriculture, forestry and fishing account for seventy-five per cent of the Gross Domestic Product(GDP) and employ about eighty per cent of the population. Since 1988 the Lao government has encouraged privately-owned family farms to produce surpluses to sell and the availability of consumer goods in rural areas has been increased to encourage this. About a third of the rice is produced by upland *swidden*, that is, slash and burn cultivation which is said to be leading to serious deforestation. In order to provide more food and to prevent deforestation, considerable emphasis has been placed on expanding irrigation, funded in the main by foreign economic aid. However, recent droughts have demonstrated the significant level of dependence on weather conditions. In addition to rice, there has been an increase in cash-crop production, with coffee assuming greater importance in the 1980s and the acreage devoted to its cultivation doubling between 1982 and 1986. In order to improve the diet of the population, there have been projects to improve and develop animal husbandry. Fish in particular forms an important part of the Lao diet and recently an important fishing industry has developed on the Nam Ngum reservoir (fifty miles north of Vientiane), which provides the major source of fish for the urban market of Vientiane. An important contribution to export earnings is made by timber; the government has made efforts to control the rate of logging and to encourage the development of plants for finishing timber in Laos.

The sale of electricity to Thailand provides a major source of export earnings. The Nam Ngum dam was built in 1971, a second phase was completed in 1978, and by 1987 its capacity had been increased to 150,000 kilowatts with five turbines operating. Almost ninety per cent is exported to Thailand under a ten-year agreement. Locally, electricity supplies only five per cent of energy needs but there are plans to increase rural electrification, partly to replace wood as one of the principal fuels in rural areas. In anticipation of increased local demand for electricity, a second major hydro-electric project was begun in 1988 at Xeset in southern Laos, funded by the Asian Development Bank, the World Bank and Sweden.

Substantial deposits of valuable minerals are present in Laos including tin, gypsum, potash, iron, coal, gold, copper, limestone, manganese and lead, but few are commercially exploited. Tin and gypsum have recently been mined with Soviet assistance and exported to the Soviet Union. The lack of an adequate transport and communications infrastructure is a handicap to economic development and much of the international economic aid has been directed to improve it. Japanese and Australian aid has been used to improve river communications and help with port construction and other infrastructure projects. The Australians are providing assistance with building a road-and-rail bridge across the Mekong linking Thailand and Laos, which is due to be completed in 1994. There are plans for a second such bridge in the south which would provide a link from Thailand via Laos to Vietnam, part of the long-envisaged trans-Asian highway. There has been talk of financing a railway in Laos by Thai companies but this seems unlikely in the near future.

The Lao economy still relies heavily on foreign aid and loans for finance, local taxation is not yet adequate to meet all the revenue needs for economic development. In 1988 a restructured banking system was announced; the two national banks, the Banque d'Etat and its subsidiary the Banque du Commerce Exterieur Lao had to change their roles as they lost their monopoly. The Banque d'Etat assumed the role of a central bank and the Banque du Commerce Exterieur Lao became a 'business' bank and used the existing branch network of the Banque d'Etat. The first foreign controlled bank, the Joint Development Bank, which is controlled by Thai business interests opened in October 1989. In November of the same year the first foreign bank to open an office in Laos was the Thai Military Bank. The Asian Development Bank has been providing aid for the reorganization of the banking system. In August 1990 the government passed a new set of economic laws relating to property ownership, contracts, inheritance, banking, and court fees.

In foreign trade imports into Laos consistently outstrip exports in value. The major imports are petroleum products, machinery, raw materials, foodstuffs, and consumer goods. The principal exports are electricity, timber, tin, gypsum, and coffee. The major trading partners have been members of the Communist bloc, however, in view of the changes occurring in those countries the future economic relations with them is unpredictable. Thailand is the most important non-communist trading partner followed by Japan, Singapore and France.

Social and economic life in Laos is improving but with the changes in economic direction social disparities in income are becoming more apparent. Thus the increase in consumer goods available has not benefitted all. The changes in the methods of income distribution mean that those in salaried posts such as teachers and health care workers have been adversely affected by inflation and the revaluation of the kip in comparison with those in private business or agriculture. This has exacerbated problems in the health and educational sector as in some cases staff have abandoned their posts. There are severe problems in the provision of medical and other health services. Much of the medical equipment is old and damaged, and in an effort to extend services nationwide, resources are now spread very thinly. In August 1991 it was reported that there were 933 hospitals in the country, with 8,244 beds and 1130 doctors. That is for every 100,000 inhabitants there are 19.37 beds and 2.6 doctors. Malaria continues to be a serious problem and there are fresh outbreaks during floods, as in the summer of 1991.

The present Lao government is endeavouring to overcome traditional inter-ethnic hostility by encouraging the spread of schooling and the use of the Lao language among the whole population. A successful adult literacy campaign has been conducted. Education is compulsory for the first five years from seven to eleven, and there has been a campaign to establish a primary school in every village, with shortages of basic necessities being met with assistance from UNICEF. Secondary education is available in middle-schools and high-schools, both courses lasting three years, but these schools are based in towns, which restricts access particularly for ethnic minorities and female students. Tertiary education is more limited and based in Vientiane, while some students study abroad. However, the number of schools has more than doubled since 1975 and in 1985 it was estimated that sixty-seven per cent of school-age children were enrolled in schools.

The future prospects for Laos seem better than in the past, although the future is difficult to predict. It is one of a number of countries dependent on the success of other parts of the world economy. The economic and political changes in its major aid partners in Eastern Europe will undoubtedly affect economic programmes in Laos. In addition, Laos relies on a general atmosphere of good relations in the international sphere to avoid becoming a pawn in the international politics of major powers. Its position as a buffer state means that it is always sensitive to developments in the neighbouring states of Vietnam and Thailand. It has begun to reconstruct its society but needs time for educational and technical developments and for trained local staff to permeate society so that it can achieve some measure of economic progress and independence.

On the use of this bibliography

Laos is a little known country with a complex history; French colonization at the end of the nineteenth century defined its boundaries to the area that we think of today as Laos. Indigenous scholarship has been hampered by the relative poverty of the country and the civil war that dogged the first twenty years of independence. Where possible works by Laotians have been included if available in English or French. Foreign scholarship has been dominated by the French but even their research is relatively sparse compared with the work on Vietnam. Thus in selecting items for the bibliography a large number of French items is included but works in English which summarize this research have also been included for the general reader. The bibliography aims to offer a broad subject coverage but it also reflects the dominance of works on the recent history of Laos and the wars fought over its territory from 1945 to 1973. Political opinion was and is severely divided over these events and an attempt has been made to offer a balanced coverage that will enable the reader to reach his own conclusions. Similarly the actions and policies of the Lao People's Democratic Republic provoke strongly partisan views. The bibliography aims to offer an introduction to major and significant sources on Laos. The subject bibliographies quoted and the bibliographies within some of the books will enable a reader to pursue a subject in depth. A feature which hampers the bibliographer of Laos is the semi-published nature of much of the material issued about the country, such work has been included where it has been relatively easily found in research libraries, much of the current material on Laos produced by teams of international experts falls into this category.

The bibliography has been arranged under thirty-four main subject headings, entries are arranged in alphabetical order of author's name within these subject groups. Full details of title and author are given for each book, together with publisher, place and date of publication and pagination, where maps or bibliography are included these are indicated. References to articles in journals contain in addition the name of the journal, volume and part number and the pages on which the article is found. It was felt significant for Laos to note within the annotations the presence of significant photographic illustrations. The annotations which accompany each entry attempt to distil something of the content and where relevant the intellectual tendency of the item. The separate author, title and subject indexes offer further means to search the bibliography. The subject index offers access to both broad headings with subdivisions and to detailed entries.

In this bibliography and in the indexes the practice has been followed of referring to Lao, Hmong, Thai, Vietnamese and Chinese authors by their full names in direct order unless because of marriage or the use of Western first names they indicate that they follow Western practice, cross-references are given to other forms of the name in the index. Spellings of personal names have been given as found in published work, thus Prince Souvanna Phouma is conventionally referred to with his name given as two words although it can be given as one word, whereas his half-brother's name Prince Souphanouvong is always given as one word. Honorifics such as Prince, Thao, Phya and Maha have been included in names but are not indexed. In the text the title of Prince is not always used when these figures are exercising a political role. Names of places in Laos have followed customary usage but this has never been exact as it represents Western forms of Lao names, some of which are in the process of changing. Names of the neighbouring countries occur in conventionalized forms, Thailand poses a problem because it was known as Siam before 1939 and so Siam and Siamese are used where these are more historically appropriate.

Acknowledgements

The gestation period of this work has been long and I wish to record my gratitude for the support of those who endured it, in particular my family. My colleagues Ian Brown and Andrew Turton both provided extremely useful help and I would also like to record my gratitude to unknown and unsung library assistants and stack attendants without whom the bibliographer would not survive. I am, however, responsible for any errors, omissions and weaknesses.

Helen Cordell
London
October 1991

Vietnam. The first essay considers its place in the nineteenth century as the focus of French ambitions for a route to China: this sets the scene for the present volume, and is largely derived from Osborne, 1975 (q.v.). The next two essays report on a field trip along the Mekong in 1957 in the region above Luang Prabang. They are intended to fill a gap in the 1950s literature on Laos. They are largely unedited accounts written by young anthropologists on their first encounter with that little known portion of Laos. There is a brief note to introduce these accounts for the reader of the 1980s. These accounts have a freshness and charm lacking in formal accounts, recounting details of village life, customs and festivals at the time. The volume is completed by the fourth essay which considers trade and transport on the Upper Mekong, the data referring to the early 1970s. Hafner identifies market centres and considers the trade between Laos and Thailand in the stretch of the river above Vientiane. His predictions for possible improved communications between Laos and Thailand in this area have been disrupted by the coolness between the two countries over the border question.

8 **Laos: its people, its society, its culture.**
Edited by Frank M. LeBar, Adrienne Suddard. New Haven,
Connecticut: HRAF Press, 1960. 3rd rev. ed. 1967. 294p. maps. bibliog.
(Survey of World Cultures).

The purpose of this work is to provide a summary in English of all the information available on Laos. It is thus a digest of previously published material, a large part of which was written in French. Its scope is the socio-economic, cultural and governmental structure of Laos. It avoids the worst pitfalls of over-simplification and is a useful introductory work. The portrait of Laos it presents is that of the traditional society as modified by French colonial rule. The 1967 revision took into account the major events which had taken place in Laos during the period 1960 to 1967. The work covers culture, historical background, geography, population and ethnic groups, religion, social structure, education, politics and government, foreign relations, economics, trade and industry, and agriculture. There are useful statistical tables for the 1950s. It is a portrait of Laos before the major disruptions of war and emigration had taken place, and should be read in conjunction with other works which provide a more up-to-date picture. Many of the chapters, such as those on religion and literature, are still valid.

9 **L'Indochine.** (Indo-China.)
Sylvain Lévi. Paris: Société des Editions Géographiques,
Maritimes, Coloniales, 1931. 2 vols. bibliogs.

An elegantly produced work, published as one of a series for the Exposition Coloniale Internationale de Paris, 1931 (International Colonial Exhibition in Paris, 1931). Volume one is a general introduction to the French territories of Indo-China, which are dealt with individually under each subject heading: the geography, people, history, religion, literature, art and archaeology. Volume two is devoted to the French administration of Indo-China and has chapters on the civil, military, legal, fiscal, postal, educational, economic, mapping and intellectual sections of the administration. There is a statistical appendix on the population of Indo-China. Both volumes are illustrated with contemporary photographs.

10 The little world of Laos.

Oden Meeker. New York: Scribner's, 1959. 256p.

Meeker was a US CARE official in Laos in the mid-1950s. His account of his experiences of Laos is most interesting now for the picture it paints of life there at that time, although he does also refer to political events. A picture essay by Homer Page, comprising thirty-two plates, complements the work.

11 Aspects du pays Lao. (Aspects of Laos.)

Thao Nhouy Abhay. Vientiane: Edition Comité Littéraire Lao, 1956. 129p.

Eleven articles on aspects of life in Laos: the ceremony of *Baci* (that is, a ceremony to ensure blessings and safety at a significant moment such as marriage, a journey or the entrance into a community – it is non-Buddhist, but performed by someone respected for their Buddhist piety and celebrated by a community, and is a feature of Lao life to which travellers frequently refer); rites of marriage and death; people's names; love poetry; Lao Buddhism; the festival of That Luang; versification; Sin Xay; some folktales; and the dance the Lam Vong. Most of the articles appear in an English version in *Kingdom of Laos: the land of the million elephants and of the white parasol* (q.v.).

12 Mission Pavie, Indochine 1879-1895. (The Pavie mission, 1879-1895.)

Auguste Pavie. Paris: Leroux, 1898-1919. 10 vols. maps.

The published record of the work of Pavie and his companions, who mapped Laos, established its boundaries, subdued Deo Van Tri and his Black flags, and helped to establish French rule in Laos. These volumes are frequently in journal form, and are illustrated with contemporary photographs, line drawings and a large number of maps. They were published in two series, *Etudes diverses* (Varied studies) and *Géographie et voyages* (Geography and travels). The three volume titles of the first series were: 1, *Recherches sur la littérature du Cambodge, et du Laos et du Siam (1898)* (Research on the literature of Cambodia, Laos and Siam), which includes the French and Lao text of two traditional tales, 'Twelve young girls' and 'Néang-Kakey'; 2, *Recherches sur l'histoire du Cambodge, du Laos et du Siam* (1898) (Research into the history of Cambodia, Laos and Siam), French translations of historical chronicles, the manuscripts for Laos having been found in Luang Prabang; 3, *Recherches sur l'histoire naturelle de l'Indo-Chine orientale* (1904) (Research on the natural history of eastern Indo-China), dealing with the prehistory of man, but the main part is a classified zoology, the material having been collected by several writers. The second series (Geography and travels) is introduced by two volumes which summarize the four principal groups of exploration, entitled *Exposé des travaux de la mission*, 1 and 2 (An account of the work of the mission); the other five volumes give detailed accounts of particular expeditions and are 3, *Voyage au Laos et chez les sauvages du sud-est de l'Indochine* (1902) (Journey to Laos and amongst the primitive tribes of the south-east of Indo-China); 4, *Voyages au centre de l'Annam et du Laos et dans les régions sauvages de l'est de l'Indochine* (1902) (Journey to the centre of Annam and Laos and to the regions of the wild tribes of the east of Indo-China), by Captain Malglaive and Captain Rivière; 5, *Voyages dans le Haut Laos et sur les frontières de Chine et de Birmanie* (1902) (Travels in Upper Laos and along the frontiers of China and Burma), by Pierre Lefèvre-Pontalis; 6, *Passage du Mé-khong au Tonkin, 1887 et 1888* (1911) (Traverse from the Mekong to Tonkin, 1887 and 1888); 7, *Journal de marche, 1888-1889 (and) Événements du Siam, 1891-1893* (1919) (Log of the march 1888-1889 (and)

Events in Siam, 1891-1893). This last volume gives Pavie's version of the Paknam incident. The atlas contains Pavie's maps with brief notes on the areas mapped.

13 **Le Laos.** (Laos.)
   Lucien de Reinach.   Paris: Charles, 1901. 2 vols.

Written by one of the earliest French administrators in Laos, published in this elegant edition, it is a study of the geography, inhabitants, social customs, languages, economy, industry, trade and political organization of Laos. The second volume, devoted to appendices, contains texts of treaties between France and Siam relating to Laos and Battambang; official reports on the status of Laos and research in the archives at Hue, notes on the cultivation of various products; and a note on the legal code of Vientiane. There are also a large number of contemporary photographs. This work provides an account of Laos in the first years of French administration and also information of the type that might be found in a gazetteer. A second revised edition was published posthumously in 1911 by Guilmoto in Paris, the text having been somewhat re-arranged and the appendices and photographs omitted.

14 **Le Laos: dieux, bonzes et montagnes.** (Laos: gods, monks and
   mountains.)
   Jean Renaud.   Paris: Redier, 1930. 158p. map. (Toutes Nos Colonies,
   no. 1).

Characterized as of little value by Lafont (*Bibliographie du Laos* [q.v.]), this is a simple account of Laos for the French in metropolitan France. The value for the modern reader is the large number of contemporary photographs of all aspects of Laos. Lack of a contents list, or a list of plates, makes it more difficult to use.

15 **Veux-tu connaître le Laos?** (Do you want to know Laos?)
   Véronique Sayasen.   Paris: Sudestasie, 1987. 16p. (Collection l'Enfant
   Bilingue).

This charming booklet for children introduces Laos through the character Monemani. On each page is a sentence in French and Lao, in script, illustrated with attractive colourful drawings. In its few pages it introduces the key aspects of the life of a rural Lao child, her village, her dress, Lao daily life and the festivals.

16 **In a little kingdom.**
   Perry Stieglitz.   Armonk, New York; London: M. E. Sharpe, 1990.
   230p. map.

Stieglitz's association with Laos began in 1959 when he was assigned, on a Fulbright grant, to teach at the Vientiane *lycée*. He later became a foreign service officer, and cultural attaché in the United States State Department, serving in Laos. This is an autobiographical account of his links with Laos from 1959 to 1968, interspersed with details of contemporary political developments. It provides a portrait of Prince Souvanna Phouma, whom Stieglitz came to know initially through a common interest in bridge, and later more intimately after his marriage to Princess Moune, Prince Souvanna Phouma's daughter. The account concludes with a chapter on developments in Laos from 1969 to 1984 when contacts with Laos were limited to family visits, and it ends with the death of Prince Souvanna Phouma from heart disease. While unashamedly autobiographical, the book provides another useful insight into the political history of Laos in this complex period. Stieglitz was a strong supporter of the neutralist position of Prince Souvanna Phouma and found himself sometimes at odds with his United States colleagues. It is an affectionate portrait of the last years of the Kingdom of Laos. A generous selection of photographs illustrate the text.

17 **Southeast Asian exodus: from tradition to resettlement, understanding refugees from Laos, Kampuchea and Vietnam in Canada.**
Edited by Elliot L. Tepper.   Ottawa: Canadian Studies Association, 1980. 230p. maps. bibliog.

Intended for those wishing to understand the refugees recently arrived in Canada, this book provides social, economic and historical background information on the countries of Indochina, as well as on the reasons for departure of the refugees and specific cultural differences that may cause problems of understanding and resettlement. Written by Canadian academics with experience of the countries, it is a useful general work of introduction.

18 **Notice sur le Laos français.** (Account of French Laos.)
Published by order of M. Paul Doumer, governor-general of Indo-China under the direction of lieutenant Colonel Tournier, chief colonial officer.   Hanoi: Schneider, 1900. 191p.

A compilation of all the current information available on Laos. It is interesting for the range of knowledge that had been acquired and consistency with later research. There is no index or contents page and so the reader must search for the information required. The subjects covered are the geography; the peoples of Laos (p. 10-124), a description of the ethnic groups including the Lao and their customs, religion and way of life; the French administration and its organization; fauna; flora; agriculture; forest resources; industries; mines; communications; and commerce. The tone is one of optimism for a prosperous economic future.

19 **In the liberated zone of Laos.**
Van Son, et al.   Hanoi: Foreign Languages Publishing House, 1968. 53p.

Reports by five North Vietnamese journalists of a visit in 1968, to the area of Laos controlled by the Pathet Lao government. Written in rather flowery prose, they describe the attempts to continue normal life despite living under air attack; the continuation of agriculture and artisanal industries; the expansion of education and literacy among people who had previously had little chance of receiving an education; festivals; a visit to the fortress of Phoukout; and stories of those who had joined the Lao Patriotic Front after having been forced to serve in the Lao special forces. These reports are complemented by that of Jacques Decornoy's 'Life in the Pathet Lao liberated zone' (q.v.).

20 **Laos: a country study.**
Donald P. Whitaker, et al. Washington, DC: US Government Printing
Office, 1971. 2nd ed. 335p. maps. bibliog. (Area Handbook Series, DA
550-58).
The 1971 edition of the *Area handbook for Laos* was reissued in 1979 with the current
title, but the work and information is rooted in 1971. It was issued again in 1985. It is a
comprehensive reference work on Laos, and does recognize the effect of the division of
the country and try to include coverage of the Lao Patriotic Front's area of
administration, if from a distance. The four broad divisions of the work are social,
political, economic and national security; the bibliography is divided into correspond-
ing sections.

Post 1975

21 **Vivre au Laos.** (To live in Laos.)
Michel Cahour. Marseille, France: Le Temps Parallèle, 1989. 148p.
(Collection 'Je Lis').
Cahour returned to Laos in 1975 with his Laotian wife and their two daughters to live
there and work with the newly established republican government. He had spent two
years in Laos from 1966 to 1968 as a teacher, and so is able to provide some idea of the
contrast in the country after 1975. Cahour tried to work in Laos as a Lao for Laos;
what he experiences is the clash of cultures and expectations which arise. Finally he
realizes that he cannot contribute as he wished and asks to leave. This work is his
reflection on the experience twelve years later. It is both a portrait of the new rulers
taking over the organization of the country and a view of Laos from the point of view
of a Westerner, one who wishes the new society well but is aware of its problems.

22 **Le partage du Mekong.** (The division of the Mekong.)
Amphay Doré. Paris: Encre, 1980. 265p. map.
Dòré recounts the events of 1973 to 1979 in Laos from the point of view of a
participant and an observer. Of Lao and French parentage, he is not only educated in
the culture of both societies, but as a trained ethnologist had made a study of Lao
society. He succeeds in providing the necessary cultural context for understanding Laos
and the events in Laos. When Doré returned to Laos, on completing his education in
France, it was his firm intention to remain there for good. Finally, circumstances made
it difficult to remain and with great sadness he was forced to choose between Lao and
French nationality and felt compelled to choose to leave Laos. This is an account of
both personal and national experience and offers an illuminating insight into the first
years of the Lao People's Democratic Republic.

23 **Laos.**
Vientiane: KPL, 1989- . quarterly.
A quarterly picture magazine published in Lao and English editions. The stories are
concerned with economic and social progress, friendly foreign relations, sport and
cultural activities. The four central pages are printed in colour, as are the four cover

pages. The topics selected are indicative of the government's view of the positive image of Laos which it wishes to project.

24 **Laos.**
Roman Ozerski, Sergei Sevruk, text by Stanislav Blazenkhov.
Moscow: Planeta, 1985. 200p. map.
A photographic essay on modern Laos illustrating the landscape, Buddhist monuments, agriculture, construction, industry, town life, education, recreation and political figures. There are some historical photographs of the Pathet Lao resistance too. This book has been published in a number of languages including English, Spanish and Russian.

25 **Cultural support to Laos: report by a SIDA-mission, March 1990.**
SIDA. Vientiane: The Author, 1990. 45p. bibliog.
SIDA, the Swedish International Development Authority, established regular project support for Laos in 1979-80, and in 1988 further support was agreed, including some in the cultural sphere. This report was written to consider areas for promoting cultural support between the two countries. After an initial survey of the social and cultural background, the authors examine the cultural policies and institutions of the Lao People's Democratic Republic. They report on the National Library, the National Folkdance and Music School, the Central Dance and Music Troupe, the Theatre Troupe, the Cinematographic Company, the School of Fine Arts, the National Museums, the Vannasin Magazine, the Tam Ting Cave and the National Committee for Social Science. They conclude with proposals for co-operation.

26 **Contemporary Laos: studies in the politics and society of the Lao People's Democratic Republic.**
Edited by Martin Stuart-Fox. St. Lucia: University of Queensland Press, 1982. 345p. map.
Intended to present a portrait of Laos in 1980, this book assembles eighteen essays by experts on Laos and South East Asia. They present an assessment of the first five years of rule by the Lao People's Revolutionary Party (LPRP) and look at various aspects of the social and political life of the country. Each essay deals succinctly with a particular topic; the first five deal with political developments, the seizure of political power and its exercise by the LPRP. Two essays deal with economic developments and foreign aid, and there are single essays on the government's radical new approach to education, its attitude to Buddhism, and the policies towards minority peoples and refugees. Aspects of international relations, the perennial problem for Laos of seeking accommodation with the neighbouring powerful states and her search for survival and identity, are dealt with in the final six essays.

27 **Laos: politics, economics and society.**
Martin Stuart-Fox. London: Pinter; Boulder, Colorado: Lynne Rienner, 1986. 220p. map. bibliog. (Marxist Regimes Series).
An analysis of politics, economics and society in Laos since 1975. The material was gathered primarily during the author's field trips to Laos when he was able to conduct extensive interviews with Lao officials. The introduction gives a historical perspective to this account of the social structure of Laos, the political and economic system, and the domestic and foreign policies of the new government. This is a comprehensive and

detailed consideration of the Lao People's Democratic Republic based on original research and a study of current sources. Basic data is given in tabulated form, very useful given the difficulty in obtaining source material, and there is also a useful glossary.

28 **Laos: beyond the revolution.**
Edited by Joseph J. Zasloff, Leonard Unger.   London: Macmillan, 1991. 348p. maps.

The origins of this volume lie in a conference organized by Zasloff and Unger in May 1988 entitled 'Current developments in Laos'. They were worried by the lack of scholarly attention paid to Laos in recent years. The book represents papers presented at the conference, in many cases updated, plus contributions from others who could not be present. They are grouped around the subjects of Lao politics, economics, society and external relations, and US policy towards Laos, both historically and in the present. The appendices contain three State Department reports to Congress on Laos, on narcotics and human rights, plus the 1988 Amnesty International report on Laos. The overall picture presented is a far more optimistic one than many, including these writers, have presented in recent publications, although they do not ignore the real economic and political difficulties which Laos faces as it tries to rebuild its society. In the economics section an *aide-mémoire* by the United Nations Development Programme provides a 1989 overview of the current Lao economy, backed by key statistics, and describes the economic potential of Laos with its principal limitations and government development strategies since 1975. Wendy Batson, who with her husband has been working in Laos on aid-related development projects, reports on the position of the ethnic minorities in Laos. Her report is mainly positive, with progress in education and government positions available to the brighter students from the ethnic minorities. Dr. Ng Shui Meng's report on social developments indicates that progress has been made, but that much of the health and education programme has been spread too thinly because of a lack of resources. An important section of Dr. Ng's paper is devoted to the position of women and the conflict between tradition and development. W. Courtland Robinson's survey of Laotian refugees in Thailand, and the response from the US and Thai governments, updates other work on the flows of refugees and the status of the camps in Thailand. He does not provide a solution to the problem itself, although he seems to be recommending a more positive effort towards dialogue with the government of Laos and aid to accompany resettlement in Laos. The concluding section deals with United States relations with Laos, chiefly from a historical perspective. Arthur Dommen's paper 'Lao nationalism and American policy, 1954-9', uses recently declassified diplomatic correspondence from the Department of State files in the National Archives, Washington, DC. Dommen's thesis is that United States policy worked against Lao nationalism in this period, as policies were influenced by European examples of Communist seizures of power.

Travellers' Accounts
and Travel Guides

29 **Voyages dans le Laos.** (Travels in Laos.)
Etienne Aymonier.   Paris: Leroux, 1895-97. 2 vols. maps. (Annales du
Musée Guimet. Bibliothèque d'Études, no. 5).

A continuation of Aymonier's travels in Cambodia. In 1882 to 1883 he traversed the
Khorat Plateau in Thailand and crossed the Mekong into Laos. He gives detailed
descriptions of the people he met, their style of life, customs and the economic basis of
their life, as well as the ruins and monuments his party found. The majority of the
travels were in modern Thailand, but they did explore in southern Laos and around
Vientiane.

30 **Cambodge Laos Vietnam.** (Cambodia, Laos, Vietnam.)
Michel Blanchard.   Paris: Arthaud, 1989. 264p. maps. bibliog. (Guide
Arthaud.)

A guide for the tourist that is very current. The author states that most visitors will
have to join organized tours in order to visit Laos, but he does give information for the
independent business or professional visitor such as that on flights both to Laos and
within Laos. The seventy-page section on Laos is divided into three parts, a wide-
ranging and well-written general introduction to all aspects of Laos and its culture,
including its gastronomy. A middle section of practical information, arranged in
alphabetical order, deals amongst other things with banks, addresses of tourist
agencies, tipping, shopping, climate, health dangers and a calendar of festivals. The
third section on exploring Laos gives information on the principal cities of Vientiane
and Luang Prabang with town plans, details of the hotels and information on the
monuments and museums to visit. Blanchard continues with information on the smaller
towns and other places to visit in Laos. He does warn of the lack of hotel
accommodation in some of the areas. He also touches briefly on areas that are not
currently open to tourism.

31 **Mémoires du Laos.** (Memories of Laos.)
Geneviève Couteau. Paris: Seghers, 1988. 336p. map. bibliog.
Established as an artist, Geneviève Couteau visited Laos in 1968 at the invitation of Prince Souvanna Phouma. She travelled widely in the area governed by the Prince and participated in many traditional ceremonies. She visited Laos for a second time in 1972 and lived in the south at the home of Prince Boun Oum, witnessing the last days of a society which was still feudal. In this lively and anecdotal account, the author brings to life a Laos now vanished, illustrated with her sketches and portraits.

32 **Quand les Français découvraient l'Indochine.** (When the French discovered Indochina.)
Charles Daney. Paris: Herscher, 1981. 175p. (Les Archives de la Société de Géographie).
A selection of historical photographs on Indo-China grouped under four themes: discovery and conquest, traditional life revealed, travel by land and water, and daily life. Daney has provided an introduction to each section and Georges Buis has provided a preface and postscript. There are brief notes on the twenty-six photographers whose work is published here.

33 **Voyage d'exploration en Indochine.** (Journey of exploration in Indochina.)
Francis Garnier, text selected and annotated by Jean-Pierre Gomane. Paris: Editions de la Découverte, 1985. 255p. map. (La Découverte Illustrée).
An abridged version of Garnier's account of the journey up the Mekong from Saigon to Yunnan between 1866 and 1868, and the return through China and by sea from Shanghai to Saigon. Several of the chapters relate to the journey of the party through Laos and an account is included of their reception by the King at Luang Prabang. Some of the original engravings have been reproduced. The editor provides an introduction and notes, and occasional linking passages to the extracts.

34 **Un voyage au Laos.** (A journey in Laos.)
E. Lefèvre. Paris: Plon, 1898. 303p. map.
Notes of his travels in Laos, both generally and when he was a member of the Commission that travelled to Muong Sing to adjudicate with the English on who should administer the area, Siam (modern Thailand) or France. These notes were written during his travels, and the impressions were recorded while they were fresh in his mind. They are intended to be both a practical guide for travellers and entertainment for the armchair traveller. There are some notes of ethnographic interest and some contemporary photographs of the people and country.

35 **A propos du 'Journal de voyage au Laos' de G. van Wuysthoff et de ses assistants.** (Concerning the travel log of G. van Wuysthoff and of his assistants.)
Paul Levy, Jacques Népote. *Péninsule*, no.13 (1986), p. 3-92. maps.
Paul Levy had conducted considerable research on the expedition of G. van Wuysthoff, and publishes it here to coincide with the publication of Jean-Claude Lejosne's translation, *Le journal de voyage de G. van Wuysthoff et de ses assistants au*

Laos (1641-1642) (q.v.). Jacques Népote provides the historical and geographical context. Professor Levy looks at three aspects of this text: the exact route of the journey and precise identification of the places mentioned; the ethnographic details; and identification of the original of the vernacular terms mentioned and their meaning. The study concludes with twenty-six maps of the Mekong made in 1941-42 by the boundary commission determining the frontier between Laos and Thailand. They are tracings of the first half of the Vientiane reaches, which have never been published and remain in manuscript. The origins of the maps and the ground they cover is described in the section 'Cartographie du Mekong', p. 90-92. This article is an important adjunct to Lejosne's translation, the maps making it a unique publication.

36 **A dragon apparent: travels in Cambodia, Laos and Vietnam.**
Norman Lewis. London: Cape, 1951. Reprinted, London: Eland
Books, 1982. 317p. map.

Describes a journey made in 1950 through Indo-China during the first Indo-Chinese war, when the French were fighting to regain control (at a time when, as the author says in the preface to the reprint edition, traditional ways were being challenged by new forms of entertainment such as the cinema, and when the microphone relayed the music of festivals). Lewis' journey in Laos took him by road from Vientiane to Luang Prabang by way of Lao and Hmong villages. He offers an impression of both French and Lao life in villages and cities, as well as his brief skirmish with the fringe of the insurgency. It is a sympathetic outsider's impression that captures this brief period in the history of Laos.

37 **Henri Mouhot's diary: travel in the central parts of Siam, Cambodia and Laos during the years 1858-61.**
Abridged and edited by Christopher Pym. Kuala Lumpur: Oxford
University Press, 1966. 160p. maps. bibliog. (Oxford in Asia Historical
Reprints).

Mouhot's expedition into Laos was his fourth and, as he died there of fever, also his last. This account is based on his diary, which was rescued and published posthumously. This new abridged edition is the first to be published in a hundred years. Mouhot was a naturalist and the account of his journey is filled with remarks on plant and animal life. His first attempt to reach Laos from Thailand was a failure, but returning with letters of introduction, he journeyed to Luang Prabang overland as the river route was considered too dangerous. He describes Luang Prabang, its population and his audience with the first and second kings. This edition is useful for the information on Mouhot which Pym provides. The full text was published as *Travels in the central parts of Indochina (Siam), Cambodia and Laos during the years 1858-1859 and 1860*, in two volumes by John Murray in 1864. It was the first travel account of Laos in modern times. The French edition of 1868, which was published after the English edition, has just been reissued as *Voyage dans les royaumes de Siam de Cambodge et Laos et autres parties centrales de l'Indo-Chine: relation extraite du journal et de la correspondance de l'auteur* (Travels in Siam, Cambodia and Laos and other central parts of Indo-China: account taken from the diary and correspondence of the author), and is edited by Ferdinand de Lanoye (Geneva: Olizane, 1989. 319p. map. [Collection Objectif Terre]). There is a brief preface by Olivier Page.

38 **Indochine: Laos, Cambodge, Viet-Nam.** (Indo-China: Laos, Caml
Viet-Nam.)
Jacques Népote.   Geneva: Olizane, 1990. 396p. maps. bibliog. (L
Guides Artou).
A guidebook which provides a brief historical and cultural background for the
time visitor. Practical information is gathered in the last section. As a ge
geographical introduction, particularly for the traveller on an organized visit, it w
be useful, but the guide by Blanchard (*Cambodge Laos Vietnam* [q.v.]) has n
practical information.

39 **River road to China: the Mekong expedition, 1866-1873.**
Milton Osborne.   London: Allen & Unwin, 1975. 249p. maps. bibliog..
The expedition, which is the subject of this book, travelled the route of the Mekong
river seeking a navigable route into south-western China. The route of the river was
not known to westerners and previous travellers had not ventured much above
Vientiane. The book is a continuous narrative with long extracts translated from the
accounts of the explorers. The author has made use of the French archives as well as
the published accounts to prepare this work. It is useful in that unlike the French
writers who favoured individual participants, he can take the detached view of an
outsider, distanced by time and nationality. The travels through Laos form a relatively
small though important part of the journey. This book forms a helpful preliminary for
those who wish to read the accounts that the French participants wrote, to which he
provides the references.

40 **Pages laotiennes: le Haut-Laos, le Moyen-Laos, le Bas-Laos.** (Laotian
pages: Upper-Laos, Central-Laos, Lower-Laos.)
A. Raquez.   Hanoi: Schneider, 1902. 537p. map.
The travel diary of Raquez, who was invited to travel through Laos by Colonel
Tournier, *Résident Supérieur* (chief colonial officer) of Laos. Raquez travelled
throughout Laos and gives a vivid picture of what he saw in the early days of the
French protectorate, illustrating the text with innumerable small photographs. He gives
detailed descriptions of the customs and dress of the various ethnic groups that he
encountered, as well as descriptions of the Lao and their way of life. He includes texts
of customary laws, p. 401-448. He refers to the recent history of the country as
appropriate. The book is published in the form of a diary, but the indexes and detailed
table of contents enable the reader to find particular topics. Raquez contributed
several articles on Laos to the *Revue Indochinoise* (q.v.) from 1902-04.

41 **Vientiane guide 1991.**
Compiled and edited by the Women's International Group.   Vientiane:
WIG, 1990. 66p. maps.
Compiled by the Women's International Group, current residents of Vientiane, this is
a collection of useful information for the resident and visitor. It provides brief
background information on Laos, but most is devoted to information essential for the
expatriate family such as health care, education, equipment to bring, shopping and
services, and leisure facilities. On many of the facing unnumbered pages are
advertisements for Lao businesses from trading companies and exporters, hotels and
guest houses, to cake shops and hairdressers. The guide concludes with a series of
street maps of Vientiane with an index of street names.

42   **Le journal de voyage de G. van Wuysthoff et de ses assistants au Laos (1641-1642).** (The travel journal or log of G. van Wuysthoff and his assistants in Laos, 1641-1642.)
Translation and commentary by Jean-Claude Lejosne.   Metz, France: Editions du Centre de Documentation du Cercle et de Recherches Laotiennes, 1987. 370p. maps. bibliog.

Gerrit van Wuysthoff, an official of the Dutch East India Company (VOC), is thought to be the first European to travel to Laos. There are references to attempts by others to visit Laos in the previous hundred years. His account and those of his two assistants, who accompanied him, are here translated in full into modern French for the first time. In addition, the translator has set the work into context with notes on the Dutch East India Company and on the trade goods, weights and measures. He also discusses the manuscript and previous published editions. There is a detailed index of the journal. Van Wuysthoff's interest was of course to open up trade for the Dutch East India Company, but his account contains useful observations on Laos and is valuable to the historian as a record which can be dated with certainty. He gives a detailed account of the ceremonial at the court of King Surya Vongsa in Vientiane, the gifts and trade goods exchanged, and a summary of conditions in Laos. Previous commentators have made much of his observations on the licentiousness of the Lao, but this in fact forms a small part of his observations and it was not directed at the court. His main preoccupations are with the possibility of conducting trade with the Lao, their trustworthiness and their ability to offer suitable trade goods. An English translation of an earlier summary of this work is published as Appendix K in *A narrative of the mission to the court of Ava in 1855*, compiled by Henry Yule (reprinted Kuala Lumpur; Oxford: Oxford University Press, 1968, p. 374-77).

Mission Pavie, Indochine 1879-1895. (The Pavie mission, 1879-1895.) *See* item no. 12.

Geography and Geology

General

43 **Les gisements miniers au Laos.** (Mineral deposits in Laos.)
Auguste Bernard. *Péninsule*, no. 20 (1990), p. 1-98. map.
A study of the tradition of mining in Laos, which suggests that there may be economically viable mineral resources to be exploited there. The first part of the study is on mines and metallurgy in Laos based on a study of earlier accounts, the second part is a statement of the currently known mineral deposits. The metals found in Laos range from gold, silver and tin to lead, iron and antimony; there are also deposits of coal, gypsum and precious stones. Bernard worked in Laos and studied the official reports, but more precise references to his sources would have been welcome.

44 **Le climat de l'Indochine et les typhons de la mer de Chine.** (The climate of Indo-China and the typhoons of the China Sea.)
E. Bruzon, P. Carton. Hanoi: Imprimerie d'Extrême-Orient, 1929. 151p. maps.
After a geographical overview of Indo-China, the authors cover temperatures, atmospheric pressures, winds, monsoons, rain, humidity, clouds and atmospheric disturbances. These are supported by an extensive range of maps and tables of observations from meteorological stations. Laos is treated within the whole work. The second half of the book deals with typhoons.

45 **Indo-China: a geographical appreciation.**
Canada: Department of Mines and Technical Surveys, Geographical
Branch. Ottawa: The Author, 1953. 88p. maps. bibliog. (Foreign
Geography Information Series, no. 6).
A useful geographical summary in English of the states of former French Indo-China.
It is easy to find specific types of information because of the divisions and sub-divisions
of the chapters. The statistical material is all pre-1950. The presentation is of a text-
book type.

46 **Review of the geology and mineral resources of Kampuchea, Laos and
Vietnam.**
H. Fontaine, D. R. Workman. In: *Geology and mineral resources of
Southeast Asia: proceedings of the third regional conference on geological
and mineral resources of Southeast Asia, Bangkok, November 14-18
1978.* Edited by Prinya Nutalaya. Bangkok: Asian Institute of
Technology, distributed by Wiley, 1979, p. 539-603. maps. bibliog.
The most comprehensive bibliography and most recent summary of the geology and
mineral resources of Laos.

47 **Geological evolution of South-east Asia.**
Charles S. Hutchison. Oxford: Clarendon Press, 1989. 368p. maps.
bibliog. (Oxford Monographs on Geology and Geophysics; no. 13).
This is a study of the effect of plate tectonics on the formation of the region. Hutchison
states, 'South-east Asia provides the world's most outstanding geological laboratory for
the study and understanding of active plate tectonics', and 'the region is also of interest
in providing evidence of relationships between tectonic evolution and economic
deposits'. Of Laos however, he comments that little new work had been possible and
that little is known still of the geology of the country. Hutchison's work is based on
published research and so the lack of research on Laos influences his coverage of the
country.

48 **Carte géologique Viet Nam – Cambodge – Laos. 1:500,000.** (Geological
map of Vietnam, Cambodia, Laos. 1:500,000.)
Dalat, Vietnam: Service Géographique National du Viet Nam, 1961-63.
24 sheets.
A set of geological maps with memoirs, here called *Notices*. The maps and accounts
are the work of E. Saurin and others of the Service Géologique de l'Indochine, first
published in 1939. The *Notices* (Memoirs), which comprise sixteen volumes, give an
explanation of the research and the maps, which have had information added from
geological research that has taken place since the 1930s. Four of the original volumes
were not republished. Five of those seen are relevant to Laos: vol. 4, Luang Prabang;
vol. 7, Vientiane; vol. 11, Hue; vol. 14, Khong; and vol. 16, Pak Nam; and each is
linked to one or more of the sheet maps. Only an 'almost complete set' of this
publication has been seen, and it is not clear if the publication of the whole work was

finished. Most of the material on Laos is available. These memoirs provide the best summary of research on the fossil remains from each layer of Laos. Research which is about to be started again in a joint Franco-Lao project.

49 **Indo-China.**
Edited by J. C. Stuttard. London: Naval Intelligence Division, 1943.
535p. maps. bibliog. (Geographical Handbook Series; B. R. 510).
Originally produced for official purposes during the Second World War, this series of books was later released from its 'restricted' classification. It is a compendium based on published sources, largely those of the French colonial authorities. It covers geology and physical features, coasts, climate, vegetation, fauna, medical services and health conditions, the people, history, government, administration, law, agriculture, forestry, fisheries, industry, labour, commerce, finance, ports, railways, roads and waterways. There are a number of useful appendices which include statistics, place-names, maps, and information on principal towns and cities, particularly ports. The information in this work is now dated, but it has not been superseded in this form. It provides an easy introduction to older sources, which were largely written in French, for any in-depth investigation of these matters.

50 **Geology of Laos, Cambodia, South Vietnam and the eastern part of Thailand.**
D. R. Workman. London: HMSO, 1977. 33p. maps. bibliog.
(Overseas Geology and Mineral Resources, no. 50).
A summary of the geology of the Lower Mekong Basin, providing a description of the stratigraphy based largely on the publications of the former Service Géologique de l'Indochine.

51 **Mineral resources of the Lower Mekong Basin and adjacent areas of Khmer Republic, Laos, Thailand and Republic of Viet-Nam.**
D. R. Workman. New York; Bangkok: United Nations, Economic Commission for Asia and the Far East, 1972. 148p. maps. bibliog.
The work is divided into a series of chapters on metallic ore minerals, fuel and industrial minerals; they are subdivided into sections on each of the countries of the region. This is a comprehensive survey from the literature of known mineral deposits and their exploitation in the region. Maps identify the sites of known significant deposits of each mineral. At this date Laos was planning, with foreign economic assistance, to train more staff to investigate the mineral resources of the region; this is now beginning to be implemented. A briefer survey of the earlier position is given in *Mining developments in Asia and the Far East: a twenty-year (1945-1965) review to commemorate the twentieth anniversary of ECAFE* (New York: United Nations, ECAFE, 1967. 136p. [Mineral Resources Development Series; no. 27]).

Atlases

52 **Atlas of physical economic and social resources of the Lower Mekong Basin.**
Prepared by the Engineer Agency for Resources Inventories and the Tennessee Valley Authority for the Committee for Coordination of Investigations of the Lower Mekong Basin. Bangkok: United Nations, ECAFE, 1968. 257 leaves.
A bilingual English-French work, the maps and the accompanying material are based on data furnished by the government agencies of the four Mekong Basin countries (Thailand, Laos, Cambodia and the Republic of South Vietnam) and other national and international organizations. The maps are grouped under major topics with appropriate subdivisions, thus under the topic 'Physical resources' there are sections on physiography, climatology and geology. The other headings are 'Human resources', which includes population, ethnography, education and health; 'The social and economic infrastructure', which includes urban development, industries, fisheries and tourism; 'Transportation and communication'; 'Developmental activities'; and 'Mapping'. The text provides statistics and factual details related to the material illustrated in the maps.

53 **Atlas of South-East Asia.**
Introduction by D. G. E. Hall. London: Macmillan; New York: St. Martin's Press, 1964. [94p.]
As a regional atlas this has to some extent been replaced recently by Ulack and Pauer's *Atlas of Southeast Asia* (q.v.). However some of the maps in this work are more detailed, and although spellings of place-names may have changed and most cities are considerably larger now, it is still useful. There is a series of topical maps for the region on climate and vegetation, which includes rainfall, population, minerals and communications. Each country or region is the subject of a series of detailed maps: Laos is included in the series on Indochina, where there are maps on climate and vegetation, agriculture, population, minerals, industries and communications. The political and physical map is of Thailand and Indo-China. There are eight historical maps of the region on the endpapers. There is a short introduction to the region as a whole, illustrated with a range of evocative and now historical photographs.

54 **Atlas de la ville de Louang Prabang.** (Atlas of the town of Luang Prabang.)
Luc Mogenet. Vientiane: Vithagna, 1973. 111p. bibliog. (Collection: Documents pour le Laos, no. 3).
There is a general introduction in words and photographs to the town of Luang Prabang. The plates are a mixture of maps, sketches, and statistical exercises on aspects of the town and the surrounding area. There are twenty detailed plans (scale 1:2500) of the districts of the town, giving place-names and administrative boundaries. This is followed by material on places of worship, administration, lighting, water, transport, demography and migration, education and housing. Housing is covered by eight sketches of various types of house, both traditional and modern, for four socio-economic groupings. The page numbering is rather deceptive, as for most of the work only every other page is printed.

55 **Itinéraires automobiles en Indochine: guide du touriste. v. 3. Annam, Laos.** (Itineraries for motorists in Indochina: tourist guide. v. 3 Annam and Laos.)
Georges Norès. Hanoi: Imprimerie d'Extrême-Orient, 1930. 144p. maps.

Designed to help the motorist plan his journey. There is an introductory section on what you need to know about Laos. This is followed by a description of each itinerary in words, indicating the features along the routes and brief information about the towns. There is all the necessary information on road conditions and the tariffs charged at ferries. Parallel to this description, there is a series of maps for each itinerary. Five of the routes are through Laos, some of them routes which link Laos with Vietnam. There is also a series of town plans, five of which are towns in Laos: Pak-sé, Savannakhet, Thakhek, Vientiane and Xieng Khouang. There is a final map of the whole area, indicating the overall arrangement of the routes described.

56 **Frontiers of Asia and Southeast Asia.**
J. R. V. Prescott, H. J. Collier, D. F. Prescott. Melbourne, Australia: Melbourne University Press, 1977. 105p. maps.

An atlas of land and maritime boundaries of Asia and South East Asia from colonial times to the present day. Three of the sections relate to Laos, referring to her boundaries with Thailand, Cambodia, Vietnam and China. There is one page of description facing the relevant map.

57 **Atlas of Southeast Asia.**
Richard Ulack, Gyula Pauer. New York: Macmillan; London: Collier Macmillan, 1989. 171p. bibliog.

The first comprehensive atlas of the region to be published since Hall's *Atlas of South-East Asia* (q.v.). The aim is to provide detailed and current maps and information, but the compilers admit that for Laos some of their information may reflect the situation before 1975 and the map of Vientiane may not be absolutely up to date. The work begins with a regional overview, and the same topics are taken up again in an entry for each of the nations of the region. The national section needs to be read in conjunction with the regional overview, where statistical comparisons for the region are made. The subjects covered are basic statistical and factual information for each country, historical overview and background, the physical environment, the economy, transport, population and culture. There is a map of Laos and Vientiane, and topical maps illustrating subjects such as economic activities or the geopolitical situation in the early 1970s as well as regional maps. There are several photographs included but not many of them deal with Laos, although they convey the general atmosphere of Southeast Asia. The entry for Laos is weaker than those for some of the other countries, but given the difficulty of obtaining current information it is understandable. The compilers admit there may be some superficial North American bias, as they presume that the atlas will be used primarily by Americans, and so for example non-metric measurements are preferred, but metric equivalents are usually provided.

Flora and Fauna

58   **Bulletin de la Société Royale des Sciences Naturelles du Laos.** (Bulletin of the Royal Society of Natural Sciences of Laos.)
Vientiane: Royal Society of Natural Sciences of Laos 1961-64. nos. 1-15.

Articles on the flora and fauna of Laos, and to a lesser extent on physical anthropology and geology. Some subjects are pursued by their authors in a series of articles distributed over a number of issues. Occasionally an important article is reprinted, for example, C. Spire 'Plantes médicinales du Laos' (Medicinal plants of Laos), no. 15 (1964), p. 48-61, was originally published in 1907.

59   **A dictionary of the economic products of the Malay Peninsula.**
I. H. Burkhill.   Kuala Lumpur: Ministry of Agriculture and Co-operatives, 1966. 2 vols. bibliog.

This is a reprint of the edition first published in 1935 by the Crown Agents for the Governments of the Straits Settlements and the Federated Malay States. Despite the use of the term Malay Peninsula in the title, this work is relevant to the whole of South East Asia. It is an alphabetically arranged dictionary of brief encyclopaedia-style entries, organized under the scientific names of flora, fauna and minerals capable of economic exploitation. Each entry consists of a brief description in a sentence or two of the item, bibliographical references if available, other forms of name, and an indication of the geographic spread of the plant, animal or mineral. Burkhill then describes what it produces and what it is used for. There are marginal notes to highlight uses such as medicinal or food. The length of entries may vary and, for example, the entry on *Laccifer*, the insect which produces stick-lac, used as a dye or resin, runs into two pages. Stick-lac is a product which has been traded from Laos since the earliest times. There is an index to lead the reader from common or local names to the form used in the entry.

60 **Riches of the wild: land mammals of South-East Asia.**
Earl of Cranbrook. Singapore: Oxford University Press, 1987. 95p.
maps, bibliog. (Images of Asia).

Based on three decades of the author's personal involvement with the study of
mammals, it is 'the first in mammology devoted to South-East Asia', written in non-
specialist language for the general reader, and aimed at all naturalists. The first chapter
introduces the environment of South East Asia, which has 'favoured the evolution of
an exceptionally rich fauna of some 660 species'. In the following chapter the mammals
are discussed group by group. It is illustrated with photographs and fine colour plates
by Commander A. M. Hughes. A checklist of the mammals gives the English and
scientific names and their geographic distribution. Pocket-sized, this would be useful
for the tourist. A study of Lao mammals in French is Jean Deuve *Les mammifères du
Laos* (The mammals of Laos) (Vientiane: Ministère d'Education Nationale, 1972.
196p.).

61 **Fish and fish dishes of Laos.**
Alan Davidson. Rutland, Vermont: Tuttle, 1975. 2nd rev. ed. 206p.
bibliog.

An account of the freshwater fish of Laos is given in the first part of the book. Each
entry gives the Lao, English and taxonomic name of each fish with a detailed drawing
to enable it to be recognized. There are notes on size, colour and other features. Each
entry has a paragraph on the special characteristics of the fish and its distribution in
South East Asia, with notes on its qualities for eating and the dishes in which it can be
used. The second part of the book contains full and detailed recipes of the principal
fish dishes of Laos and useful hints on the other ingredients needed.

62 **Serpents du Laos.** (Snakes of Laos.)
J. Deuve. Paris: ORSTOM, 1970. 251p. maps. bibliog. (Mémoires de
l'ORSTOM; no. 39).

A description of ninety-six species of snake found in Laos and frequently in the
neighbouring countries. The first part of the book deals with general aspects of snakes,
vernacular names, and the topic of poisonous snakes and their poisons. The second
part deals with snakes by species. The author's bibliography refers to the period 1937-
70, with a few earlier works. For an earlier survey of published work see, R. Bourret
Les serpents de l'Indochine (The snakes of Indo-China) (Toulouse, France: Henri
Basuyeau, 1936).

63 **Flore du Cambodge, du Laos et du Vietnam.** (Flora of Cambodia, Laos
and Vietnam.)
Paris: Museum National d'Histoire Naturelle, 1960- . maps.

Of this work in progress, twenty-five fascicules have already been published, and it is
estimated that this represents about twenty per cent of the work needed to complete it.
It is based on articles which examine a particular class of plant, illustrated with plates
and maps. It is based largely on the collections of the Herbarium of the Phanerogamy
Laboratory of the Natural History Museum, Paris. It continues the work of the *Flore
générale de l'Indochine* (General flora of Indo-China) (Paris: Masson, 1907-51. 9 vols.).
The revision was necessitated by the acquisition of new collections of plant material
and the need for a greater conformity to international norms.

Flora and Fauna

64 **Vegetables in South-East Asia.**
G. A. C. Herklots. London: George Allen & Unwin, 1972. 525p. bibliog.

The first part of the book is devoted to the broad topic of vegetable cultivation, including considerations of climate, pests and weeds. The second part is a detailed description of vegetables grouped in broad classes, arranged under their common English-language name. Each entry provides the scientific name and one or more vernacular names. It normally includes details on the area of origin, a description, information on cultivation and occasionally notes. Line drawings are provided for many specimens. There is an index of both scientific and popular English names.

65 **Plants from the markets of Thailand: descriptions and uses of 241 wild and cultivated plants, with 341 colour photographs.**
Christiane Jacquat. Bangkok: Editions Duang Kamol, 1990. 251p. map. bibliog.

While caution must be exercised in extrapolating from the Thai experience to the Lao, this is a useful reference source for information in English on material traced in Lao sources. The colour illustrations of the plants and the way they are used and decorated are excellent. The material is arranged by species, and gives both botanical and local names, a short description of the plant and its uses, and sometimes recipes. There is also an index of scientific and Thai names in romanization.

66 **A field guide to the birds of South-East Asia: covering Burma, Malaya, Thailand, Cambodia, Vietnam, Laos and Hong Kong.**
Ben F. King, Edward C. Dickinson. London: Collins, 1975. 480p. maps. bibliog.

Covering all 1,198 species known to have occurred in the region, the main body of the text is devoted to the description of each species grouped according to the bird family to which it belongs. Most entries are concerned with physical description but may include details on a bird's call, its range, its distribution and its habitat. The book lacks a distribution index, but the authors planned to publish it elsewhere. Black and white drawings and coloured plates assist the task of identification. There is an index of scientific and popular names.

67 **Nature and life in Southeast Asia.**
Edited by Tatuo Kira, Tadao Umesao. Kyoto, Japan: Fauna and Flora Research Society, 1961-67. 5 vols.

The reports of Japanese field trips to South East Asia are contained in this series. Thailand was the main area of concern to the groups, but some of the material is of wider application.

68 **Coléoptères scarabéides de l'Indochine.** (Scarabeid beetles of Indo-China.)

Renaud Paulian. Paris: Larose, 1945. 228p. map. bibliog. (Faune de l'Empire Française, no. 3).

Scarabeid beetles found in Indo-China are analysed in family groups and arranged by subspecies. There are bibliographical references attached to each entry, with more general studies collected in a bibliography at the end. The species are illustrated and geographical distribution is indicated at the end of each entry.

69 **Medicinal plants of East and Southeast Asia: attributed properties and uses.**

Compiled by Lily M. Perry, with the assistance of Judith Metzger.

Cambridge, Massachusetts: MIT Press, 1980. 620p. bibliog.

The main sequence of this listing is by family of plants, arranged in alphabetical order, subdivided by the members of that family. The entry describes its officinal (medical) uses and gives the bibliographical reference to the source for this statement. The use in different parts of East and South East Asia is found within the entry. There are indexes to the therapeutic properties ascribed to the plants, an index to various disorders and an index of scientific names. This is a useful English-language complement to A. Pételot, *Les plantes médicinales du Cambodge, du Laos et du Viêtnam* (q.v.).

70 **Les plantes médicinales du Cambodge, du Laos et du Viêtnam.**

(Medicinal plants of Cambodia, Laos and Vietnam.)

Alfred Pételot. Saigon, Vietnam: Centre de Recherches Scientifiques et Techniques, 1952-54. 4 vols. (Archives des Recherches Agronomiques au Cambodge, au Laos, et au Viêtnam, nos. 14, 18, 22-23).

The first three volumes list the medicinal plants according to their botanical family, and the fourth volume acts as an index to the whole work giving lists according to therapeutic properties, botanical, common, vernacular and Chinese names of the plants. Each entry provides scientific, popular and Chinese names for the plants, a botanical description and the medicinal properties and usage. Pételot refers to the previous major works for the region in this field. He notes in his preface that the climate of the mountain areas of Laos and North Vietnam is similar to that of southern China, and that in more peaceful times the Chinese had come to restock with supplies of medicinal products.

71 **Phytonomie et taxinomie botanique lao.** (Plant names and Lao botanic taxonomy.)

Richard Pottier. *Asie du Sud-Est et Monde Insulindien: Bulletin du Centre de Documentation et de Recherche (CeDRASEMI)* (South East Asia and the Island World: Bulletin of the Centre for Documentation and Research [CeDRASEMI]) vol. 7, no. 1 (1976), p. 21-29.

An explanation of the derivation of plant names in Lao. Pottier is at pains to explain that unless the structure is understood, a literal translation can give a false impression. Names are brief and include a classificatory element, but Lao taxonomy differs considerably from scientific taxonomy.

Flora and Fauna

72　**Common snakes of South East Asia and Hong Kong.**
　　Frank F. Reitinger, Jerry K. S. Lee.　Hong Kong: Heinemann, 1978.
　　114p. bibliog.
There is a general introduction to snakes followed by the entries for snakes listed under their common English-language name. Each entry by snake contains its scientific name, size, description, colour, habitat, food, breeding, distribution, field identification and habits. There is an index of the names of snakes, both common and scientific. The regional distribution is indicated on a chart at the end of the book; more than half are found in Laos. A good selection of line drawings and coloured plates help with the identification of particular snakes.

73　**A garden of eden: plant life in South-East Asia.**
　　W. Veevers-Carter.　Singapore: Oxford University Press, 1986. 59p.
　　bibliog. (Images of Asia).
In this book for the traveller or general reader, Veevers-Carter surveys different types of plants in each chapter. Relevant chapters are those on the trees of the monsoon forest, timber trees, medicinal spices, the sacred lotus and the temple trees, the grasses, and the palms. The information provided is brief, but there are excellent figures and sixteen coloured plates to amplify the text.

74　**Bibliographie botanique indochinoise de 1955 à 1969.** (Indochinese
　　botanical bibliography, 1955-69.)
　　Jules Vidal.　*Bulletin de la Société des Études Indochinoises*, n.s. 47,
　　no. 4 (1972), p. 655-748.
This bibliography continues A. Pételot's *Bibliographie botanique de l'Indochine* (Indochinese botanical bibliography) (1958). It is an alphabetical index of authors and titles, with a subject and taxonomic index of over one thousand entries. A supplement for the years 1970 to 1985 has also been published, *Bibliographie botanique indochinoise de 1970 à 1985* (Indochinese botanical bibliography, 1970 to 1985) by J. E. Vidal, Y. Vidal and Pham Hoang Ho (Paris: Museum National d'Histoire Naturelle, Laboratoire de Phanérogamie, 1988. 132p.).

75　**Contribution à l'ethnobotanique des Hmong du Laos.** (Contribution to
　　the ethnobotany of the Hmong of Laos.)
　　Jules Vidal, Jacques Lemoine.　*Journal d'Agriculture Tropicale et de*
　　Botanique Appliquée, vol. 17, nos. 1-4 (1970), p. 1-59. map. bibliog.
In the first section there is a discussion of the Hmong and plants and their use. There follows an alphabetic list of plants according to their Hmong name, with the scientific name and a brief remark on use and any bibliographic references. There are indexes according to family of plants, scientific names, popular names and uses.

76 **Noms vernaculaires de plantes (Lao, Mèo, Kha) en usage au Laos.**
(Vernacular names for plants (Lao, Hmong, Lao Theung) used in Laos.)
Jules Vidal. *Bulletin de l'Ecole Française d'Extrême-Orient*, vol. 49
no. 2 (1959), p. 435-608. map. bibliog.

Plants play an important part in the life of the peoples of Laos; they are used for food, medicines, manufactures and religious ceremonies. Vidal has compiled a list in Lao, both romanized and in Lao script of names used for plants, with the scientific name. An indication is given of the region in Laos where the term was collected. There is a second list of the scientific names and the Lao equivalents. There are photographic illustrations of a small selection of the plants.

77 **La vegetation du Laos.** (Vegetation of Laos.)
Jules Vidal. Toulouse, France: Douladoure, 1956-60. 2 vols. (Travaux du Laboratoire Forestière de Toulouse. Vol. 5, Géographie Forestière du Monde. Section 1, Asia; vol. 1, East Asia, no. 1).

In volume one Vidal provides a study of the physical environment of Laos, giving a summary of the geographical and geological features and soils. This is followed by a survey of climatic conditions, which lead to the author's conclusions about the probable ecological outcome for Laos. In volume two Vidal discusses the vegetation in the various regions of Laos. Volume one was republished in Laos under the same title in 1972 (Vientiane: Vithagna [Documents pour le Laos, no. 1]).

Prehistory and Archaeology

78 **La naissance du monde selon les traditions lao: le mythe du Khun Bulom.**
(The birth of the world according to Lao traditions: the myth of Khun
Borom.)
Charles Archaimbault.   In: *La naissance du monde: Égypte ancienne,
Sumer, Akkad, Hourrites et Hittites, Canaan, Israel, Turcs et Mongols,
Iran préislamique, Inde, Siam, Laos, Tibet, Chine.* (The birth of the
world: ancient Egypt, Sumer, Akkad, Hurrians and Hittites, Canaan,
Israel, Turks and Mongols, Pre-islamic Iran, India, Siam, Laos, Tibet,
China).   Paris: Éditions du Seuil, 1959, p. 383-416. map. bibliog. (Les
Sources Orientales, no. 1).

Archaimbault introduces the myths of the origin of the world in Laos and provides
translations of significant extracts from them. He covers the versions in the annals, in
the *nithan*, a poetic literary form, and the oral tradition. He discusses the Luang
Prabang tradition and makes a comparison among the traditions.

79 **The Pa Mong archaeological survey programmes, 1973-1975.**
Donn Bayard.   Otago, New Zealand: Department of Anthropology,
University of Otago, 1980. 175p. maps. bibliog. (University of Otago
Studies in Prehistoric Anthropology, vol. 13).

In advance of the Pa Mong Project, the plan to build a dam at Pa Mong across the
Mekong River, archaeological research was done in the areas of Laos and Thailand
which would be flooded after the construction of such a dam. Bayard presents the full
final report of the research. Twenty-seven sites were surveyed in Laos of varied
historical periods, and a full archaeological summary is given. Many of the finds were
taken to New Zealand for later analysis. A brief review of the implications of the
Mekong Project for archaeology is given in *Archaeology and the Mekong Project*
(Bangkok: Secretariat of the Committee for the Co-ordination of Investigations of the
Lower Mekong Basin, 1973. 10p. maps).

80 **Man's conquest of the Pacific: the prehistory of Southeast Asia and Oceania.**
Peter Bellwood. Auckland, New Zealand: Collins, 1978. 462p. maps. bibliog.

There is a great lack of material on Laotian prehistory because there have been few archaeological excavations in the country. This book covers the work that has been done; its value is that it sets this in the regional context of work on South East Asia, and brings together a synthesis of the research on the region. There are useful illustrations and photographs to complement the text.

81 **Mégalithes du Haut-Laos, Hua Pan, Tran Ninh.** (Megaliths of Upper Laos, Hua Pan and Tran Ninh.)
Madeleine Colani. Paris: Editions d'Art et d'Histoire, 1935. 2 vols. (Publications de l'École Française d'Extrême-Orient, no. 25-26).

This is the fundamental and authoritative work on the megalithic remains in Upper Laos in the area known as the 'Plain of Jars'. The work is based on three expeditions made between 1931 and 1933 and describes the finding of the menhirs of Hua Pan (or Houa Phan) and the jars of Tran Ninh (or the Plain of Jars). The work is lavishly illustrated with photographs and drawings which illustrate Colani's findings. It was summarized in English in Erik Seidenfaden's article 'The peoples of the Menhirs and the Jars', *Journal of the Thailand Research Society*, vol. 34, no. 1 (1943), p. 49-58. Colani updated this research in 'Nouvelles jarres au Tran-ninh site de Song Meng' (New jars in Tran-ninh, the site of Song Meng), *Bulletin de l'École Francaise d'Extrême-Orient*, vol. 40, no. 2 (1940), p. 495-96. She reports on new finds of monolithic jars at three sites; many have lids decorated with animals.

82 **Recherches sur le préhistorique indochinois.** (Research on Indochinese prehistory.)
Madeleine Colani. *Bulletin de l'École Française d'Extrême-Orient*, vol. 30, nos. 3-4 (1930), p. 299-422. maps. bibliog.

A survey of the research into the prehistory of Indo-China to 1930. Divided onto three sections, it provides an overall view of recent discoveries, an account of recent research and a discussion of the principal finds. Although the bulk of this research had taken place in modern Vietnam, there are brief references to Laos. Its relevance lies in the discussions of Hoa Binh and Bac Son whose cultures have contributed the terms Hoabinhian and Bacsonian to descriptions of prehistoric cultures of this region.

83 **La culture lao et ses origines: des faits nouveaux.** (Lao culture and its origins: some new facts.)
Pierre-Marie Gagneux. *Asie du Sud-Est et Monde Insulindien: Bulletin du Centre de Documentation et de Recherche (CeDRASEMI)* (South East Asia and the Island World: Bulletin of the Centre for Documentation and Research [CeDRASEMI]), vol. 9, nos. 1-2 (1978), p. 179-189. bibliog.

Gagneux proposes a hypothesis, based on the new archaeological evidence, that contradicts previous views of the history of Laos from the sixth to the eleventh century. He suggests that this area was a zone of Mon high culture, broken into a number of Buddhist kingdoms, of which Dvâravatî would have been the most powerful; further, that the Tai invaders of the twelfth and thirteenth centuries, far from destroying the local culture, assimilated it, only imposing their own language and a number of political innovations but leaving the Mon religious, social and economic substratum untouched. Gagneux suggests a number of areas of study which could confirm or disprove his hypothesis.

84 **Les sites anciens de la plaine de Vientiane: VIIe-XIe siècles.** (Ancient sites of the Vientiane Plain: 7th-11th centuries.)
Pierre-Marie Gagneux. *Péninsule*, nos. 11-12 (1985-86), p. 27-111.

A report of the archaeological research conducted by the author since 1974, in collaboration with the Historical Monuments Service of Laos. It is a French translation of the report presented in 1975 to the Lao. It sets out to record the recent archaeological discoveries in the Vientiane Plain and to suggest future areas of research. This research he suggests should provoke a total re-evaluation of the history of Laos before the thirteenth century. There is a list of sites identified as likely to be of interest. Gagneux suggests some possible conclusions on this period of art and history. Three appendices give an inventory of statuary finds that have been identified, a collection of sketches of the principal finds, and a list grouped by district (*Muong*) of the sites and finds. A geographical index in Lao script and a bibliography complete the report.

85 **Indochina.**
Bernard Philippe Groslier. London: Barrie & Jenkins, 1970. 283p. maps. bibliog. (Ancient Civilizations).

A general study for the layperson of the early history of mainland South East Asia. Groslier provides a path through the scholarly evidence of archaeologists and historians. The lack of detailed archaeological work in the region makes is difficult to offer more than surmises in some cases. This is a broad survey, and for Laos it must be taken as indicative of the history of the area before the foundation of Fa Ngum's Kingdom of Lan Xang rather than a definitive account.

86 **The archaeology of mainland Southeast Asia, from 10,000 B.C. to the fall of Angkor.**
Charles Higham. Cambridge, England: Cambridge University Press, 1989. 387p. maps. bibliog. (Cambridge World Archaeology).

A broad survey of the archaeology of South East Asia. The introduction discusses the development of archaeology as a subject of study and provides information on the foundation and early work of the Ecole Française d'Extrême-Orient. The reader will find little that makes direct reference to the modern political area of Laos, as the kingdom did not come into existence until the end of the period covered here. Nonetheless there is much that is of general relevance. In the section on the uplands of Laos, Higham suggests that Colani's (q.v.) hypothesis may be correct, that the society associated with the jar burials controlled exchange routes.

87   **Histoire abrégée de l'archéologie indochinoise jusqu'à 1950.** (A brief history of Indochinese archaeology up to 1950.)
Louis Malleret.   *Asian Perspectives: a Journal of Archaeology and Prehistory of Asia and the Pacific*, vol. 12 (1969), p. 43-68. bibliog.
A brief history of archaeological research in Indo-China, with full bibliographical references to some of the published sources in which it is described. Cambodia receives the lion's share of the coverage as one would expect, but Laos figures in the section with Thailand. Malleret concludes with a brief outline of the prehistory of the region.

88   **Les recherches préhistoriques au Cambodge, Laos, et Viet Nam (1877-1966).** (Research on the prehistory of Cambodia, Laos and Vietnam, 1877-1966.)
E. Saurin.   *Asian Perspectives: a Journal of Archaeology and Prehistory of Asia and the Pacific*, vol. 12 (1969), p. 27-41. bibliog.
A survey of the largely French excavations and literature on the prehistory of the region. Most of the finds in Laos have been in Upper Laos; from the finds of Fromaget of hominid and other remains of the quaternary, traces of Hoabinhian, Mesolithic, Neolithic and Iron Age cultures have been found. This article is a brief chronological guide to the scope of the literature on the subject.

89   **Les origines du Laos.** (The origins of Laos.)
Vo Thu Tinh.   Paris: Dong Nam A, 1983. 95p. map. bibliog.
The aim of this work is to offer a synthesis of work in French, Lao, Vietnamese, Thai and English on the origins of Laos. It begins with a detailed retelling of the myths of the origin of Laos; it briefly covers the archaeological evidence, as well as the Lao annals and the evidence from neighbouring countries, which corroborate the story of the foundation of the kingdom of Laos by Fa-Ngum in 1353. A useful compilation, it was previously published in the *Bulletin des Amis du Royaume Lao* (q.v.) between 1970 and 1973.

Aspects socio-économiques du Laos médiéval. (Some socio-economic aspects of mediaeval Laos.)
See item no. 369.

History

General

90　**The indianized states of Southeast Asia.**
　　G. Coedès.　Honolulu, Hawaii: East-West Center Press, 1968. 403p.
　　maps.

A history of the region from the beginning of the Christian era to about 1500 AD. It deals with the rise and decline of several empires on the mainland, some of which extended their influence into southern and central Laos. The exact extent of this rule and its influence still awaits detailed research in Laos, but this volume provides useful indicative material. It also provides information on the culture which Fa Ngum brought from the Angkorian court to his newly-founded kingdom of Lan Xang. Coedès deals briefly with the founding of Lan Xang and refers to the historical sources in which it is recounted. This work should be read in conjunction with Coedès' *The making of South East Asia*, (q.v.).

91　**The making of South East Asia.**
　　G. Coedès.　London: Routledge & Kegan Paul, 1966. 268p. map.
　　bibliog.

Laos as a kingdom did not come into identifiable being until the fourteenth century. In this work the history of Laos from the fourteenth to the nineteenth century is covered, along with the history of the other mainland South East Asian states. In the first half of the work, which considers the earlier history of the region, some of the regions which now form part of Laos are dealt with in the sections on prehistory and early history. The value of this work is its treatment of the mainland of South East Asia as a whole in the period before the evolution of the present kingdoms, and it continues up to the period of European colonization. There are illustrations of significant architectural monuments.

92 **Encyclopedia of Asian history.**
Edited by Ainslie T. Embree, prepared under the auspices of the Asia
Society. New York: Charles Scribner's Sons; London: Collier
Macmillan, 1988. 4 vols. maps.
Written by acknowledged experts in their field, this is a highly accessible and yet
authoritative encyclopaedia. There are entries for history under several headings
including Laos, Lan Sang, Champassak, Luang Prabang and Sieng Khwang. In
addition there are biographical entries for several important figures such as Souvanna
Phouma and Souphanouvong; there are also entries for important movements such as
the Lao Issara and the Pathet Lao. Reference is made at the end of each entry to
related subjects and to the principal works on the subject. Each entry is signed. In
addition there is a considerable amount of material on South East Asia in the general
entries on education or women for example, but these are very broad in coverage and
scarcely consider Laos in a useful way.

93 **A history of South-East Asia.**
D. G. E. Hall. London: Macmillan, 1981. 4th ed. 1070p. maps.
bibliog.
The standard general history of South East Asia, this work covers the period from the
first populations in the region to the beginnings of independence for the colonized
countries. The history of Laos is so intertwined with that of its neighbours that this is a
useful source for the history of the region. It also gives the history of Laos in a concise
form.

94 **Histoire du Laos français: essai d'une étude chronologique des
principautés laotiennes.** (History of French Laos: an attempt at a
chronological study of the Laotian principalities.)
Paul Le Boulanger. Farnborough, England: Gregg International, 1969.
381p. bibliog.
A survey of Laotian history from 1353 to the establishment of French rule in 1893. Its
object was to present a coherent and uninterrupted account of the history of Laos. Le
Boulanger has been criticized for not analysing the sources he used critically and for
using only a limited number of the Lao annals. Despite its weaknesses and its
limitation to political history, this work has not yet been superseded.

95 **Histoire du Laos.** (History of Laos.)
Paul Levy. Paris: Presses Universitaires de France, 1974. 128p. maps.
bibliog. (Que Sais-je?, no. 1549).
A succint history of Laos from prehistoric times to 1973. This series is designed to meet
the need for information by the general public. Each topic is dealt with briefly but
clearly and provides a useful introduction. The author indicates clearly the
bibliographical sources necessary to pursue subjects in further detail.

96 **History of Laos: from the days of Nan-Chao right down to the present day showing how the Thai/Lao were split up into various branches . . . .**
M. L. Manich Jumsai. Bangkok: Chalermnit, 1971. 2nd ed. 325p. map. bibliog.

An interesting history of Laos because it has been written by a Thai, who has been able to use different sources and has a different perspective on the history of the region. It is based on research in Paris and Laos. It is the only history of Laos in English which offers a continuous narrative from the origins of the Lao and Thai up to about 1965. This account is rather oversimplified, and it is interesting as a reflection of the Thai perception of the region's history and evolution. A fifty-four page bibliography is appended to the main part of the book.

97 **Chronological table of the history of Laos.**
A. R. Mathieu. In: *Kingdom of Laos: the land of the million elephants and of the white parasol.* Compiled by René de Berval. Saigon, Vietnam: France Asie, 1959, p. 32-49.

Presents the history of Laos from 1316 to 1955 in a tabulated chronology of kings, rulers and chief events. The article also refers to the key features of the period prior to the fourteenth century.

98 **History of Laos.**
Maha Sila Viravong, translated by the US Joint Publications Research Service. New York: Paragon Book Reprint Corp., 1964. 147p.

This work is translated from volume one of the *Phong savadan lao* (Lao annals or chronicle) published in Vientiane in 1957. It covers the history of the Lao and Laos from the ninth century BC to the middle of the nineteenth century AD. This is history told in the style of the annals; it is a chronicle of the rulers and the territory they governed and the major events which influenced their reigns. It is valuable as a Lao source for the history of their country. The chapters on the early period before the establishment of Fa-Ngum's reign give an account of social ranks and administrative organization, with details of social and economic life.

99 **Thailand: a short history.**
David K. Wyatt. New Haven, Connecticut; London: Yale University Press, 1984. 351p. maps. bibliog.

This work is included in a bibliography of Laos for two reasons. Firstly, it provides the history of relations between Thailand and Laos up to the 1980s, including the defeat of Chao Anou, King of Vientiane, in 1827 and the deportation of the Lao population over the following two decades. Wyatt does not mention in this context the removal of the Emerald Buddha from Vientiane to Bangkok. Secondly, in the first three chapters Wyatt discusses more generally the history of the Tai, of whom the Lao are a branch. Before the founding of Lan Chang the whole region was subject to population movement and rule by different suzerains. Wyatt summarizes current archaeological and linguistic research as well as the study of the annals to provide a comprehensible idea of the probable history of the area, which still requires considerable research.

Eighteenth to twentieth century

100 **La Légion en Indochine, 1885-1955.** (The French Foreign Legion in
Indo-China, 1885-1955.)
Alain Gandy.   Paris: Presses de la Cité, 1988. 191p. maps. (Collection
'Troupes de choc').
An illustrated history of the French Foreign Legion in Indo-China, written by a career
army officer. The material on Laos cannot be identified immediately as there is no
index, and it forms a small part of the action. This work complements more general
histories and provides detail of one facet of Indo-China's history. The majority of the
work is devoted to the last four years of the First Indochinese War, culminating in the
battle of Diên Biên Phu, and the last months of defeat, imprisonment and retreat.

101 **Pavatsat Lao (Lao history), vol. 3: *1893 thoeng patchuban* (1893 to the
present.)**
Kasuang Su'ksa lae Kila. Sathaban Khongkhwa Witthayasat
Sangkhom.   [Vientiane]: Kasuang Su'ksa lae Kila, 1989. 558p. bibliog.
This is the first volume to be published of a projected three-volume history of Laos
written in Lao and compiled by members of the Institute of Social Sciences, within the
Ministry of Education and Sports. It is of particular significance as it is the first Lao
history written since the advent of Republican government.

102 **French colonialism in Laos, 1893-1945.**
Alfred W. McCoy.   In: *Laos: war and revolution.*   Edited by Nina S.
Adams, Alfred W. McCoy.   New York: Harper & Row, 1970, p. 67-
98.
A succinct survey of this period of Laos' history which considers, in a critical light, the
way the French administered Laos, the economic development, or rather lack of it,
under French rule, the rebellions against the French, and the new relationship between
the people of Laos and France provoked by the Japanese occupation in 1941.

103 **160 years ago: Lao chronicles and annals on Siam and the Lao.**
Mayoury and Pheuiphanh Ngaosyvathn.   In: *Proceedings of the
International Conference on Thai Studies, Canberra, 3-6 July 1987.*
Compiled by Ann Buller.   Canberra: Australian National University,
1987, vol. 3, pt. 2, p. 467-76.
An examination of the background to the sack of Vientiane, 1827, by two Lao
scholars. They have used Lao chronicles and they have re-examined other sources from
a Lao perspective. For the general reader it is rather undigested, but it is worth
pursuing for those seriously interested in this period. The poor standards of
proofreading in these conference papers as a whole is particularly acute in this paper
and adds to the difficulties in using it. There are copious notes which allude to the
sources, but it makes tracing the bibliographical references difficult, and whether
sources are written in Thai or Lao has not been made explicit.

104 **À la conquête des coeurs: le pays des millions d'éléphants et du parasol blanc, les 'Pavillons noirs' – Déo Van Tri.** (To the winning of hearts: the land of millions of elephants and the white parasol, the 'Black flags' and Déo Van Tri.)
Auguste Pavie, introduction and notes by André Masson. Paris: Presses Universitaires de France, 1947. 381p. maps. (Colonies et empires, 2; Série: Les Classiques de la Colonisation, no. 16).

Published to mark the anniversary of Pavie's birth, this is based on his diary written while he was travelling through Laos from 1887 to the beginning of 1889, and from which he compiled the reports he sent back to Paris and Saigon. Pavie was sent as the new French vice-consul to the court of Luang Prabang. At the time when the French were extending their rule in Vietnam, the Thais sought to seize the territories of Laos, while their rivals the Vietnamese were occupied. They had sent an élite expeditionary force of troops ahead of Pavie. At the same time, the treaty of 1885 between France and Annam (the Vietnamese court) had left a number of armed bands marauding in Vietnam and Laos, largely displaced Chinese from Yunnan and usually known by the name of the colour of their flags. At the time of Pavie's arrival the Thais had taken several of these bandit leaders hostage but when their fellows, led by Deo Van Tri, threatened and later occupied Luang Prabang, the Thais fled. Pavie's party saved the old King Oun Kham who asked for French protection. This diary recounts Pavie's travels in Laos and the events he witnessed, and several encounters with the 'Black flags' who he brought to submission and forced to return to China. His account of what he saw and the ethnic groups has been borne out by later academic researchers. This edition is made more useful by Masson's introduction and notes.

105 **In search of Southeast Asia: a modern history.**
Edited by David Joel Steinberg. Honolulu, Hawaii: University of Hawaii Press, 1987. rev. ed. 590p. maps. bibliog.

A regional history from the eighteenth century to the present, which examines the way in which the states still living in a traditional style at the outset of the narrative met the external forces of international trade and colonialism and emerged as the present nation states of the region. Laos receives relatively brief but coherent treatment; its history can be seen in the context of that of its neighbours. Here it is argued that Laos as a nation existed only from the declaration of independence in 1945 and, in view of the divisions of civil war and old rivalries, one state did not exist until the takeover of power by the Pathet Lao in December 1975.

106 **Siam under Rama III, 1824-1851.**
Walter F. Vella. New York: J. J.Augustin for the Association of Asian Studies, 1957. 180p. maps. bibliog. (Monographs of the Association for Asian Studies, no. 4).

Vella's study of the reign of King Rama III of Siam, modern Thailand, has been included because he deals with the revolt of Vientiane, here transcribed as Wiangchan, p. 79-91. In 1778 Vientiane became a vassal state of Siam and its ruler Chao Anu felt by 1826 that the Siamese preoccupation with the Burmese threat offered a propitious moment for revolt. Vella gives a good and clear account of the events, the Siamese reprisals and the subsequent efforts to secure their eastern boundary against further Lao revolt or incursions from Annam, modern Vietnam. Vella's account uses Thai historical sources, which have been the basis for most discussion of these events.

Mayoury and Pheuiphanh Ngaosyvathn (q.v.) have presented a preliminary study which provides a different view from that of the Siamese chroniclers and historians.

107 **Siam and Laos, 1767-1827.**
David K. Wyatt. *Journal of Southeast Asian History*, vol. 4, no. 2 (Sept. 1963), p. 13-32.

An examination of the events which led up to the Vientiane rebellion in 1827 based on Thai and Lao documents and chronicles. Wyatt's thesis is that the rebellion was rooted in a long period of increasingly active Thai involvement in Lao affairs. This is an episode where the position of Laos as a buffer state and transit point for the Burmese invasions of Siam is crucial to its fate. The rebellion of Chao Anu in Vientiane is seen as a revolt against an increasing Thai encroachment on Vientiane and the political fragmentation of Laos. The result of the revolt was the abolition of the Kindom of Vientiane, the removal of its population to Laos and the direct administration of its former territories by the Thai. This a good chronological account of the events of these important sixty years which set the seal on the fate of Laos, its people and its boundaries.

Second World War and Lao Issara

108 **La présence militaire française en Indochine 1940-1945.** (The French military presence in Indo-China 1940-1945.)
Claude Hesse d'Alzon. Vincennes, France: Publications du Service Historique de l'Armée de Terre, 1988. 375p. maps. bibliog.

A history of the French armed forces in Indo-China for the period 1940 to 1945. One of the early chapters is devoted to the Thai conflict, when the Thai demands for the restoration of territory in Laos on the west bank of the Mékong and other territory in Cambodia erupted into armed conflict. Hesse d'Alzon deals with the military action and the Japanese intervention to produce an armistice and treaty. Much of the remainder of the work deals with the efforts of the resistance within Indo-China and the work of the forces parachuted into Indo-China. Laos figures quite prominently in parachute drops of troops and as a secure zone close to the Chinese border. After the Japanese *coup de force* in March 1945 a few French soldiers escaped to join the underground struggle, although most were imprisoned by the Japanese. There are several appendices which provide a chronology of events, 1939-45, a list of the legislative texts and regulations concerning the defence of the colonies and Indo-China in particular, numerous lists of military organization, details of regiments, and insignia, and a list of the operations of the special forces, their parachute drops and so on.

109 **L'Indochine française, 1940-1945.** (French Indo-China, 1940-1945.)
Pierre Brocheux, William J. Duiker, Claude Hesse d'Alzon, Paul
Isoart, Masaya Shiraishi. Paris: Presses Universitaires de France,
1982. 244p. maps. bibliog. (Collection Travaux et Recherches de
l'Institut du Droit de la Paix et du Développement de l'Université de
Nice).
A collaborative research project which used recently accessible archive sources as well
as recent research to study the subject of French Indo-China during the Second World
War at the level of governmental decision-making and action. Isoart writes about the
part played by De Gaulle's policies in 1944 and after, which undid the work of Decoux
and triggered off the war which only ended in 1954. Hesse d'Alzon's research is
concerned with the role of the French armed forces in Indo-China between 1939 and
1945. Duiker writes on the United States' policies towards Indo-China at this period
and Shiraishi writes on the Japanese presence in Indo-China from 1940-45. It should be
noted that the fifth paper by Brocheux is only concerned with Vietnam. This is a book
for the serious historian and, without any indexes or complete bibliography, cannot be
accessed easily, although the material merits attention.

110 **Guérilla au Laos.** (Guerilla in Laos.)
Michel Caply. Paris: Presses de la Cité, 1966. 347p.
The story of the resistance organized with the aid of the Allies against the Japanese in
Laos. Told as a continuous narrative, Caply has based his account on interviews with
surviving French and Lao participants and the records which are extant. In the last
third of the book he writes of the re-establishment of French authority after the
Japanese capitulation.

111 **La libération du Laos, 1945-1946.** (The liberation of Laos, 1945-1946.)
General Jean Boucher de Crèvecoeur. Vincennes, France: Service
Historique de l'Armée de Terre, 1985. 234p. maps. (Documents,
no. 1).
Based on contemporary documents, this work was written in 1947 by one of the chief
participants; it has been published virtually unamended. De Crèvecoeur was the head
of French clandestine forces in India and became the commander of the French forces
in Laos; he used the archives of both these units to write his account, archives which
have now almost entirely vanished. It is an account of the harrying of the Japanese,
after their takeover of power in Indo-China by force on March 9 1945, by five hundred
men in Laos, two hundred Europeans, mainly French, and three hundred Indo-
Chinese. The main task of this group was to wait for the Japanese capitulation and to
seize the centres of power for France, but this they were unable to achieve against the
Lao Issara movement. The book recounts in detail the military actions which resulted
finally in the restoration of French authority. It provides insights into the action of the
British and US allies in this difficult period. It is valuable as a documentary source.

112 **SOE in the Far East.**
Charles Cruickshank.   Oxford: Oxford University Press, 1983.
285p. maps. bibliog.
A history of Special Operations Executive in Asia, one of the official histories of the
Second World War, which gave its author free access to official documents. One of the
chapters in part 2, 'Special operations', deals with work in French Indochina. Dislike
of the French colonial regime by Roosevelt, and Churchill's animosity towards De
Gaulle meant that, while there was considerable preparatory work, SOE was able to
contribute little to the resistance movement or to assist the French army *in situ* to resist
the Japanese after the coup of March 1945. The principal interest of this account is the
revelation of the processes involved at the highest levels of command.

113 **Lao Issara: the memoirs of Oun Sananikone.**
Translated by John B. Murdoch and '3264'; edited and with an
introduction by David K. Wyatt.   Ithaca, New York: Cornell
University, Department of Asian Studies, Southeast Asia Program,
1975. 60p. maps, bibliog. (Data Paper Series, no. 100).
A unique account, by a major participant, of the origins of the Lao Issara in 1944-46.
This is a valuable contribution to our knowledge of what is a confused period in Lao
history. In these pages appear many of the Lao who play an important part in Lao
politics. This work is not complete; it begins in the middle of Oun's memoir and is
written after a considerable lapse of time from the events, but it has the liveliness of
the account of a participant. It complements the memoir *Iron man of Laos Prince
Phetsarath Ratanavongsa* (q.v.).

114 **Iron man of Laos Prince Phetsarath Ratanavongsa.**
By '3349', translated by John B. Murdoch, edited by David K. Wyatt.
Ithaca, New York: Cornell University, Department of Asian Studies,
Southeast Asia Program, 1978. 111p. (Data Paper Series, no. 110).
The autobiography of Prince Phetsarath, who was head of the Lao civil service, Prime
Minister and Viceroy of the Kingdom Of Luang Prabang during the Second World
War, leader of the Lao resistance to the French in 1946, exiled for eleven years to
Thailand, and mediator between his younger brothers Prince Souvanna Phouma and
Prince Souphanouvong. Although not named as the author, Prince Phetsarath would
appear to be the writer of this work which reflects his ideas and judgements. Murdoch
has prepared a selective translation, omitting mainly descriptive accounts of journeys,
lists of people and the full text of the Geneva agreement on Laos of 1954. The text
deals with Prince Phetsarath's education, including his studies in France, the Japanese
occupation, the fight for freedom, his exile, and his return to help restore peace in
Laos. There are sketches of three important figures in modern Lao history, Prince
Souphanouvong, Boun Kong Manivong, and Bong Souvannavong. Murdoch has
provided a useful introduction to the historical events in this work.

115   **Le destin de l'Indochine: souvenirs et documents 1941-1951.**
(Indochina's destiny: memories and documents, 1941-1951.)
G. Sabattier.   Paris: Plon, 1952. 466p. maps.

General Sabattier's book attempts to set the record straight on his own part and that of
the French armed forces in Indo-China between 1941 and 1945. He was in the south of
France at the time of the armistice with Germany and he was ordered to go to Indo-
China as quickly as possible. There he was initially occupied with the forces in the west
trying to resist the Siamese advance into Cambodia and western Laos. The Japanese
brought about the armistice and peace treaty of May 1941 between the two parties;
France was forced to cede the territories of Laos west of the Mekong as well as the
provinces of Battambang and the northern parts of Siem Reap and Kompong Thom in
Cambodia. He deals with the situation of the army in Indo-China under the uneasy
relationship with the Japanese, the resistance that was organized, and the army
operations which took place after the Japanese coup in March 1945. The army's
operations were strenthened by joint action with the Allies after the establishment of
peace in Europe. Action in Laos was in the north designed to deny access to the
Japanese across the plains to the south, as well as to keep open the routes to China
where Free French forces were established. He concludes with his observations on the
mistakes in French policy in the region between 1946 and 1951.

The First Indochinese War (1946-54) and the Geneva Conference (1954)

116   **Mourir au Laos.** (To die in Laos.)
Erwan Bergot.   Paris: Éditions France-Empire, 1965. 267p. maps.

An account by a survivor of a mobile franco-vietnamese unit in the First Indochinese
War of his withdrawal into Laos. The text is amplified by contemporary photographs.
Bergot has collected the accounts of others from this war amongst those in his *Héros
oubliés* (Forgotten heroes) (Paris: Grasset, 1975. 390p.).

117   **La guerre d'Indochine, 1945-1954: textes et documents.** (The
Indochinese War 1945-1954: documentation and texts.)
Gilbert Bodinier.   Vincennes, France: Service Historique de l'Armée
de Terre, 1987- . 2 vols. to date. maps. bibliog.

Volume one, entitled *Le retour de la France en Indochine, 1945-1946* (The return of
France to Indo-china, 1945-1946), and volume two *Indochine 1947, règlement politique
ou solution militaire?* (Indo-China 1947, political rule or military solution?), have been
published to date and future volumes are planned for each year of the war. The work is
a selection of major documents on the First Indochinese War, now that the archives
have been declassified, accompanied by explanatory documentation, a chronology,
explanation of the organization of the military forces used, biographies of key figures,
maps and bibliographies. Laos obviously figures less than Vietnam in these records,
but they provide a summary of the material in the archives.

118   The Geneva Conference of 1954 on Indochina.
James Cable.   New York: St. Martin's Press, 1986. 179p. bibliog.

The author, one of the British delegates to the Conference, treats this subject from the
point of view of British diplomacy. He has used those public records which have now
been released under the thirty-year rule, although several files from this period remain
closed. An account of the negotiations both inside and outside the conference, this is a
clear depiction of this complex matter, particular emphasis being given to the part
played by Britain. The text of the final declaration of the Geneva Conference, 21st July
1954, is reproduced here as an appendix.

119   The war in Indo-China, 1945-54.
Jacques Dalloz.   Dublin: Gill & Macmillan; Savage, Maryland: Barnes
& Noble, 1990. 280p. maps. bibliog.

A translation of *Guerre d'Indochine, 1945-54* (Paris: Seuil, 1987). A very readable,
narrative, political history of the First Indochinese War. It is prefaced by two chapters
which set the scene for the events which followed the close of the Second World War
in Indochina and the restoration of French rule. Laos as always within Indo-China
plays a relatively small part within this narrative, but it is always clearly set in the
context of contemporary events in the rest of Indo-China.

120   End of a war: Indochina 1954.
Philippe Devillers, Jean Lacouture.   London: Pall Mall Press, 1969.
412p. map. bibliog.

A translation of the work published in French in 1960, but with the third section
rewritten and brought up to date. The title did not offer a judgement that the war had
ended but is rather a description of the subject, that is, how a war is brought to an end
and the 'tentative possibilities of coexistence are created'. Laos plays a relatively small
part in this narrative and does not figure in the third section. Half the book is
concerned with the manoeuvres of each party at the Geneva Conference. It provides a
detailed account of the negotiations. In the French edition, the third section provides a
sketch of Laos, Cambodia and Vietnam in 1960, that is, *La fin d'une guerre: Indochine
1954* (The end of a war: Indo-china 1954) (Paris: Editions du Seuil, 1960).

121   The emancipation of French Indochina.
Donald Lancaster.   New York: Octagon , 1974. 445p. map. bibliog.

First published in 1961 by Oxford University Press, this work deals extensively with
events in Vietnam and less fully with those in Laos and Cambodia. It is based on
extensive reading and discussions with French and Vietnamese in Saigon, where
Lancaster served in the British Legation from 1950 to 1954. It is a political history of
the Indo-Chinese states; it sets the scene for events after the restoration of French rule
in 1946 and is a detailed study of the events up to the Geneva Conference of 1954 and
the immediate aftermath. It emphasizes the position of Laos as a buffer state that was
rarely able to act independently of events in neighbouring countries.

122   **La première guerre d'Indochine, 1945-1954: bibliographie.** (The First
Indochinese War, 1945-1954: a bibliography.)
Alain Ruscio.   Paris: L'Harmattan, 1987. 286p.
The author of this bibliography has devoted his own researches to the subject of the
First Indochinese War. It contains 2,356 references to works which range from simple
eyewitness accounts to detailed historical studies. The work is arranged in topical
chapters broken up under various subheadings. Where relevant there is a distinction
made between contemporary documentation and accounts of witnesses and studies of a
particular theme. The concluding chapter covers literary works and films dealing with
the war. There are indexes to subjects and authors.

123   **The 1954 Geneva Conference on Indo-China and Korea.**
United Kingdom, with a new introduction by Kenneth T. Young.
New York, Greenwood Press, 1968. 168p., 42p.
A re-publication of the two British Parliamentary Command papers *Documents relating to
the discussion of Korea and Indo-China at the Geneva Conference, April 27-June 15, 1954*
(London: HMSO, 1954. 168p. [Miscellaneous, no. 1] [Cmd. 9186]) and *Further documents relating to the discussion of Indo-China at the Geneva Conference, June 16-July 21,
1954* (London: HMSO, 1954. 42p. [Miscellaneous, no. 20] [Cmd. 9239]). Young provides
a useful introduction to this collection of contemporary documents.

1945- .

124   **Laos.**
Australia: Department of External Affairs.   Canberra: The Author,
1970. 204p. bibliog. (Select Documents on International Affairs, no. 16).
'This selection of documents tracing the history of Laos since the Second World War,
attempts to show how Laotian political groups and the international community have
viewed Laotian problems over the years, and how domestic and international aspects
have interacted upon each other'. The selection of 214 documents traces the history of
Laos from the Constitution of 1947 to a statement by Richard Nixon in December
1969. The emphasis is placed on events surrounding the two Geneva Conferences and
the efforts to establish international political agreement in the mid- and late-1950s, the
conflicts between Lao political groups in 1962 and 1963, and the events of the late
1960s. Many of the documents are only presented as extracts and all are given in
English, translated where necessary from French or Lao.

125   **Second Indochina War: Cambodia and Laos today.**
Wilfred Burchett.   London: Lorrimer, 1970. 160p. map.
This is the most complete summary of Burchett's writing on Laos, occupying more
than two-thirds of this volume. He traces Lao wars of insurrection back to the early
years of French occupation; only with the Japanese occupation did they become
organized on a national basis. He contrasts the United States' view that a power
vacuum was created in Laos with the departure of the French, with the view of the
people of Laos of a struggle for independence from foreign domination. This is a

largely chronological account of events in Laos from 1941 to 1970. He offers a very different view of Kou Voravong's murder from that in Jean Deuve's *Un episode oublié de l'histoire du Laos: le complot de Chinaimo* (q.v.). He quotes extensively from Roger Hilsman's *To move a nation* (q.v.), but frequently to put a very different interpretation on his points. Burchett's position is quite clear; he supported the Pathet Lao, and in this he presents a view of events and the United States' role in them that contrasts forcefully with that in most of the other works.

126 **The wars in Vietnam, Cambodia and Laos, 1945-1982: a bibliographic guide.**
Richard Dean Burns, Milton Leitenberg. Santa Barbara, California: ABC-Clio Information Services, 1984. 290p. maps. (War/Peace Bibliography Series, no. 18).
This bibliography covers the First, Second and Third Indochinese Wars; that is, the First from 1946 to 1954; the Second, also frequently called the Vietnam War, from 1961 to 1975; and the Third, which is used to describe the disputes between Vietnam and Kampuchea (Cambodia) in 1977 which culminated in the invasion of Kampuchea by Vietnam at the end of 1978 and the fighting between Vietnam and China which broke out along the border in 1979. The work is well organized into chapters on specific themes, which have brief introductions and many subheadings to facilitate use. The entries are not annotated unless the titles do not convey the content, or the work represents a very specific viewpoint. There is useful material on the wars in Laos, and the topics covered are: the United States and the politics of intervention; Congress, international law and negotiations; strategy, tactics and support efforts; combat operations; the costs of war; the war at home (i.e. the United States); and works on particular periods and episodes of fighting.

127 **Marxism and the history of the nationalist movements in Laos.**
C. J. Christie. *Journal of Southeast Asian studies*, vol. 10, no. 1 (Mar. 1979) p. 146-58.
A study of Lao nationalism and the nationalist credentials of the Pathet Lao. Christie outlines the emergence of modern nationalism in Laos from 1945, to the success of the Pathet Lao in redefining the nature of Lao nationalism to include the ethnic minorities of Laos, and to their emergence as the preservers of Lao nationalism and directors of the movement of national liberation.

128 **Un épisode oublié de l'histoire du Laos: le complot de Chinaimo, 1954-1955.** (A forgotten episode in the history of Laos: the Chinaimo conspiracy.)
Jean Deuve. Paris: Centre d'Histoire et Civilisations de la Péninsule Indochinoise, 1986. 152p. maps. (Travaux du Centre d'Histoire et Civilisations de la Péninsule Indochinoise).
A detailed study of events in Laos, which were overshadowed by the negotiations at the Geneva Conference. The author traces the apparent plotting based around the military camp and village of Chinaimo, close to Vientiane. He discloses the work of infiltration by the *Bureau Spécial*. At the time the opposition accused the government of fabricating the plot to discredit the forces of opposition. There were acts of terrorism and the Defence Minister Kou Vouravong was fatally wounded in an attack on the home of Phoui Sananikone, Foreign Minister. Here the conspiracy is described

as the secret services unravelled it and followed it on a day by day basis, as they infiltrated it. Their work is described in detail and only the identity of agents still alive is concealed. In an appendix the evidence of some of those involved in the plot, who gave information on their return from exile, is given in translation. This work should be read with Deuve's *Le royaume du Laos, 1949-1965* (q.v.).

129 **Le royaume du Laos, 1949-1965: histoire événementielle de l'indépendance à la guerre américaine.** (The kingdom of Laos, 1949-1965: history of events from independence to the American war.) Jean Deuve. Paris: École Française d'Extrême-Orient, 1984. 387p. maps. bibliog. (Travaux du Centre d'Histoire et Civilisation de la Péninsule Indochinoise) (Publications hors Série de l'EFEO).

As the author's subtitle suggests, this is a narrative history of events from 1949 to 1965; events to which the author was a witness as adviser to the Lao government on security matters. This is a history of the political events of the period. There are several useful appendices, a selection of documents, a chronology of events, and biographical notes on the important Lao figures mentioned in the text.

130 **'How the dominoes fell': Southeast Asia in perspective.** John H. Esterline, Mae H. Esterline. Lanham, Maryland: Hamilton Press, 1986. 492p. maps. bibliog.

A history of South East Asia with a chapter on each country, including one on Laos, p. 105-34. Its purpose is to deal with political history from the earliest times with a more detailed account of events from 1945 to 1985, looking at the 'characteristics of indigenous and colonial political cultures, the influence of nationalism and the impact of the Vietnam war on the region'. It provides a readable, if simplified, account of the history of Laos concentrating on the most recent forty years.

131 **Interim reports of the International Comission for Supervision and Control in Laos.** International Commission for Supervision and Control in Laos. Presented . . . to Parliament . . . . London: HMSO, 1955-58. 1st to 4th: 77p. (Cmd. 9445), 57p. (Cmd. 9630), 94p. (Cmnd. 314), 159p. (Cmnd. 541).

The first in this series of reports deals with the establishment and organization of the International Commission, the regroupment and withdrawal of forces, the special convention regarding the Vietnamese People's Volunteers settled in Laos, and all the other problems such as prisoners of war to be dealt with at the end of a war. The report is backed by appendices of evidence and detail including complaints made by various parties and important speeches made by key figures. It covers the period August 11 1954 to December 31 1954. The second report, January 1 1955 to June 30 1955, continues in the same vein as the first. The third and fourth reports, July 1 1955 to May 16 1957, and May 17 1957 to May 31 1958, contain chronologies of important events in the periods covered by the reports. They also cover the negotiations which led to elections and the achievement of the aims of the Geneva Conference; the final sentence of the introduction to the fourth report reads, 'As a result of these developments, peace has at last been restored to Laos'. The appendices contain the agreements achieved at the time, as well as official correspondence between Prince Souvanna Phouma, the Prime Minister and Prince Souphannouvong.

132 **Pawns of war: Cambodia and Laos.**
Arnold R. Isaacs, Gordon Hardy, MacAlister Brown, editors of the
Boston Publishing Co.. Boston, Massachusetts: Boston Publishing
Co., 1987. 192p. map. bibliog. (The Vietnam Experience).
A history of the war in Laos and Cambodia from 1945 to the 1980s. Written for the
general reader, it offers a continuous text lavishly illustrated with good contemporary
photographs. The writers are strongly against the new republican government of Laos
and the Pathet Lao. In the same series, *South Vietnam on trial mid-1970 to 1972* (by
David Fulghum, Terence Maitland, editors of the Boston Publishing Co.. Boston,
Massachusetts: Boston Publishing Co., 1984. 192p. maps. bibliog. [The Vietnam
experience]) has a chapter (p. 68-97) on the Lam Son 719 campaign, when the war in
South Vietnam spilled over into Laos. It is in the same style, with many photographs
and a map of the campaign area.

133 **The politics of heroin in Southeast Asia.**
Alfred W. McCoy, Cathleen B. Read, Leonard P. Adams II. New
York: Harper & Row, 1972. 464p. maps.
The role of opium in the history of modern Laos is here interwoven with the history of
the other countries in South East Asia. The opium trade was tapped as a source of
secret revenue to finance guerilla forces by the French in Laos, and was continued by
the CIA. The story is a complicated one involving both political and criminal
ambitions. When conditions made dealing in opium difficult, because of its bulk, the
solution was its conversion to heroin. When the disruption by fighting in Laos severely
reduced the amount of opium available, Laos became the exit point for opium grown
in Burma. McCoy gives detailed accounts of how revenues from this trade were used to
finance guerilla units, an aspect of the wars in Laos which is avoided or skated over in
other accounts. He also gives a coherent account of the split between the Hmong clans
which resulted in some fighting with the Pathet Lao and some with the Royal Lao
Government forces. This book uses both printed sources and an extensive series of
interviews with those involved over the previous twenty-five years.

134 **Power struggle in South-East Asia.**
Oey Hong Lee. Zug, Switzerland: Inter Documentation Co., 1976.
614p. map. bibliog. (Bibliotheca Asiatica, no. 13).
Oey presents a view of the political history of South East Asia through a history of the
power struggles in each country. In Laos this is characterized as the struggle between
nationalism and foreign intervention. It is a history of the competing struggles for
independence from 1945 to 1975, with the creation of the Lao People's Democratic
Republic. A collection of relevant documents has been reproduced on the microfiches
which accompany this book. For Laos, there are eleven, all associated with the
negotation of the cease-fire in 1973 and the transition to a republican government, and
all taken from the *Summary of world broadcasts: Far East* (q.v.).

135 **Laos and the victorious struggle of the Lao people against U.S. neo-
colonialism.**
Phoumi Vongvichit. [n.p.]: Neo Lao Haksat, 1969. 228p. map.
A fundamental work that provides an understanding of the Lao Patriotic Front. The
author was Secretary-General of the Lao Patriotic Front at the time of writing and was
most recently acting President of Laos. Based on official documents of the Front, it is a

history of the struggle for independence and a critique of the role of France and the United States in preventing the existence of a genuinely independent Laos. He discusses the role of economic aid in the creation of a new social class, that of the comprador bourgeoisie, inextricably linked with the the United States' presence in Laos. This new economic class created its own links with the armed forces and other sources of power. The strategies and philosophy of the Lao Patriotic Front are contrasted favourably with the economic exploitation experienced in the area of Laos under the control of the Royal Lao Government. In *Douze années d'intervention et d'aggression des impérialistes américains au Laos* (q.v.) rather fuller details are given of the events used by Phoumi Vongvichit in his discussion of the war. In 1988 the work was reissued without changes; a copy of the French edition has been seen: *Le Laos et la lutte victorieuse du peuple lao contre le neo-colonialisme americain* (1988. 157p.).

136 **Independence and political rivalry in Laos 1945-61.**
E. H. S. Simmonds. In: *Politics in Southern Asia.* Edited by Saul Rose. London: Macmillan, 1963, p. 164-99.
An essay on the political history of Laos from 1945 to 1962, which clearly chronicles the events. It is valuable as later work has tended to skate over this period more briefly, and yet many of the key figures and the key events in Lao history were prominent at this time and both the actors and events influenced later Lao history. It examines the social and psychological factors which exerted an influence on the world of Lao politicians.

137 **Storm over Laos: a contemporary history.**
Sisouk Na Champassak. New York: Praeger, 1961. 202p.
An insider's view of Laotian history from 1945. Sisouk was an influential member of the Comité pour la Défense des Interêts Nationaux (Committee for the Defence of National Interests). The work concentrates on the period after the Geneva Conference of 1954, in which Sisouk was an active participant in various government posts. He tries to present an objective analysis of events, and he does not fail to criticize aspects of the US presence such as the spread of corruption, but he has no sympathy for the Pathet Lao. Valuable as a historical source, this work offers the chance to hear a Lao voice on Laos' history.

138 **Vietnam, Laos and Cambodia: chronology of events 1945-68.**
United Kingdom: Central Office of Information. London: British Information Services, 1968. [151]p. map.
A chronology presented in tabulated form, from the Japanese *coup de force* in 1945 to the opening of talks between the United States and Vietnam in Paris, May 1968.

139 **Documents relating to the British involvement in the Indo-China conflict, 1945-1965.**
United Kingdom: Foreign Office. London: HMSO, 1965. 268p. bibliog. (Cmnd. 2834) (Miscellaneous, no. 25, 1965).
This volume 'is meant to explain how Britain came to be concerned with Indo-China and to describe the policies pursued by successive British Governments since 1945'. The selection of 174 documents is preceded by a background narrative of the British role in events from 1945-65, which clarifies where each of the documents fits into

events and policy. The bibliography is of previous British official publications on the subject.

140 **Tribal politics in Indochina: the role of Highland tribes in the internationalization of internal wars.**
Gary D. Wekkin. In: *Conflict and stability in Southeast Asia.* Edited by Mark W. Zacher, R. Stephen Milne. Garden City, New York: Doubleday/Anchor, 1973, p. 121-47. maps.
A study of the effect that the disaffection of the semi-nomadic ethnic groups in the highland regions of Laos had on the internationalization of the wars in the region. He considers the reason for the alienation of the Lao Theung and Hill Tai in the area that became the territorial base of the Pathet Lao. It was an alienation that went back to the period of French colonial rule and the treatment they received from the lowland Lao. The Pathet Lao promised them political autonomy; social and political equality for all ethnic groups was part of their political platform. The traditional hostility between the ethnic minorities is not part of Wekkin's subject.

The Second Indochinese War and the Geneva Conference (1961-62)

141 **Voices from the Plain of Jars: life under an air war.**
Compiled and with an introduction and preface by Fred Branfman.
New York: Harper & Row, 1972. 160p. maps.
The Plain of Jars, site of the funeral urns of a megalithic society in Laos, was home to about 130,000-170,000 people in the 1950s. The plain and Xieng Khouang were the home of the Lao Phuan and the hills around to the ethnic minorities of Laos. The Plain of Jars provides a strategic route north and south and has been contested through the centuries. From 1964 to 1969 it was the scene of increasingly severe bombing raids by United States planes, mostly based in Thailand. This bombing campaign, which was not officially admitted until 1970, forced a large portion of the surviving population to be resettled as refugees around Vientiane, a lowland area that they found too hot, and where they were given poor land to cultivate and little material help. In this book, sixteen of the autobiographies collected by the compilers are reproduced. They recount the experience of life under periods of continual aerial bombardment, the attempts to continue farming at night, and the tragedy which all encountered. Branfman is concerned to demonstrate that modern techniques of war intrude on the lives of ordinary people who have no power to combat it or to stop it. This book portrays the experience of war of the peasant, and not the global view of most histories.

142 **The furtive war: the United States in Vietnam and Laos.**
Wilfred G. Burchett.   New York: International Publishers, 1963.
224p.

Burchett, an Australian journalist, specialized in reporting foreign wars; the second part of this work, p. 161-217, is called 'Laos in perspective'. In a rather anecdotal style Burchett looks at events between the assassination of Kou Vouravong in September 1954 and the full-scale war which had developed by April 1963. It is the history of the civil war of the Royal Lao Government against the Pathet Lao, which resulted in an international war. Burchett offers the perspective of the Pathet Lao whom he met and interviewed, and this is where its interest lies.

143 **Mekong upstream.**
W. G. Burchett.   Hanoi: Red River Publishing House, 1957. 324p.
maps.

Based on two visits to Laos in 1956 and 1957, the author recounts (p. 213-324) the historical background to the current situation in Laos. The interest of this work lies in his record of interviews with members of the Pathet Lao and his sympathetic exploration of the reasons for their opposition to both the government in Vientiane and previously to the French colonial government. He visited a Pathet Lao stronghold and describes daily life and social organization under their administration. Twelve pages of photographs illustrate his text.

144 **Battle of Vientiane of 1960: with historical background leading to the battle.**
Chalermnit Press Correspondent.   Bangkok: [Chalermnit], 1961. 109p.
map.

It is hazarded that the author of this account is the well-known Thai writer Manich Jumsai. The first thirty-three pages provide a journalistic account of the battle, and the rest of the work attempts to provide the background to Kong Le's coup, in which the author tries to fill in the facts of the events. It is a difficult narrative to follow, and it is made more difficult by typographical errors which give the year as 1961 when it would seem that 1960 is intended. It does offer a Thai view of the events and provides information on the fate of Thais at the time. It includes a considerable number of contemporary photographs, including portraits of some of the key participants such as Kong Le and Quinim Pholsena.

145 **At war with Asia.**
Noam Chomsky.   London: Fontana/Collins, 1971. 282p.

The fourth chapter of this volume is devoted to Laos (p. 145-200). Chomsky's account is based on his observations and interviews during a week in Laos in 1970, and his use of published sources and congressional hearings. His purpose is to make clear his view of the United States' role, in support of the Royal Lao Government against the Pathet Lao. His analysis of the role of the press in reporting on the war in Laos from 1958, and on Laos since 1975, is pursued in the chapter on Laos in *After the cataclysm: postwar Indochina and the reconstruction of imperial ideology* (Noam Chomsky, Edward S. Herman.   Nottingham, England: Spokesman, 1979. 392p.).

146 **Conflict in Laos: the politics of neutralization.**
Arthur J. Dommen. New York: Praeger, 1971. rev. ed. 454p. maps.
bibliog.
Dommen is a journalist with many years experience in the Indo-China region. He traces the origins and development of the war in Laos, both in its own right and as part of the larger conflict in Indo-China. This is a detailed account of military and political events, to which have been added four chapters in the revised edition, with the result that the detail of his account of the earlier years has not been lost because of the necessity to cover events of the early 1960s. Dommen's views have changed somewhat between the two editions; by 1971 he sees the aims of Vietnam as having a more profound part to play in any future settlement for Laos.

147 **Anatomy of a crisis: the Laotian crisis of 1960-1961.**
Bernard B. Fall, edited with an epilogue by Roger M. Smith. Garden City, New York: Doubleday, 1969. 283p. maps. bibliog.
A critique of US foreign policy in Laos, the outcome of which was the polarization of political groupings in Laos and the impossibility of a peaceful solution to Laos' problems because the United States transferred its support from the neutralist camp to an opportunist right-wing group. The 'crisis' is set in its historical context by a survey of the history of Laos up to the 1958 elections. The events of the next three years are covered in detail; the account is closely linked to the sources from both sides of the political divide. The author produces a closely argued and highly readable study of this period.

148 **The prevailing wind: witness in Indo-China.**
Michael Field. London: Methuen, 1965. 392p. map.
A personal record of the events of 1956 to 1963 in Indo-China, where the author served as foreign correspondent for a London newspaper. Three separate sections deal with the events in each of the three former French dependencies. The events in Laos are dealt with in a relatively brief account, but it is coherent and clear and provides many observations by Field on the key actors in this period in Laos. The author would obviously prefer a non-communist solution to the Laotian problem, but he provides a more neutral account than that of Lao or American writers.

149 **Conflict in Indo-China: a reader on the widening war in Laos and Cambodia.**
Edited by Marvin Gettleman, Susan Gettleman, Lawrence Kaplan, Carol Kaplan. New York: Random House, 1970. 461p. maps. bibliog.
An anthology of extracts compiled 'to further scholarly interest in Southeast Asia, and more importantly, to help bring peace to that strife-torn region'. The range of material is wide: official documents, speeches, texts of international agreements, monitored radio broadcasts, congressional hearings, scholarly articles, and journalistic analyses; some items first published in French have been translated into English. This book is not a substitute for reading the original items, but it makes accessible many that would not be easily available and alerts the reader to sources that might be missed. The readings are grouped under subject headings with an editors' introduction: 'Early heritage and colonialism', 'Independence and the Geneva accords of 1954', 'The struggle for neutrality in Laos', 'The furtive war in Laos', and two more sections on Cambodia. It is perhaps about the last section, 'The furtive war in Laos', that the

editors felt most strongly. In this section there is, Richard Nixon's statement 'The situation in Laos: the case for escalation (March 6, 1970)'; Peter Dale Scott's reply and rebuttal 'Laos: the story Nixon won't tell'; Carl Strock on the creation of refugees by US bombing between 1968 and 1970; extracts from the 1969 congressional hearings, 'Exploring the U.S. role in Laos: hearings of the Symington Committee (October, 1969); the monitored broadcast statement, 'Lao Patriotic Front's "five points" (March 6, 1970)'; and Madeline Riffaud's 'Interview with Prince Souphanouvong in the liberated zone of Laos (March, 1970)', in which he gives his opinion of Nixon's statement of March 6, 1970.

150 **American policy toward Laos.**
Martin E. Goldstein. Rutherford, New Jersey: Fairleigh Dickinson University Press, 1973. 347p. maps. bibliog.

A study of the relations between the United State and Laos, with the emphasis on events between 1954 and 1962 and the role of the United States. Based on first-hand accounts and the available documentation, Goldstein attempts to unravel those events analytically and to concentrate on the aspects of US policy which influenced them. He endeavours to explain what led to the Lao factions and to the agreement reached by the great powers at the second Geneva Conference.

151 **A half-way house for the half-brothers: Burchett on Laos.**
Geoffrey C. Gunn. In: *Burchett reporting the other side of the world, 1939-1983.* Edited by Ben Kiernan. London: Quartet Books, 1986, p. 270-78.

In a book of essays on Burchett's work as a war correspondent, this brief essay presents Burchett's reporting and writing on Laos in chronological order. It is an appraisal of his work as a journalist and it is fleshed out with extracts from letters to his father. It points out the significance of Burchett's writing as a lone voice bringing the world's attention to the war in Laos.

152 **Laos crisis, 1960-61.**
David K. Hall. In: *The limits of coercive diplomacy: Laos, Cuba, Vietnam.* Alexander L. George, David K. Hall, William E. Simons. Boston, Massachusetts: Little Brown, 1971, p. 36-85. bibliog.

An account from the perspective of the United States administration of the Laos crisis of 1960 to 1961. Their efforts were directed at defending Thailand and SEATO (the South-East Asia Treaty Organization), and so their objectives were to maintain the Royal Lao Government in place and neither to permit nor countenance any further Pathet Lao advance in Laos. It is a useful review of published work, and an analysis from the perspective of the discipline of International Relations of the options available to the United States government and its motivation. Hall concludes that President Kennedy subtly coerced the communists to hold back and refrain from overrunning the Royal Lao Government areas, that the President had reduced the goal of the Eisenhower administration, and that the compromise for which he was prepared to settle was consonant with the limited military means that both the previous administration and he were prepared to employ. Hall is more cautious in his interpretation of the results, but he argues that the existence of the International Control Commission and mechanism of the Geneva Conference made the outcome possible. The introductory and concluding chapters of the work by A. L. George set this essay into its disciplinary and contemporary context.

153 The key to failure: Laos and the Vietnam War.

Norman B. Hannah. Lanham, Maryland: Madison Books, 1987.
335p. maps.

An attempt to understand why the United States lost the Vietnam War. The author has identified an 'algorithmic error' in United States strategy. This related to the Geneva accords on Laos in 1962. The United States agreed to the recognition of Laos as a neutral state. Within the following year they came to a tacit agreement with the North Vietnamese, by which North Vietnam agreed not to launch ground attacks against western Laos, if the United States did not launch ground attacks against the Laotian panhandle, that is the southern third of Laos. This provided real protection to the main supply route between the North and South of Vietnam, the Ho Chi Minh trail. This proved to be the massive failure in logic which Hannah maintains caused the United States lack of success. Hannah's major premise is that the role of the Geneva accords of 1962 in United States strategy for Indo-China, not just for Laos, was 'comprehensive, ubiquitous, determinative, enduring – and disastrous'. This book examines the steps in the Second Indochinese War in which the strands of United States policy in Laos, Cambodia and Vietnam, instead of uniting to form a strong knotted rope, blocked activity and were only unravelled by the North Vietnamese victory. This is a study of the formulation and application of the United States' strategic premise of counter-insurgency, and on the development of an alternative strategy of territorial defence, by an author who in one capacity or another in the United States foreign service from 1962 was involved with Indo-China.

154 To move a nation: the politics of foreign policy in the administration of John F. Kennedy.

Roger Hilsman. Garden City, New York: Doubleday, 1967. 602p.
maps.

One of the case studies in this very readable book is on United States foreign policy towards Laos, written by a participant in the Kennedy administration. Eisenhower stated that Laos was one of the hardest problems he was handing over to Kennedy. The problem, which had been a long time in the making, is clearly outlined here. On the eve of Kennedy's inauguration as President the government of Souvanna Phouma in Laos, established after the coup led by Kong Le, was ousted by General Phoumi Nosavan. This developed into armed struggle between the government forces and the Pathet Lao, now joined by Kong Le and his supporters. A decision on action had to be made by the United States, and Kennedy came out in support of a neutral and independent Laos and accepted the British proposal for a new Geneva Conference on Laos. Hilsman chronicles the diplomatic, political and military manoeuvring for power and solutions in the United States administration, and the views and actions which governed the United States response to the crisis. Hilsman sees Laos as a success of sorts for Kennedy's policy of a neutral Laos: governed by the 1962 Geneva accords, an uneasy peace established, and the United States not committed to military involvement but at the same time retaining this as a threat.

155 Wider war: the struggle for Cambodia, Thailand, and Laos.

Donald Kirk. New York: Praeger, 1971. 305p. maps. bibliog.

Kirk sees the Second Indochinese War as a continuation of the historic struggles for control of the buffer states of Laos and Cambodia, and he prophesies that even at the end of the war the struggle for territorial dominion will not end. The section on Laos provides a useful summary of the history of the war and looks at the attempts to find peace and the United States' involvement. It is helpful to have the coverage of events in Cambodia and Thailand, because these undoubtedly coloured the views and hence the actions of the United States in Laos.

156 **North Vietnam and the Pathet Lao: partners in the struggle for Laos.**
Paul F. Langer, Joseph J. Zasloff.   Cambridge, Massachusetts:
Harvard University Press, 1970. 262p. maps. bibliog.

Focusing on the role of North Vietnam in Laos, this work traces the part played by North Vietnam in the Lao revolutionary struggles from the beginnings in the 1940s. Much of the evidence for the North Vietnamese role is taken from the testimony of defectors; this confirms the belief of the writers that North Vietnamese support played a vital part in the ability of the Pathet Lao to maintain the insurgency. Interviews with a number of Pathet Lao defectors are also used to provide detail on the organization of political and military life in the Pathet Lao area.

157 **International Conference on the settlement of the Laotian question, 1961-2.**
George Modelski.   Canberra: Australian National University, Research School of Pacific Studies, Department of International Relations, 1962. 156p. map. bibliog. (Working Paper, no. 2).

This working paper presents a summary record of proceedings of the International Conference and the basic documents from it. This second Geneva Conference on Laos established , at the end of its proceedings, the protocol for the neutrality of Laos, 1962. The work begins with a commentary which looks at the events leading up to the Conference, its work, the negotiations and the outcome.

158 **Douze années d'intervention et d'aggression des impérialistes américains au Laos.** (Twelve years of intervention and aggression in Laos by the American imperialists.)
[n.p.]: Neo Lao Haksat, 1966. 135p. map.

Published on the occasion of the fourth anniversary of the signature of the Geneva accords, this work looks at the way American neo-colonialism has attacked the rights of Laos to independence, which was guaranteed by the Geneva agreements of 1954 and 1962. It examines the role of US aid and the roads which were built with it, as well as the US military bases built in Thailand on the border with Laos. The build up of US military and civilian advisers in Laos, and the agencies for which they worked, is examined. In a work published by the Lao Patriotic Front, hostility to US intervention is to be expected, but the documentation used frequently originated from the US agencies themselves.

159 **Un quart de siècle de lutte opiniâtre et victorieuse.** (Quarter of a century of stubborn and victorious struggle.)
[n.p.]: Neo Lao Haksat, 1970. 108p. map. (Laos, no. 1).

A selection of articles compiled and published by the Lao Patriotic Front on the occasion of the twenty-fifth anniversary of their struggle for the independence of Laos. The main article, which gives the volume its title, is by Kaysone Phomvihane summarizing the key points of the military and political struggle. There is also a chronological summary of the principal events in that struggle over those years and a summary of the political, military and economic achievements of the Lao Patriotic Front. Prince Souphanouvong, President of the Central Committee and later first President of Laos, introduces the book with an appeal rallying the supporters. On the twenty-sixth anniversary he published *Serious bankruptcy of Nixon doctrine in Laos* ([n.p.]: Neo Lao Haksat, 1971. 29p.), a further critique of the United States prosecution of 'intensified special war'.

160 Laos and the super powers.
Perala Ratnam. New Delhi: Tulsi Publishing, 1980. 167p.

Based on his personal observations and study over a three-year period, Ratnam tries to answer the question of why Laos has failed to attain stability, peace or economic growth since its independence. He gives a detailed analysis of the forces which influenced major events up to the abdication of the King and the declaration of a republic in Laos. His perspective is that of Laos as a pawn caught up in the rivalry between the superpowers, which, by determined resistance, has demonstrated the limitations of these powers. He sees a neutralist position as offering the best hope for peace and stability in Laos. Ratnam was the Indian ambassador in Laos and he gives an eyewitness account of the Kong Le coup in 1960, p. 73-125.

161 An international history of the Vietnam War.
R. B. Smith. London: Macmillan, 1983- . vol. 1- .

Laos might seem marginal in this work, and yet one suggestion which Professor Smith offers is that 'One possible interpretation of the "origins" of the second war in Vietnam is that it arose . . . . from the consequences of American policy in Laos' (vol. 1, p. 80). The coverage of Laos, though brief, in volumes one and two which deal with the years 1955-61 and 1961-65, sets out clearly the policy and interests of all the governments that came to be involved in Laos and its fate. One useful feature is the chronological table of events at key moments, enabling the reader to keep track of the detail.

162 Thai-American relations in the Laotian crisis of 1960-1962.
Surachai Sirikrai. Ann Arbor, Michigan: University Microfilms, 1981. 384p. bibliog. (UM: 8008569).

A doctoral thesis presented in 1979 to the State University of New York, Binghamton. Surachai presents a view of Laotian history from 1945 to 1962 viewed from Thailand and the United States. The foreign relations of Thailand and the United States are played out against the backdrop of the events in Laos. This work offers another useful perspective on this period of the history of Laos.

163 Laos: the escalation of a secret war.
Sandra C. Taylor. In: *The Vietnam War as history*. Edited by Elizabeth Jane Errington, B. J. C. McKercher. New York: Praeger, 1990, p. 73-90.

Unlike the Vietnam War, the United States was able to keep its military operations in Laos secret for many years. Allegations of covert operations and a secret war were denied and were poorly covered in the world's press. Here Professor Taylor amplifies the accounts of events presented previously by partisans of the right and the left with material from recently opened but still censored documentary sources of the first years of the Lyndon Johnson administration. Her thesis is that 'the U. S. government relegated Laos to a diplomatic backwater yet condoned in piecemeal fashion the escalation of a secret war, emphasizing always that the conflict be kept hidden from the rest of the world in order to preserve the fiction of the Geneva Accords while maintaining pressure on the communist Pathet Lao and those the United States saw as the real aggressor, the Vietminh'.

164 **Notes of a witness: Laos and the Second Indochinese War.**
Marek Thee. New York: Random House, 1973. 435p. map.

The author, whose original name was Gdanskí, was a member of the International Commission for Supervision and Control in Laos, and this work is based largely on the notes that he made then. The main emphasis of the book is on the events of 1961-62, and it is a history based on observation and interviews. Thee was able to cross the political divide and meet both sides in the conflict, which enhances and enriches this account.

165 **Laos: buffer state or battleground.**
Hugh Toye. London: Oxford University Press, 1968. 245p. maps. bibliog.

In this book Toye's aim is to relate the problems of Laos in the mid-1960s to their historical origins. He had spent the years 1960-62 in Laos, a critical period in its history. After a brief survey of the history to 1940, Toye assesses the impact of the Japanese occupation, the First Indochinese War (1946-54), the problem of neutrality, the Laotian civil war, and the Geneva Conference of 1961-62 on Laos' position as a buffer state between Thailand and Vietnam. His conclusion is rather pessimistic about a possible peaceful outcome for Laos, given her traditional role as a buffer state and the unlikely prospect of a neutral Laos achieving international recognition.

Military operations and organization

166 **Development and employment of fixed-wing gunships 1962-1972.**
Jack S. Ballard. Washington, DC: United States Air Force, Office of Air Force History, 1982. 326p. maps. bibliog. (The United States Air Force in Southeast Asia).

A history of the evolution of the fixed-wing gunship and the tactics developed for its use in counter-insurgency. One of the main theatres in which it was used was Laos, over the Plain of Jars and the Ho Chi Minh trail and in the campaign Lam Son 719.

167 **The United States Air Force in Southeast Asia, 1961-1973.**
Edited by Carl Berger. Washington, DC: Office of Air History, 1977. 381p.

A heavily illustrated book covering every aspect of Air Force operations in South East Asia. Written in a detached style, it talks of sorties and tonnage of bombs dropped. For the civilian reaction it would need to be read in conjunction with other material such as F. Branfman, *Voices from the Plain of Jars* (q.v.).

168 **The war in Laos, 1960-75.**
Kenneth Conboy. London: Osprey Publishing, 1989. 48p. map.
(Osprey Men-at-Arms Series, no. 217).

A work which is essentially concerned with uniforms, insignia and equipment used by the various armed forces in Laos during the fifteen years of war. The text covers Laotian government forces, the government allied forces (that is pro-government guerilla forces, who were mainly Hmong), Thai volunteer forces, United States Military Assistance groups and more briefly, the Pathet Lao and the North Vietnamese Army. The work is illustrated with contemporary photographs and coloured plates of the uniforms by Simon McCouaig, and there are detailed notes on the plates at the end. There is a concise chronological history to introduce the work which chronicles the military engagements which followed the failure of the first coalition government. A companion work that is also relevant, and the definitive work for uniforms and insignia, is Gordon L. Rottman, *U.S. Army Special Forces, 1952-84* (London: Osprey Publishing, 1985. 64p. bibliog. [Osprey Elite Series, no. 4]).

169 **The air war in Indochina.**
Edited by Raphael Littauer, Norman Uphoff. Boston, Massachusetts: Beacon Press, 1972. rev. ed. 289p. maps. bibliog.

A study sponsored by the Peace Studies Program of the Center for International Studies and the Program on Science, Technology and Society at Cornell University. Based on interviews and discussions with over eighty consultants and access to transcripts obtained in Indo-China, the work looks at the objectives and activity of different air campaigns in Indo-China and offers an evaluation. One chapter looks at the campaign in southern Laos, to place an interdiction on the Ho Chi Minh trail, and another considers the air war in northern Laos. In the south air sorties rose to an average of over 200 a day in 1968 and 1969, and in the north they rose to an average of over 300 a day in 1969. The study concludes that the air campaigns resulted in very short-term success, but created large scale destruction and made a quarter to a third of the population refugees. There are statistical summaries of the evidence gathered. Other chapters offer consideration of the wider effects of air war.

170 **A historic victory of the Lao patriotic forces on Highway 9-southern Laos.**
[n.p.]: Neo Lao Haksat, 1971? 106p. maps. (In Laos, no. 2).

This is an account of the operation called Dewey Canyon II and later called Lam Son 719 by the Americans, a series of battles fought around Ban Dong in Laos close to Khe Sanh on the Vietnamese side of the border, as told by the Lao Patriotic Front. It was a battle of forty days from the date that the United States and South Vietnamese forces first crossed the frontier into Laos; the details are recounted in stirring language. An account told from the other side is given in Keith Nolan's *Into Laos: the story of Dewey Canyon II/Lam Son 719; Vietnam 1971* (q.v.). The text was also published in French as *Victoire historique des forces patriotiques lao sur la route no. 9 – Sud Laos* (Historic victory of the Lao patriotic forces on Route no. 9 in southern Laos) [n.p.]: Neo Lao Haksat, 1971? 114p. maps. [Au pays du pays Laos; no. 2].

171 **Phoukout stronghold.**
[n.p.]: Neo Lao Haksat Publications, 1967. 22p. map.
Phoukout, a fortress built into the Kout peak in Xieng Khouang province was the Pathet Lao base to defend the Plain of Jars and Route no. 7, the chief route into their base at Sam Neua. This pamphlet is an account of the virtual siege of the fort over three years and the resistance to air and land attack. Stories of individual courage and initiative are interwoven with the detailed account. There are also eight pages of photographs to illustrate the text.

172 **Into Laos: the story of Dewey Canyon II/ Lam Son 719; Vietnam 1971.**
Keith William Nolan. Novato, California: Presidio, 1986. 388p. map. bibliog.
The last major operation fought by the Americans in Vietnam was the 1971 invasion of Laos. This is a detailed account of the military operations of that campaign, intended to prevent the North Vietnamese from using Laos, particularly the Ho Chi Minh trail, as a spring board for attacking southern Vietnam. Based on research amongst officials, records and participants, the dry details are filled out with the experiences of individual combatants.

173 **Air America: the true story of the CIA's mercenary fliers in covert operations from pre-war China to present day Nicaragua.**
Christopher Robbins. London: Corgi Books, 1988. 352p. bibliog.
Air America is the everyday name used to refer to airlines with various names which have operated since 1947 in association with the Central Intelligence Agency, the CIA. Robbins seeks to tease out the history of this secret air force; it is told largely in terms of the pilots' own stories and from the perspective of pilots. The criminal activities which are often laid at the door of Air America pilots are dealt with lightly as the activities of a small minority. He passes no judgements on the morality of their actions, stressing that the pilots believed they were acting in the interests of the United States. The activities of Air America in Laos are covered in two chapters, plus references in other chapters such as the one devoted to opium. The style and tone of this book is journalistic and impressionistic, but while the official record is closed a more rigorous approach is difficult. This is a revised and updated edition of the work first published as *The invisible air force: the true story of the CIA's secret airlines.*

174 **The ravens: the men who flew in America's secret war in Laos.**
Christopher Robbins. New York: Crown, 1987. 420p. bibliog.
The operation known as the Steve Canyon Program in the United States Air Force was a covert airborne operation in Laos from 1966 to 1972. The author has reconstructed the background to the events and provides an impression of the experiences of the combatants in an operation which is still covered by full secrecy classification. A collection of photographs illustrates the story.

175 **Green berets at war: U.S. Army Special Forces in Southeast Asia 1956-1975.**
Shelby L. Stanton. Novato, California: Presidio Press, 1985. 360p. maps. bibliog.

A history of United States commando operations in South East Asia. Chapter two on Laos deals with the period from 1959 to 1962. Special Forces were first sent disguised as contracted civilian specialists; only in 1961 with the establishment of the United States Military Assistance Advisory Group could they wear uniforms, and they were then designated White Star. Details of their work with the Lao Army and the Hmong guerilla units are recounted, including their part in assisting the defeat of Kong Le's troops. In Laos the Special Forces developed patterns of training and operation which they used elsewhere. Most of the rest of the work deals with operations in Vietnam, but from the details given in the list of those 'Missing in action' and the honour citations, many of these operations spilled over into Laos. A full study of commando operations in Laos was published in a technical memorandum, *Case study of U.S. counterinsurgency operations in Laos, 1955-1962* (McLean, Virginia: RAC Publications, 1964 [Research Analysis Corporation Technical Memorandum; RAC-T-435]).

Personal narratives

176 **Captive on the Ho Chi Minh trail.**
Marjorie Clark. Chicago: Moody Press, 1974. 160p.

Two missionaries in Laos, Lloyd Oppel, a Canadian and Sam Mattix, an American, were captured in Laos. This is the story of their capture and imprisonment for five months first by the Lao and then by the North Vietnamese in the 'Hanoi Hilton'.

177 **Escape from Laos.**
Dieter Dengler. San Rafael, California; London: Presidio Press, 1979. 211p. maps.

The story of a United States naval pilot shot down in 1966 over Laos and held prisoner for some months in Laos before his escape and subsequent rescue by United States helicopter. This is a fluently written autobiographical account of a man determined to survive. The set-backs and hardships are recounted in graphic detail.

178 **My secret war.**
Richard S. Drury. Fallbrook, California: Aero Publishers, 1979. 2nd ed. 224p. map.

A personal account by a fighter-pilot of his year based in Thailand, 1969-70, flying bombing missions into Laos: an operation that was officially denied for some months. It was mainly written at the time of the events, after missions. Drury is fanatical about aeroplanes, passionate about flying, and committed to the work he was doing. There are detailed accounts of missions flown, targets tackled, and rescues of bailed-out pilots. His dislike of paperwork and regulations for their own sake is also clearly stated. Thirty pages of photographs show details of the aeroplanes and formations, damage received from anti-aircraft fire, and other points from his text.

179 **In the valley of the Mekong: an American in Laos.**
Matt J. Menger. Paterson, New Jersey: St. Anthony Guild Press,
1970. 226p. map.

Menger, a member of the Order of Mary the Immaculate, was the first American missionary to go to Laos, and served there from 1957. In this book we follow him through his first steps in learning Lao, ministering to extremely remote communities in Laos, and finally his work in Vientiane as director of Catholic relief services. He gives a personal firsthand account of the Kong Le coup in Vientiane and the subsequent coups and counter-coups of Laos. His descriptions of the life of the Lao and Hmong villagers is more evocative than some scientific descriptions. In his travels he used all the available forms of transport and so one has a user's view of communications in Laos. He writes sympathetically of the people of Laos, and the missionary attitude that the indigenous beliefs are pagan and that civilization is using a fork to eat and a handkerchief to blow the nose, surfaces infrequently. Menger's book *Slowly climbs the sun* (New York: Twin Circle, 1973. 228p.) is more of a descriptive travel book about Laos.

180 **Mister Pop.**
Don A. Schanche. New York: David McKay, 1970. 310p. map.

This is the story of Edgar Buell, an Indiana farmer who, in his forties, went to work in Laos in 1960 for the International Voluntary Services (IVS) as a field worker and stayed for nine years. He was sent initially to a settlement on the Plain of Jars, to a model farming project that proved to be a well-equipped failure. Buell studied the farming methods of the Lao, Lao Theung and the Hmong of the area and introduced practical innovations such as the provision of steel tips for the ploughs. Within a year most of the team of IVS workers was withdrawn as conflict in the area grew, and then Buell and the one remaining IVS worker used the bulldozer left by an agricultural project to assist in practical road and dam construction. Eventually Buell was pulled back to Vientiane as Royal Government control of the Plain of Jars was lost to the Pathet Lao. He spent the rest of his time in Laos organizing programmes of relief for the Hmong refugees; what began as temporary assistance became a systematized $10 million-a-year programme. This is a rather anecdotal account, but apart from Buell's work it covers the organization of the Hmong rebel army during the period of Kong Le's coup, the nature of the Hmong refugee movements as whole villages followed the withdrawal of guerillas to mountains where there was no food or shelter available, and the covert operations of the United States military and its recruitment of agents among the Hmong.

181 **Reported to be alive.**
Grant Wolfkill, Jerry A. Rose. London: W. H. Allen, 1966. 303p.

Wolfkill, a cameraman for NBC, and two Air America pilots were captured in May 1961 on the day the cease-fire came into operation. Nonetheless, they were held captive for fifteen months and this account details their marches across country to prison, the transfer between prisons during this time, and their treatment while in prison, as well as their own efforts to keep sane and occupied.

1975- .

182 Power in Indo China since 1975: a report and appendices.
Australia: Joint Committee on Foreign Affairs and Defence,
Parliament of the Commonwealth of Australia. Canberra, Australia:
Australian Government Publishing Service, 1981. 129p. map.
The terms of reference of the sub-committee on Indo-China were to report on 'the changing power structure in Indo China since 1975 and its effects on Australia and the region'. In the light of their investigations, they made recommendations for future Australian foreign policy towards the region. The report considers government and politics since 1975, the economy, the military situation, and foreign relations. Although this is a brief account it provides useful information simply, and offers points of comparison with neighbouring countries. Appendix 1 is a useful chronology of events from April 1975 to February 1981.

183 Bohica.
Scott Barnes, Melva Libb. Canton, Ohio: Bohica Corporation, 1987.
c. 700p.
An extraordinary story of a mission to rescue United States military personnel, who had been reported as missing in action and were now believed to be imprisoned in Laos. Barnes' story, and the accusations of dirty tricks played by elements associated with the United States administration, leave the reader to decide whether this is a tall story or a true chronicle of events. Barnes appears to be sincere and more than half the book is documentary material in a series of appendices.

184 The yellow rainmakers: are chemical weapons being used in Southeast Asia?
Grant Evans. London: Verso, 1983. 202p. map.
In 1979, reports were received of 'yellow rain' that was devastating the mountain peoples in the north of Laos. The United States State Department claimed that it was a chemical weapon being used to end the anti-government resistance of the remnants of the Hmong secret army. These accusations were published formally as *Chemical warfare in Southeast Asia and Afghanistan: report to the Congress from Secretary of State Alexander M. Haig Jr., March 22 1982* (Alexander M. Haig. Washington, DC: United States, Department of State, 1982. 30p.). Grant Evans examined the evidence produced and interviewed refugee Hmong in Thailand and Laos. Evans considers that panic and fear among the Hmong were manipulated, that while riot-control gases may have been used there is no physical evidence, which bears scientific examination, to support the accusation that toxins were used against any populations in Laos.

185 Résistances en Indochine, 1975-1980. (Opposition in Indo-China, 1975-1980.)
Bernard Hamel. Paris: IREP, 1981. 277p. maps. bibliog.
Hamel, a journalist, seeks to record the tragedy of the 'liberation' of Indo-China, that is the opposition to the new governments which could only be expressed in resistance movements that seemed to be largely ignored internationally. He states his intention to keep to the facts without concealing his sympathies for the resistance movements. The work is in three parts: the birth of resistance movements, the early years, the present

and likely fate for them. Material on Laos is interspersed with material on Vietnam and Cambodia. It is a mixture of unattributed quotation from Lao and French individuals that he deems to be valuable sources, and a linking narrative. It provides in an impressionistic manner some indication of the opposition to the government in Laos in the first five years of the republic, but it does not provide hard documentary facts. In the *Country profile* for 1986 the Economist Intelligence Unit was able to state 'by 1986 most armed opposition had ceased'.

186 **Indochina Chronology.**
Berkeley, California: Institute of East Asian Studies, University of California, 1982- . quarterly.
Designed to provide reliable and complete data about current events in and related to Indo-China for researchers, students and others, such as journalists. It provides a chronology of significant events in the three countries of Indo-China, and the source of the item. There is a bibliographical section which summarizes relevant, recently published monographs and periodical articles, and contains information on research projects, films and conferences.

187 **Indochina's refugees: oral histories from Laos, Cambodia and Vietnam.**
Joanna C. Scott. Jefferson, North Carolina; London: McFarland, 1989. 312p. maps.
Based on interviews with refugees at the Philippine Refugee Processing Centre at Bataan in the Philippines, conducted by the author between October 1985 and May 1986. These refugees were all undergoing intensive language training and cultural orientation before joining family and friends in the United States. The twelve Lao interviewed were all imprisoned after 1975 in seminar camps; they were all members of the armed forces of the Royal Lao Government, or government officials. Two of those interviewed are the wives of men imprisoned, who joined their husbands in the seminar camps when they had no other means of support. Apart from the account of their own experiences they try to record and recall the fate of other occupants of the camps. In an appendix the author gives the names of those recalled as having been present in four camps in the Viengxay area. They give a particular view of events in Laos after 1975.

Local history and annals

188 **Les annales de l'ancien royaume de S'ieng Khwang.** (The annals of the former kingdom of Xieng Khouang.)
Charles Archaimbault. *Bulletin de l'École Française d'Extrême-Orient*, vol. 53, no. 2 (1967), p. 557-673. maps. bibliog.
Xieng Khouang was the realm of the Phuan a Tai group inhabiting the higher plateaux east and north of Vientiane. Archaimbault discovered four manuscripts of their annals in Luang Prabang. Three are believed to date from 1925 when they were sent to Luang Prabang on the order of the vice-king; the fourth is dated 1952. Archaimbault provides a brief introduction and a French translation of these annals. In addition he adds the biography of a Phuan provincial chief, born in 1918, which he took down in 1965.

There are also genealogical tables derived from the annals, and some pages of the manuscripts are reproduced in photographs.

189   **Contribution a l'étude d'un cycle de légendes lau.** (Contribution to the study of a cycle of Lao legends.)
Charles Archaimbault.   Paris: École Française d'Extrême-Orient, 1980. 441p. (Publications de l'École Française d'Extrême-Orient, vol. 119).

Based on Lao manuscripts which are reproduced in facsimile in this work, the study considers five Lao legends which deal with events at the dawn of Lao history. There is a consideration of the oral and manuscript traditions in which they have survived, as well as a translation or summary in French of each of the texts.

190   **L'histoire de Campasak.** (The history of Champassak).
Charles Archaimbault.   *Journal Asiatique*, vol. 249, no. 4 (1961), p. 519-95. map.

A reconstruction of the history of Champassak in southern Laos. It is based on epigraphic sources and manuscript annals. Archaimbault links these with the legends that have accrued about the history of the former kingdom.

191   **Stèle de Vat Phou, près de Bassac [Laos].** (The stele of Vat Phu, near Bassak [Laos].)
A. Barth.   *Bulletin de l'École Française d'Extrême-Orient*, vol. 2, no. 3 (1902), p. 235-40.

The stele or inscription column of Vat Phu is a document of the Khmer ruler King Jayavarman I, dated 664 and 667 AD. It indicates the northern extent of the Khmer empire at that date. Barth provides a description, a transcription and a translation of the inscription. A facsimile of it is also provided.

192   **La perception des mouvements millénaristes du Sud et Centre Laos (fin du XIXe siècle-milieu du XXe siècle) depuis la décolonisation.** (The perception of millenarist movements in south and central Laos (end of the 19th-mid-20th century) since decolonization.)
B. Gay.   In: *Premier symposium franco-soviétique sur l'Asie du Sud-Est (Moscow, 1989)* (First French-Soviet symposium on South East Asia [Moscow, 1989]).   Edited by R. V. Pozner, O. V. Rybina.
Moscow: Institut Vostokvedeniiya, 1990, p. 229-40. bibliog.

Gay first outlines the principal events in the movements that he characterizes as millenarist, based on his research in the French archives and in Laos in 1986 and 1987. He identifies three phases: the first in the Bolovens Plateau between 1895 and 1898; the second a long-running movement centred on the Bolovens Plateau from 1899 to 1937; and the third in Savannakhet from 1899 to 1903. Lao historiography, which did not get established until after 1975, has tended to place four kinds of interpretation on these movements; political, basically anti-colonial struggles; political but using the manipulation of religious beliefs; religious and political; and social and superstitious. Gay outlines the key features and authors of these arguments. It is unfortunate that the bibliographical citation is not more systematic as it will be rather difficult to follow up Gay's work. At one point it is not clear if there is a misprint or a lack of a citation.

193 **Minority manipulation in colonial Indochina: lessons and legacies.**
Geoffrey C. Gunn. *Bulletin of Concerned Asian scholars*, vol. 19, no. 3 (1987), p. 20-28. maps.
A study of ethnohistory in the colonial period, focused on the montagnards of the Laos-Annam frontier. This area in southern Laos, where it borders central Vietnam, was one of the last areas of French colonial penetration. Gunn discusses the case of the sub-group of the Kha, now known as Lao Theung, the Kha Leu, who bestraddled the border and had historically paid tribute to the ruler of Annam, while being technically under the suzerainty of Vientiane. Gunn outlines the 'Scandal of Saravane', an abuse of power by the colonial administrators in the region, which gave rise to an improved policy for minorities, which, however, was never fully implemented. One of the keys to the problem was the undefined nature of the border, which the current Vietnamese and Lao governments defined in a treaty of 1977, and a protocol of 1978.

194 **Les rois de Champassak.** (The kings of Champassak.)
Pierre Lintingre. Paksé, Laos: Inspection Générale du Royaume, 1972. [66]p.
The object of the author is to demonstrate the continuity of the royal line of Champassak through history. It is a summary of the history of Champassak and a critical study of the writings of others on the subject. This brief work is illustrated with material on Prince Boun Oum and his family, and monuments and inscriptions from the Paksé area.

195 **The That Phanom chronicle: a shrine history and its interpretation.**
Edited and translated by James B. Pruess. Ithaca, New York: Cornell University, Southeast Asia Program, 1976. 76p. map. bibliog. (Data Paper, no. 104).
The shrine of the That Phanom relic is situated on the west bank of the Mekong River in modern Thailand. The area was under the suzerainty of the kingdom of Lan Xang, and it has long served as a symbol of the identity of the Lao in modern Laos and the Lao of Thailand. Pruess provides a translation of a history of the shrine, itself based on a manuscript, which offers an example of local Buddhist historiography. He provides a useful introduction which explains the genre of literature and the content of this work. The work translated refers largely to the period of Lan Xang history, although the last chapter relates to the twentieth century.

196 **Contribution à l'histoire du royaume de Luang Prabang.** (A contribution to the history of the kingdom of Luang Prabang.)
Saveng Phinith. Paris: École Française d'Extrême-Orient, 1987. 477p. maps. bibliog. (Publications de l'École Française d'Extrême-Orient, no. 141).
In this work Saveng supplies an annotated translation of a Lao manuscript written in 1870 at the request of the father of the second king for the King of Siam (modern Thailand). The text gives the history of Luang Prabang from its legendary origins to the period of its existence as a dependency of Siam, that is up to the eve of the French

protectorate. Saveng's study of this text compares the account given with other sources which exist for Lao history, and the analytical indexes and chronology enable the user to handle what was written as a continuous text. There is a facsimile reproduction of the manuscript for those who wish to use the Lao text.

197   **A culture in search of survival: the Phuan of Thailand and Laos.**
Snit Smuckarn, Kennon Breazeale. New Haven, Connecticut: Yale University, Southeast Asia Studies, 1988. 279p. maps. bibliog.
(Monograph Series/Yale University Southeast Asia Studies, no. 31).
A study of the Phuan, the Tai-speaking population of the province and kingdom of Xieng Khwang in Laos, who were deported in large numbers during the nineteenth century to Thailand. The first half of the work is an examination of Phuan history, in particular the deportations and the efforts to survive in Laos; the second half examines Phuan culture as it survives in Thailand. Snit Smuckarn is a Phuan native of the district studied in Thailand, as well as Director of the Research Centre at the National Institute of Development Administration in Bangkok. The historical background is reconstructed from the national archives of Thailand, France and the United Kingdom, as well as published works. Phuan manuscripts have not survived in large numbers and many that were held in the National Library, Manuscripts Division, in Thailand were lost in a fire, although some extracts had been published. The history of the Phuan was recorded in the late nineteenth century, and a study of these annals has been prepared by Charles Archaimbault, 'Les annales de l'ancien royaume de S'ieng Khwang' (The annals of the former kingdom of Xieng Khwang) (q.v.). The fate of the Phuan documented here fills an important gap in the study of the history of Laos and the competing rivalries of Thailand and Vietnam, succeeded by the competing rivalries of Britain and France. It was dynastic rivalry among the Phuan that gave these external powers the opportunity to exert their influence. The study of Phuan culture in Thailand which has survived for between four and eight generations gives some indication of the strength which enabled it to maintain a separate identity and separate state within Laos.

160 years ago: Lao chronicles and annals on Siam and the Lao.
See item no. 103.

Population and Demography

198 **Population resettlement in the Mekong River Basin: Papers of the third Carolina Geographical Symposium.**
Edited by L. A. Peter Gosling. Chapel Hill, North Carolina: University of North Carolina at Chapel Hill, Department of Geography, 1979. 135p. maps. bibliog. (Studies in Geography, no. 10).
The papers in this volume consider the effects of the creation of reservoirs along the tributaries of the Mekong, and the effect on the people who have to be resettled. These papers were preparatory work for a study on the effects of building a dam across the Mekong at Pa Mong near Vientiane in Laos. The contributions which refer specifically to Laos are: R. Paul Lightfoot, 'Spatial distribution and cohesion of resettled communities'; Maxine E. Olson, 'Village cohesion in Laos: the effects of the war refugee experience'; and Theodore Fuller, Faryal Ross-Sheriff, 'Urban resettlement of reservoir evacuees in Thailand and Laos'. The commentaries on the articles draw out relevant points for the planning of the Pa Mong dam and reservoir.

199 **Demographic materials on the Khmer Republic, Laos and Vietnam.**
Ng Shui Meng. Singapore: Institute of Southeast Asian Studies, 1974. 54p. bibliog. (Library Bulletin, no. 8).
An unannotated bibliography dealing with the material by topics: demographic materials and analyses, rural/urban population, minority groups, labour, and refugees. There is an index of authors, but no index to help identify the material relating specifically to Laos. It complements the author's study *The population of Indochina* (q.v.)

204 **Bibliography of the peoples and cultures of mainland Southeast Asia.**
John F. Embree, Lillian Ota Dotson. New Haven, Connecticut: Yale
University, 1950. 821p.

Although now over forty years old, this book has not been revised or superseded. It
provides a very comprehensive literature survey of material published up to 1950 on
physical anthropology, demography, archaeology, ethnology, cultural history, social
organization, law, religion, language, literature, writing and folklore for each of the
countries and their major population. There are separate sections in the bibliography
for works on the multitude of ethnic groups. There are brief annotations provided if
the title of a book or article does not indicate its content. This bibliography should be
used in conjunction with the work of Frank M. Lebar, Gerald C. Hickey and John K.
Musgrove, *Ethnic groups of mainland Southeast Asia*, (New Haven, Connecticut:
Human Relations Area Files Press, 1964).

205 **Sur les sentiers laotiens. (On Lao paths.)**
E. Guillemet. Amiens, France: Yvert, 1929. 2nd ed. 280p. map.

An account of six months in Upper Laos with the French expeditionary force in 1915
and 1916, sent to settle a rebellion raised by the Chinese from Yunnan in Phong Saly.
This volume is valuable for the considerable number of observations on the ethnic
groups of the region; there are also photographs, but the quality is not always good.
This work was first published in Hanoi in 1921. With a fellow officer, Captain O'Kelly,
Guillemet wrote a further book about the expedition *En colonne dans le Haut-Laos:
notes de voyage, 1915-1916* (In column in Upper Laos: travel notes, 1915-1916) (Hanoi:
Imprimerie d'Extrême-Orient, 1926).

206 **Compass for fields afar: essays in social anthropology.**
Karl Gustav Izikowitz. Gothenburg, Sweden: Acta Universitatis
Gothoburgensis, 1985. 313p. maps. bibliog. (Gothenburg Studies in
Social Anthropology, no. 7).

A collection of Izikowitz's essays spanning over fifty years and published in a number
of journals and reassembled here in homage to this eminent anthropologist. Seven of
the twelve essays have direct bearing on his research in Laos. Several derive from his
work on the Lamet, the others from his work on Tai peoples in Laos and the wider
area.

207 **Southeast Asian tribes, minorities, and nations.**
Edited by Peter Kunstadter. Princeton, New Jersey: Princeton
University Press, 1967. 2 vols.

The section on Laos is found in volume one; the maps and index in volume two. The
introduction, an article by Joel M. Halpern and Peter Kunstadter, describes the
distribution of ethnic groups in Laos and the general position of the minorities in
relation to the Royal Lao Government and the Pathet Lao. They also consider the
shifting settlement pattern of the ethnic minorities which had a long historical
precedent, aggravated by more recent political events. There is a table of ethnic
groups, their population size, location and language by Halpern, based on official Lao
sources. The other papers on Laos are 'Government and the hill tribes of Laos' by
G. M. T. Osborn, a picture of the conditions in which the tribal peoples live and the
action taken to alleviate their poor social conditions; 'The Meo of Xieng Khouang
Province, Laos' by G. Linwood Barney, is a study based on field work between 1950

and 1954 when Barney was engaged in linguistic and missionary work in Laos – it is a broad survey of the life of the Meo (now usually called the Hmong). The final brief article, 'U.S. aid to hill tribe refugees in Laos' by James Thomas Ward, gives a general description of the refugee relief programme of the US Agency for International Development, with particular reference to aid to the Meo (Hmong) refugees in Xieng Khouang Province, 1963-65. In volume two there is a study of the Yao or Iu Mien in Thailand, 'Anatomy and integration of social systems: the Iu Mien 'Yao' or 'Man' mountain populations and their neighbours' by Peter Kandre. It is a study of the way the Yao have adapted both to the outside world and amongst themselves in their new home in Thailand; most of the Yao had migrated to Thailand from Laos after 1945.

208 **Peoples of the golden triangle: six tribes in Thailand.**
Paul Lewis, Elaine Lewis. London: Thames & Hudson, 1984. 300p. maps. bibliog.

A photographic essay with brief notes on six ethnic groups and their subdivisions; the groups covered are the Hmong, Yao or Mien, Lahu and Akha who also live in Laos, as well as the Karen and Lisu who largely live in Burma. The work discusses the family life, religion and customs of each group, with more detail given on particulars of the costumes and ornaments worn by each of them. Undoubtedly the life of the groups described has been affected by their settlement in Thailand and their contact with a more commercial economy than that of Laos or Burma. The detail and the quality of the photographs make this an outstanding source of information, particularly for costume. The text, while brief, is excellent.

209 **Ethnic groups of French Indochina.**
Conceived and produced by Louis Malleret. Washington, DC: US Joint Publications Research Service, 1962. 110p. bibliog.

A translation of *Groupes ethniques de l'Indochine française* (Saigon, Vietnam: Société des Études Indochinoises, 1937. 62p.). The original edition contains one hundred plates and an ethnographic map, which were not reproduced in this working translation, although they are referred to at the appropriate point and so can be used together. The work is arranged according to ethnic groups and subgroups. Each brief entry indicates the geographical area inhabited, size of the group, clothing worn, hairstyles, form of agriculture, beliefs, and customs, with relevant bibliographical references. The features of the costumes illustrated in the photographs are discussed. The interest of this work is that it provides valuable information that can be attached to a particular date, because the photographs were taken at a ceremony to inaugurate the Trans-Indochina Railway and at an assembly of ethnic groups in Saigon. Although worn for a ceremonial occasion, the costumes can be identified with this particular period. The record of the geographical distribution of the ethnic groups is valuable too, as since this date there has been both natural movement and large-scale movement caused by the disruption of the wars since 1945.

210 **Sud-Est Asiatico.** (South East Asia.)
Antonio Marazzi. Novara, Italy: Istituto Geografico De Agostini, 1981. 120p. map. bibliog. (Popoli Nel Mondo).

This volume is included because of its exceptionally fine photographs of the life and peoples of South East Asia. The section on Laos covers the Lao, the Lao Theung, the Lao Tai and the Lao Soung. More information on the Meo or Hmong and the Yao is found in the section on Thailand. The text is brief and intended for the general reader, but it is sound.

The Hmong

211   **I am a shaman: a Hmong life story with ethnographic commentary.**
Dwight Conquergood, Paja Thao.   Minneapolis, Minnesota: Center
for Urban and Regional Affairs, University of Minnesota, 1989. 90p.,
bibliog. (Southeast Asian Refugee Studies, Occasional Paper, no. 8).
An account of Hmong shamanism told by Paja Thao, a Hmong shaman from Laos; he
recounted his story, translated here, six months after he arrived in the United States
and nine years after he had left Laos. Conquergood, an ethnographer, has provided
commentary and material to put it into context. This monograph forms an integral part
of the documentary film *Between two worlds: the Hmong shaman in America*, produced
by Dwight Conquergood and Taggart Siegel (Chicago: Siegel Productions; New York:
Third World Newsreel, 1985).

212   **The Hmong in the West: observations, reports, papers of the 1981**
Hmong Research Conference, University of Minnesota.
Edited by Bruce T. Downing, Douglas P. Olney.   Minneapolis,
Minnesota: Southeast Asian Refugee Studies Project, Center for Urban
and Regional Affairs, University of Minnesota, 1981. 401p.
The conference papers published here were written in an attempt to pin down
knowledge of the Hmong and to understand their problems and successes in settling
down in the United States. Inevitably it was necessary to describe aspects of Hmong
life in Laos, thus this work provides information on marriage customs, birth customs,
myths and legends, and language. For those interested in the Hmong outside Laos
there are papers on learning English and the problems of settlement in the United
States.

213   **The Hmong in transition.**
Edited by Glenn L. Hendricks, Bruce T. Downing, Amos S. Deinard.
New York: Centre for Migration Studies, 1986. 464p. map. bibliog.
This volume contains the papers presented at the second Hmong Research Conference
held at the University of Minnesota, November 1983. They fall into two categories:
those which deal with Hmong culture generally, or in the context of Laos; and those
which discuss problems of adaptation and settlement in the United States. The four
subject groups are 'Hmong culture and change', 'Adapting to a new society',
'Language and literacy', and 'Health care issues'.

214 **History of the Hmong.**
Jean Mottin. Bangkok: Odeon Store, 1980. 63p. maps. bibliog.
This short history of the Hmong begins when they lived in China and follows their spread into Vietnam, Laos and Thailand, which began in the early nineteenth century. They migrated south because Chinese repression against their uprisings and Chinese assertion of power became overwhelming. Mottin has composed his history from available published sources and he recounts it in a rather anecdotal style. He accuses the Hmong of a poor knowledge of their own history, but others have commented on their great ability to recall past events in what is still an oral-based tradition.

215 **A bibliography of the Hmong (Miao) of Southeast Asia and the Hmong refugees in the United States.**
Compiled by Douglas P. Olney. Minneapolis, Minnesota: Center for Urban and Regional Affairs, University of Minnesota, 1983. rev. ed. 75p. (Southeast Asian Refugee Studies, Occasional Papers, no. 1).
About a third of this bibliography is devoted to Hmong ethnography and the rest is on language, resettlement issues and a selection of newspaper articles. There are over nine hundred items listed.

216 **The Hmong: an annotated bibliography, 1983-1987.**
Compiled by J. Christina Smith. Minneapolis, Minnesota: Center for Urban and Regional Affairs, University of Minnesota, 1988. 67p. (Southeast Asian Refugee Studies, Occasional Papers, no. 7).
This bibliography is complementary to the earlier bibliography of Olney, *A bibliography of the Hmong (Miao) of Southeast Asia and the Hmong refugees in the United States* (q.v.). There are over three hundred entries; a large proportion deal with the Hmong in the new environment that they have entered as refugees from Laos.

217 **Sovereignty and rebellion: the White Hmong of northern Thailand.**
Nicholas Tapp. Singapore; Oxford: Oxford University Press, 1989. 238p. maps. bibliog.
A study of the current position of a Hmong opium-growing village in northern Thailand. Based on field work in a village, it is a micro-study of certain aspects of White Hmong culture, in particular geomancy, messianism and literacy. The author endeavours to relate one central legend to all other aspects of White Hmong cultural and socio-economic organization. While this is a study of a village of White Hmong who have been settled in Thailand for a long time, there is a great deal of material about the Hmong in general, including those of Laos. The last chapter focuses on the fate of the refugee Hmong from Laos both in Thailand and overseas. Appendix 1 is a helpful bibliographic essay on previous work on the Hmong, and the bibliography to the book as a whole is particularly thorough.

200 **The population of Indochina: some preliminary observations.**
Ng Shui Meng. Singapore: Institute of Southeast Asian Studies, 1974.
126p. bibliog. (Field Report Series, no. 7).
An historical survey of what is known of the population of Indo-China based on
published sources. Miss Ng discusses the population estimates of the colonial and post-
independence period and the reliability of the statistical sources. For Laos this work is
based on a series of estimates made by governmental and international agencies. The
first official census in Laos took place in 1985. For a fuller bibliography on the subject
see Miss Ng's *Demographic materials on the Khmer Republic, Laos and Vietnam* (q.v.).

201 **Population trends and policies in Laos (Lao People's Democratic
Republic) and Cambodia (Democratic Kampuchea).**
In: *International Population Conference/Congrès International de la
Population. New Delhi, September 20-27 1989.* Liège, Belgium:
International Institute for Scientific Study of Population, 1989, vol. 1,
p. 145-53.
Discusses current population trends and policies in Laos and Cambodia, and provides
an overview of the demographic situation in both countries.

202 **La population du Laos en 1943 dans son milieu géographique.** (The
population of Laos in 1943 in its geographical environment.)
Eric Pietrantoni. *Bulletin de la Société des Études Indochinoises*, new
series, vol. 32, no. 3 (1957), p. 223-43. map.
The work is based on Pietrantoni's own observations in Laos between 1931 and 1945,
and on archives in the office of the *Résident Supérieur* (chief colonial officer) in
Vientiane. He offers a picture of the distribution of the population in both the rural
and urban areas and looks at the reasons for growth, some of which he attributes to
immigration. In a previous article he had analysed the population for the earlier
period: 'La population du Laos de 1915 à 1945' (The population of Laos from 1915 to
1945) (*Bulletin de la Société des Études Indochinoises*, new series, vol. 28, no. 1 (1953),
p. 25-38).

Ethnic Groups

General

203　**Hill farms and padi fields: life in mainland Southeast Asia.**
Robbins Burling.　Englewood Cliffs, New Jersey: Prentice-Hall, 1965.
180p. map. bibliog.
A brief survey of human habitation of mainland South East Asia. Burling sets out to present a coherent synthesis of the subject, with specific examples that illustrate the different types of social organization which exist concurrently in modern South East Asia. The only specifically Laotian element is the brief section on the Lamet, but the general survey of how agricultural society has evolved is relevant to Laos. In trying to cover such a broad canvas the book runs the risk of over-simplification but it is a useful starting point. Burling's work offers an impressionistic view of the enthography which is treated systematically in *Ethnic groups of mainland Southeast Asia*, by Frank M. Lebar, Gerald C. Hickey, John K. Musgrave (New Haven, Connecticut: Human Relations Area Files Press, 1964. 288p. map. bibliog). It is based on published and unpublished field-work research. The compilers have retained the tribal/language system of grouping ethnic groups. An encyclopaedia-style entry is given for each group and covers the linguistic and territorial identification, demography and history; settlement pattern and housing; economy; marriage and family; sociopolitical organization; religion; beliefs in the supernatural and ideas on death and the afterlife. The sources are cited at the end of each section and these are given in full in the bibliography. In each entry the variant names used for each group are given and there are indexes to these forms. Many of the entries for Laos are based on the unpublished research notes of Professor Lafont. A map indicates the physical location of the peoples. Undoubtedly there has been much movement of the minority groups in Laos since this work was compiled but it will be some time before this work is replaced.

Other ethnic groups

218 **Akha and Miao: problems of applied ethnography in Further India.**
Hugo Adolf Bernatzik.   New Haven, Connecticut: Human Relations
Area Files, 1970. 772p. map. bibliog.
Based on the author's expedition to South East Asia in 1936-37, his study here is of the
Akha and Miao (also known as Hmong) groups in Thailand. This study also refers to
the published work on these groups, both of which are found in Laos. This is a classic
ethnographic study based on fieldwork and extensive reading of the literature available
up to the date of its original publication in 1947. Originally published as *Akha und
Meau* (Innsbruck, Austria: Wagnerische Universitäts-Buchdruckerei, 1947. 2 vols.).

219 **The spirits of the yellow leaves.**
Hugo Adolf Bernatzik.   London: Robert Hale, 1958. 222p. maps.
An account of Bernatzik's travels in Thailand and the immediate cross-border areas to
trace the original populations of the regions. In the frontier area between Thailand and
Laos, he sought the Yumbri, or Phi Tong Luang, the 'spirits of the yellow leaves'.
These people, who inhabit the densest forest, live by hunting and gathering forest
produce, some of which they exchange with neighbouring ethnic groups. Bernatzik's
account is in two parts: the more anecdotal diary account of his attemps to contact the
Yumbri; and his 'Monograph on the Phi Tong Luang' (p. 130-67) in which he sets out a
systematic account of their life as he was able to ascertain it. There are some
photographs of the Yumbri. The Yumbri in central Laos are considered in the article
'Les sauvages de la Nam-om' (The wild men of the Nam-om) by A. Fraisse (*Bulletin de
la Société des Études Indochinoises*, vol. 24, no. 1 (1949), p. 27-36. maps.). This group,
who had been thought to be on the point of disappearance, have been discovered to be
more numerous recently. A more recent survey of the Phi Tong Luang in Thailand is
contained in Surin Pookajorn, *Archaeological research of the Hoabinhian culture or
technocomplex and its comparison with ethnoarchaeology of the Phi Tong Luang, a
hunter-gatherer group of Thailand* (Tübingen Verlag Archaeologica Venatoria, 1988.
275, [82]p., maps. bibliog. [Archaeologica Venatoria, Band 9 (1988)]).

220 **Frontier land systems in southernmost China: a comparative study of
agrarian problems and social orgainization among the Pai Yi people of
Yunnan and the Kamba people of Sikang.**
Chen Han-Seng.   New York: Institute of Pacific Relations, 1949.
156p.
The Pai Yi, known as Yi or Lolo in Laos and Burma, are far more numerous in
Yunnan in China. The first part of this study (p. 1-71) is devoted to them. It discusses
how they moved to this part of China and their social organization, in particular land
tenure and agricultural organization. The chapters on tribute, rent, trade and usury
refer specifically to systems in China.

221 **From Lawa to Mon, from Saa' to Thai: historical and anthropological aspects of Southeast Asian social spaces.**
Georges Condominas. Canberra: Australian National University, Research School of Pacific Studies, 1990. 114p. maps. bibliog. (Occasional Paper of the Department of Anthropology, Research School of Pacific Studies, Australian National University).
These are two essays translated into English from Condominas' larger work *Espace social à propos de l'Asie de Sud-Est* (Social space with regard to South East Asia, published by Flammarion (Paris: 1980. 541p.)). The second essay is 'Essay on the evolution of Thai political systems'. In it Condominas surveys the literature on the Tai peoples who inhabit the area between Vietnam and Laos, as well as the wider Tai groupings, to offer his analysis of the political system, particularly of rulers, alliances and social organization.

222 **Ethnic groups in the valley of the Nam Song and the Nam Lik: their geographical distribution and some aspects of social change.**
Keiji Iwata, edited by Joel M. Halpern. Los Angeles: University of California, Department of Anthropology, c.1960. 33 leaves. maps. (Laos Project Paper; no. 15).
A translation and condensation of the article which was first published in the *Minzokokugaku Kenkyu/Japanese Journal of Ethnology*, vol. 23, nos. 1-2 (1959). It is a study of the village Ban Pha Tangand and the surrounding district, situated between Vientiane and Luang Prabang, where the author lived for four months in 1958. It is a study of the social organization and kinship of the Tai, Hmong, Yao and Khmu in the area. The distribution of the populations from mountain slope to valley floor conforms to the model for the region described by Robbins Burling in *Hill farms and padi fields* (q.v.).

223 **Minority groups in northern Laos: especially the Yao.**
Keiji Iwata, edited by Joel Halpern. Los Angeles: University of California, Department of Anthropology, c.1961. 33 leaves. maps. (Laos Project Paper, no. 16).
A translation and condensation of the article which was first published in *Shilin*, no. 1 (1960). It is a study of the Yao in a village between Vientiane and Luang Prabang, close to the Lao village where the author lived for four months. It is a descriptive study of the village and its agriculture, the families who inhabited the village, and their religion and ceremonies. He also considers their relationships with the other neighbouring ethnic groups.

224 **Lamet: hill peasants in French Indochina.**
Karl Gustav Izikowitz. New York: AMS Press, 1979. 379p. maps.
A reprint of Izikowitz's work first published in 1951, to which has been added Rodney Needham's 'Alliance and classification among the Lamet', first published in *Sociologus*, vol. 10, no. 2 (1960). A standard work on the Lamet, an ethnic group of Laos, the study is based on the author's fieldwork in 1937. The Lamet are a society of *swidden* (slash and burn) cultivators in northern Laos, and in this pioneering study Izikowitz describes all aspects of their economic and social life. Photographs and sketches illustrate his descriptions.

225 **Deux tribus de la région de Phongsaly: Laos septentrional.** (Two tribes from the region of Phongsaly: northern Laos.)
Henri Roux. *Bulletin de l'École Française d'Extrême-Orient*, vol. 24, nos. 3-4, p. 373-500. map.

Roux presents here the notes he made and collected while he commanded the 5th Military Territory in the north of Laos. The two tribes are the Akha and the P'u-Noi, sometimes known more fully as the Kha Pai P'u Noi. The two are treated separately and he systematically covers the same topics for each; that is, a general description of the group and their habitat, their physical characteristics and costume, historical legends, customs and practices relating to kinship, housing, birth, funerals and death, dreams, prohibitions, festivals, measurement and language. For each he gives examples of vocabulary and texts in Akha or P'u Noi with a French translation. There are photographic plates illustrating both tribes. This remains one of the few descriptions of the P'u Noi, while other published work on the Akha has mainly been on Akha from other areas. This region has been one of those in Laos most disrupted by war since 1950, and so this account has value as a record of a style of life which has been altered by external forces.

226 **Les Nya Hön: étude ethnographique d'une population du Plateau des Bolovens (Sud-Laos).** (An ethnographic study of the Nya Hön, an ethnic group of the Boloven Plateau in southern Laos.)
Barbara Wall. Vientiane: Vithagna, 1975. 228p. maps. bibliog. (Documents pour le Laos, no. 6).

A study of the Nya Hön, a Mon-Khmer-speaking ethnic group. It is based on five months fieldwork conducted in 1967. This is a descriptive, rather than an analytical study, of these *swidden* (or slash and burn) cultivators. Life in the village is covered in its social, economic and spiritual aspects as well as the agricultural practices. The work concludes with a brief sketch of Nya Hön grammar and a vocabulary of the language.

Languages

General

227 **Mainland South-East Asia, Peninsular Malaysia and Andaman and Nicobar Islands.**
Edited by D. Bradley, G. Benjamin, Stephen A. Wurm. In: *Language Atlas Pacific Area*. Edited by Stephen A. Wurm, Shiro Hattori. Canberra: Australian Academy of the Humanities in collaboration with the Japan Academy, 1981, maps. 35-37, 2 accompanying text sheets. bibliog. (Pacific Linguistics: Series C, no. 66).

As the editors state, 'the area covered by the three maps in this set is one of the linguistically most complex parts of the world'. The maps chart the disposition of the speakers of the languages of the area; the text clarifies this. The data for Laos is based on both published and unpublished research. The text explains the maps, the language classifications and migrations, and discusses the sources listed in the bibliography. The geographical area of Laos is covered in two of the maps. The final sheet provides an index to the material in the maps and text.

228 **Thailand and Laos.**
William J.Gedney. In: *Current trends in linguistics. Vol. 2, Linguistics in East and South East Asia*. Edited by Thomas A. Sebeok. The Hague, Netherlands: Mouton, 1967, p. 782-814. bibliog.

A survey of linguistic studies of Thailand and Laos to the date of writing. This bibliographical essay looks at descriptive studies, traditional studies and the lexicography of Lao as well as historical, comparative and dialect studies of the Tai family of languages. Full details of the works cited are provided in the bibliography.

229 **A Tai festschrift for William J. Gedney on the occasion of his fifth cycle of life birthday anniversary, April 4 1975.**
Edited by Thomas W. Gething. Honolulu, Hawaii: University of Hawaii, Southeast Asian Studies Program, 1975. 183 leaves. bibliog. (Southeast Asia Working Papers).

Three of the papers in this volume are relevant to Laos: 'Two types of semantic contrast between Thai and Lao' by Thomas W. Gething (ff. 43-54); 'Lam Khon Savan: a traditional form and a contemporary theme' by Carol J. Compton (ff. 55-82), providing an example of a *lam* (sung poem) in the Khon Savan style from Savannakhet, in English translation and romanized transcription; and 'Syllabic m in Tai-Lue and neighbouring Tai dialects' by John S. Hartmann (ff. 112-27).

230 **Studies in Tai linguistics in honor of William J. Gedney.**
Edited by Jimmy G. Harris, James R. Chamberlain. Bangkok: Central Institute of English Language, 1975. 409p. bibliog.

Three contributions are relevant to Laos: 'A new look at the history and classification of the Tai languages' by James R. Chamberlain, (p. 49-66); 'Location in Thai and Lao' by Thomas W. Gething, (p. 196-201); and 'Rhyme, reduplication, etc. in Lao' by G. E. Roffe, on style in discourse, containing a large number of examples collected by Roffe.

231 **Bibliography and index of mainland Southeast Asian languages and linguistics.**
Franklin E. Huffman. New Haven, Connecticut: Yale University Press, 1986. 640p.

The body of the bibliography is a master list of about 10,000 items arranged alphabetically by author; added to these are book reviews of particular items. Annotations are only given to explain titles which are unclear. Access to the bibliography is via the language and subject index, where entries are grouped under the names of languages or countries and then subdivided by topics such as grammar, dictionaries and dialects. The coverage is very wide, and apart from monographic and journal literature, Huffman indexes articles in composite works which have formed a significant part of recent publishing.

Lao language: dictionaries and grammars

232 **Lao for beginners: an introduction to the spoken and written language of Laos.**
Tatsuo Hoshino, Russell Marcus. Rutland, Vermont: Tuttle, 1981. 209p.

Designed for the beginner, this book teaches the user to speak and read Lao through a series of exercises. Lao script is used throughout alongside phonetic transcriptions so that the student can progress to reading Lao script. A brief grammatical summary is provided (p. 141-56) and a glossary in transcription. This book can be used by an individual, or it could be used with a Lao speaker to assist with pronunciation. It is complemented by the *English-Lao, Lao-English dictionary* (q.v.).

233 **Grammaire laotienne.** (Lao grammar.)
J.-J. Hospitalier. Paris: Imprimerie Nationale, 1937. 270p.

A grammar of the Lao language produced by Hospitalier who had worked as an educationist in Laos. The fonts for the Lao script were specially struck for this work. It deals with Lao script, the sounds, the tonal system and the grammatical structure. This was not intended as a self-instructional work.

234 **Lao-English dictionary.**
Allen D. Kerr. Washington, DC: Catholic University of America Press, 1972. 2 vols. (Publications in Languages of Asia, no. 2).

Compiled over a period of twelve years, of which eight were spent in Laos, this dictionary is based on material gathered from native speakers, recent vernacular publications and other published dictionaries. The compiler describes it as 'the first reasonably comprehensive dictionary of the Lao language'. Spelling was based on the royal directive to the Comité Littéraire Lao; in some cases Kerr has had to make a choice. The entries give the words in Lao script, in a romanized form and in an English definition.

235 **English-Lao, Lao-English dictionary.**
Edited by Russell Marcus, chief compiler. Rutland, Vermont: Tuttle, 1983. rev. ed. 416p.

This pocket dictionary gives one-word equivalents rather than examples of usage. The English-Lao section provides definitions in phonetic transcriptions and Lao script. Useful for its compactness, it complements *Lao for beginners* (q.v.).

236 **The Lao language.**
L. N. Morev, A. A. Moskalyov, Y. Y. Plam. Moscow: Nauka, 1979. 129p. bibliog. (Languages of Asia and Africa).

A description of the Lao language, its phonology, writing system, the formation of words, and its syntax. This work is essentially for linguists and students of language rather than for those seeking a system of self-instruction. The authors attempt to set down the language in what has been and continues to be a period of change. Uniform phonetic, grammatical or lexical standards are not yet established, although now that the country is unified there are more favourable conditions in which to establish them. The description given here is based on the Vientiane dialect as the most representative of all the dialects of modern Lao, and on original material from contemporary Lao newspapers, magazines and novels. Linguistic points were clarified with native speakers in Laos and the Soviet Union. The work was first published in Russian in this series in 1972.

237 **Elements de grammaire laotienne.** (Rudiments of Lao grammar.)
Pierre Somchine Nginn. Vientiane: Comité Littéraire Lao, 1965. 2nd ed. 98p.

A descriptive grammar which goes through the parts of speech, and states what they are and how they are used. In view of the changes in the political system, the section on personal pronouns has a historical significance and would be valuable when reading contemporary writing.

238 **Dictionnaire laotien-français.** (Lao-French dictionary.)
Marc Reinhorn. Paris: Editions du Centre National de la Recherche Scientifique, 1970. 2 vols. maps. bibliog. (Atlas Ethnolinguistique: 4. Série, Dictionnaires).

Reinhorn has worked on the Lao language since 1943, and this is the fourth version of a Lao-French dictionary he has published; it is a considerably enlarged version. Entries are given in Lao script, a romanized form, and a definition in French. It is the dictionary which most current writers on Laos cite as their point of reference on matters of language.

239 **Grammaire de la langue lao.** (Grammar of the Lao language.)
Marc Reinhorn. Paris: Samuelian, 1980. 204p. bibliog.

A descriptive grammar of the Lao language. Unlike some of his predecessors, Reinhorn is concerned with analysing Lao in categories that make sense in the context of Lao, and not to fit it to the model of a totally different language. Terms are given both in Lao script and in a romanized transcription, which reproduces the written language exactly; this makes it difficult to read initially. The work concludes with two chapters on prosody and versification.

240 **Lao: basic course.**
Warren G. Yates, Souksomboun Sayasithsena. Washington, DC: Foreign Service Institute, 1970-71. 2 vols. (Foreign Service Institute Basic Course Series).

Volume one provides introductory material in modern spoken Lao for the student who wishes to achieve proficiency. It is a set of guidelines for conversation with a native-speaking instructor and uses the Vientiane dialect as its basis, as that is the language of official government communications. There are eighty-five units, called cycles, that cover various points of grammar. Volume two is a set of readings in Lao on various topics to provide material to enable the student to obtain greater proficiency. The topics covered are those that would have been likely to be of interest to Americans going to Laos in 1970. A set of tapes for volume two could also be obtained from the publisher.

Other languages: dictionaries and grammars

241 **Dictionnaire hmong (meo blanc)-français.** (White Hmong-French dictionary.)
Yves Bertrais, Fr. Charrier. Vientiane: Mission Catholique, 1964. c. 600p.

Based on the work of a team of people, Fathers Bertrais and Charrier are named as the compilers. However, because of the typography of the title-page, this work is frequently cited as the work of one author Yves Bertrais-Charrier. The collection of the data for this dictionary took place over eight months in 1961, as previous work had been destroyed. The language studied is principally that of the White Hmong settled around Luang Prabang. The arrangement is by key terms; under these are listed phrases and expressions in which they are used. This work was reissued in 1979 by the Assumption Press, Bangkok.

242 **White Meo-English dictionary.**
Compiled by Ernest E. Heimbach. Ithaca, New York: Cornell University, Southeast Asia Program, 1969. 497p. bibliog.

A White Hmong-English dictionary based on material collected while the compiler was working as a missionary among the White Hmong in Thailand between 1954 and 1963. Most entries give two or more examples of usage, and a series of appendices provide information on specialized vocabulary, useful expressions, proverbs, and kinship charts with terminology.

243 **English-Mong-English dictionary – Phoo txhais lug Aakiv-Moob-Aakiv.**
Compiled by Lang Xiong, William J. Xiong, Nao Leng Xiong. [Milwaukee, Wisconsin: The Authors, 1983.] 570p.

Aimed at helping the Hmong in the United States with English, this dictionary of nearly 28,000 entries gives detailed explanations, or definitions in Hmong of English words. A complementary list of Hmong words is given with briefer definitions in English. A basic Hmong grammar is given in a ten-page appendix. There is no information given to indicate which Hmong dialect forms the basis of this dictionary.

244 **Yao-English dictionary.**
Compiled by Silvia J. Lombard, edited by Herbert C. Purnell. Ithaca, New York: Cornell University, Department of Southeast Asian Studies, Southeast Asia Program, 1968. 363p. bibliog. (Data Paper, no. 69).

This dictionary is based largely on material gathered among the Yao people of Thailand between 1952 and 1966, where Lombard worked as a missionary. Some more material was gained from other missionaries working with the Yao. It is a dictionary of the dialect of the Iu Mien, or Highland Yao, found in both Laos and Thailand. It is presented in the roman orthography used among the Yao in Thailand since 1954. The dictionary gives words and definitions in English, which are usually followed by

examples of usage. There are five appendices on specific aspects of language usage, that is, numbers, kinship terminology, names, proverbs and idioms, and classifiers, or counting words.

245 **Dictionary of Mong Njua: a Miao (Meo) language of Southeast Asia.**
Thomas Amis Lyman. The Hague, Netherlands: Mouton, 1974. 403p. bibliog. (Janua Linguarum: Series Practica, no. 123).

Based on a study of the language of the Hmong Njua, or Green Miao, people settled in Thailand, this is a Hmong-English dictionary. There are appendices on specific topics of vocabulary such as time and colour. Lyman has published a number of other works on the language and culture of this group, listed in the bibliography of this work, and in 1979 he published *Grammar of Mong Njua (Green Miao): a descriptive linguistic study* privately.

246 **Papers in South-East Asian linguistics, no. 10: Khmu a minority language of Thailand.**
Suwilai Premsirat. Canberra: Australian National University, 1987. 190p. map. bibliog. (Pacific Linguistics: Series A, no. 75).

Khmu is a language spoken by a large part of the population of northern Laos and also a small minority group in north and northeast Thailand. This is the group which were called 'Kha' by the lowland Lao. The language belongs to the Mon-Khmer group of languages. This study is based on the dialect spoken by a group who left Laos for Thailand about twenty years before. The book contains two studies: 'A Khmu grammar' (p. 1-143) and 'A study of Thai and Khmu cutting words' (p. 145-90). This is a study for linguists rather than those seeking a self-instructional system.

247 **White Hmong language lessons.**
Doris Whitelock. Minneapolis, Minnesota: Southeast Asian Refugee Studies Project, Center for Urban and Regional Affairs, University of Minnesota, 1982. rev. ed. 126p. (Southeast Asian Refugee Studies Occasional Paper, no. 2).

Written originally to help missionaries working with the Hmong, these were revised slightly and republished to help people working with the refugee Hmong. The lessons are designed for self-instruction with the assistance of a Hmong informant to provide the sound of the language for imitation. The vocabulary is linked to village life in the mountains. When first devised there were tapes to expand the content, but these were lost, although there were plans to try and replace them.

Scripts and writing systems

248 **Les écritures lao et leur évolution du XVe au XIXe siècles.** (Lao scripts
and their evolution from the 15th to the 19th centuries.)
Pierre-Marie Gagneux. *ASEMI: Asie du Sud-Est et Monde
Insulindien* (ASEMI: South East Asia and the Island World), vol. 14,
no. 1-2 (1983), p. 74-95. bibliog.

The result of his studies of Lao inscriptions, Gagneux offers a study of the
development of Lao script in a historical span. He concludes that there is a strong
thread of continuity in the scripts, permitting the reading of inscriptions through the
centuries. He also concludes that there is no simple way of dating texts from the script,
but a more detailed study is needed of quite a number of consonants before
conclusions can be reached. He gives a comparative table of the alphabet found
between 1491 and 1819.

249 **Mother of writing: the origin and development of a Hmong messianic
script.**
William A. Smalley, Chia Koua Vang, Gnia Yee Yang. Chicago:
University of Chicago Press, 1990. 221p. bibliog.

Shong Lue Yang, a Hmong, claimed to be descended of God with the mission of
delivering the first true Hmong alphabet. He was believed by many and attracted a
following of thousands. Here the story of how he developed his writing system through
four stages is told. This is complemented by a discussion of other systems devised for
writing Hmong, and the search for a means of dissemination of Shong Lue Yang's
script. A fuller account of the life of Shong Lue Yang by two of his followers is given in
The life of Shong Lue Yang: Hmong 'Mother of writing' by Chia Koua Yang, Gnia Yee
Yang, William A. Smalley (Minneapolis, Minnesota: University of Minnesota, Center
for Urban and Regional Affairs, 1990. 191p. [Southeast Asian Refugee Studies
Occasional Papers, no. 9]), written in Hmong in two scripts and with an English
translation.

Personal names

250 **Lao personal names.**
Central Intelligence Agency. [Washington, DC: The Author] 1967.
65 leaves.

Originally produced for use by US government agencies, copies have since been
supplied for the use of the general public. It begins with a brief introduction to the Lao
language and the problems produced by the need to reproduce it in a romanized form.
There is an analysis of the structure of Lao names; that is, both personal or given
names and family names and their normal arrangement in alphabetical listings, which is
by given name. The larger part of this book is devoted to the appendices which
provide transliteration tables, a list of Lao family names with alternative romanizations, and a list of Lao given names, also with popular romanizations. The final

appendix, headed 'Lao titles', deals with forms of address and honorifics used in conversation, as well as the more specific titles used by Buddhist clerics, the Lao nobility, royalty, officials and military personnel.

251 People's names.
Thao Nhouy Abhay.   In: *Kingdom of Laos: land of the million elephants and of the white parasol.* Compiled by René de Berval. Saigon, Vietnam: France Asie, 1959, p. 190-93.
Surnames were not introduced into Laos until 1944. Here the author discusses titles and names used in Laos, and their meaning.

Religion and
Shamanism

252 **Religious structures in Laos.**
Charles Archaimbault. *Journal of the Siam Society*, vol. 52, part 1
(1964), p. 57-74.
This article, which summarizes Archaimbault's work over a number of years, offers an
analysis of official Lao rites in which the relationships between myth, rite and history,
particularly as expressed in the annals, are exposed with clarity. It was the study of
rites that formed the starting point for Archaimbault's ethnological work: ceremonies
that he observed on more than one occasion and performed in different areas of Laos
between 1951 and 1956. There are eight photographic plates illustrating some of the
ceremonies.

253 **Structures religieuses lao: rites et mythes.** (Lao religious structures:
myths and rites.)
Charles Archaimbault. Vientiane: Vithagna, 1973. 289p. bibliog.
(Documents pour le Laos, vol. 2).
A collection of ten of Archaimbault's articles republished to ensure a wider circulation
of his work. As the editor of this work states, it was the study of rites performed in
Laos between 1951 and 1956 that formed the starting point for Archaimbault's
ethnological work. The articles deal with those beliefs and ceremonies that relate to
the foundation of the world and the founding of the Lao kingdom on the one hand,
and those which relate to the ceremonies of daily life, fishing, agriculture and death on
the other.

254 **The way of the monk and the way of the world: Buddhism in Thailand, Laos and Cambodia.**
Jane Bunnag. In: *The world of Buddhism: Buddhist monks and nuns in society and culture.* Edited by H. Bechert, R. Gombrich. London: Thames & Hudson, 1984, p. 159-70. bibliog.
As the title suggests, this is a study of Buddhist monkhood and a history of the advent of Buddhism to Thailand, Laos and Cambodia. It deals with the role of the monk, his life, when and how he enters the Sangha, or monkhood, individual pilgrimages and pastoral aspects of the monk's role. The rest of the volume is devoted to Buddhism in other regions. The first essay by Etienne Lamotte, 'The Buddha, his teachings and his Sangha' (p. 41-58) gives the history of the foundation of the first order of monks in the Buddha's lifetime.

255 **Notes sur le bouddhisme populaire lao en milieu rural lao.** (Notes on Lao popular Buddhism in Lao rural society.)
Georges Condominas. *Archives de Sociologie des Religions*, nos. 25 & 26 (1968), p. 81-110; p. 111-50. map.
Condominas discusses the practice of Buddhism in Laos in the rural setting; his study is based on the Vientiane Plain area of Laos. He covers the role of the *vat* (monastery) and the monks, the social duties linked to the monastery, festivals and gifts in the Buddhist community, and the duties linked to the cult of the *Phi* (spirits). His study is sociological rather than religious in its approach; there are thirty-seven photographs illustrating his work. These articles were republished in the *Bulletin des Amis du Royaume Lao*, no. 9 (1973), p. 27-120.

256 **Phiban cults in rural Laos.**
Georges Condominas. In: *Change and persistence in Thai society: essays in honor of Lauriston Sharp.* Edited by G. William Skinner, A. Thomas Kirsch. Ithaca, New York; London: Cornell University Press, 1975, p. 252-73. bibliog.
A briefer version in English of some of Condominas' work on Buddhism in the rural Lao community. Linked with Buddhism, and not antagonistic to it, is the cult of spirits. This operates at several levels, from the spirits of the territory that reside in the capital to the spirits of the village, the *Phiban*. After a brief survey of the former, Condominas concentrates on the village level, dealing with the sanctuary of the *Phiban*, the master of the cult, and the rituals and ceremonies, particularly the Rocket festival, associated with it.

257 **Lokapâla: génies, totems et sorciers du Nord Laos.** (Lokapâla: spirits, totems and sorcerers of north Laos.)
Henri Deydier. Paris: Plon, 1954. 242p. maps.
Inspired by a desire to understand the origins of the differences between Lao Buddhism and that of India, Deydier travelled in northern Laos, close to the Chinese border, where he observed the religious practices and beliefs of the Tai, which he describes. He also provides a certain amount of information on Buddhism and the religious festivals in Luang Prabang. His photographs illustrate the text. A manuscript copy of an English translation of the text by the late Simon Jervis-Reed has been

deposited in the library of the School of Oriental and African Studies, University of London.

258 **Un après-goût de bonheur: une ethnologie de la spiritualité lao.** (An aftertaste of happiness: Lao religion, an ethnological approach.) Amphay Doré. Vientiane: Vithagna, 1974. 99p. (Documents pour le Laos, no. 4).

An autobiographical account of Buddhist monastic life. The author, of Lao and French parentage and French education, recounts his own observations of monastic life and the daily life of monks, as well as his experience of two of the schools of Buddhist meditation, Samâtri and Vipassanâ.

259 **Les cetiya de sable au Laos et en Thaïlande: les textes.** (Sand chedis in Laos and Thailand: the texts.) Louis Gabaude. Paris: École Française d'Extrême-Orient, 1979. 338p. bibliog. (Publications de l'École Française d'Extrême-Orient, vol. 118).

The building of sand *chedis* (also known as stupas, mounts or hills), is a Buddhist practice widely spread in Burma, Thailand, Laos, Cambodia and Malaysia. Gabaude has studied Thailand and Laos together, because of the close cultural affinities. In a brief survey he outlines the occasions on which this ceremony takes place; these fall into two groups, the fortunate or happy occasions, and those to counteract misfortune. There are, in addition, exceptional circumstances which can cause the ceremony to take place, for example to ensure the future happiness of a defunct spouse, or on the occasion of the offering of new robes to the monks. Gabaude outlines the details of the construction of the *chedis* and the religious ceremonies associated with them. The main part of the work is the collection of texts, written and spoken, which he collected. These are texts recited by monks or laymen at the Buddhist ceremonies associated with the building of sand *chedis*. They are annotated and translated by Gabaude and there are facsimiles printed of the manuscripts. They are, he states, samples which reveal the principal character of this literature. A fuller study of the practice is promised, but does not appear to have been published yet.

260 **The golden peninsula: culture and adaptation in mainland Southeast Asia.** Charles F.Keyes. New York: Macmillan; London: Collier Macmillan, 1977. 370p. maps.

A general survey of the cultural traditions of mainland South East Asia. The author deals with the development of Theravada Buddhism in these societies, its influence on rural village life, and the changing society of the cities. It is valuable in bringing out those elements which are common to these societies and for pointing out the local variations. The survey of Buddhism covers the actual practice of the religion and the way it relates to the basic doctrines.

261 **Introduction du bouddhisme au Laos.** (The introduction of Buddhism into Laos.)
Pierre-Bernard Lafont. In: *Présence du Bouddhisme* (The presence of Buddhism), special issue of *France-Asie*, vol. 16 (1959), p. 889-92.
Textual evidence does not indicate the presence of Buddhism in Laos prior to the fourteenth century. The manner in which Buddhism was introduced into Laos is a subject of conjecture. There is evidence both of statuary and inscriptions from the previous centuries attributable to the Khmer and Khmerized settlements in Laos. The Lao chronicles suggest that Theravada Buddhism was introduced into Laos with the establishment of a unified Lao kingdom under Fa Ngum, which Professor Lafont suggests reflects the reality of experience for the majority of the population.

262 **Yao religion and society.**
Jacques Lemoine. In: *Highlanders of Thailand.* Edited by John McKinnon, Wanat Bhruksasri. Kuala Lumpur: Oxford University Press, 1983, p. 195-211. maps. bibliog.
A summary of what can be said with certainty about Yao religion and society, based on the author's own research among the Yao of Laos and Thailand. He describes in detail the myths of origin of the Yao, and refers to the sources for further study. He summarizes the religious life of the Yao through descriptions of the key ceremonies in the life of a Yao man. This in turn reflects the key features of social and economic organization to which Lemoine refers.

263 **Allons faire le tour du ciel et de la terre: le chamanisme des Hmong vu dans les textes.** (Lets make the journey round the heavens and the earth: Hmong shamanism as seen through the texts.)
Jean Mottin. Bangkok: White Lotus, 1982. 559p.
The texts referred to in the title are the recitations of the Hmong shamans that the author collected in tape recordings and has transcribed. The texts are produced when the shaman is in a trance-like state and cannot be produced in the cold light of day from memory. Mottin discusses the beliefs of the Hmong and the way in which healing comes about by appeal to the spirits and the appurtenances of the ceremonies. The second and larger part of the book sets out the texts of the services; the transcribed Hmong text and its French translation are on facing pages. There is an extensive glossary of the Hmong terms associated with these practices, and sketches of some of the objects to aid comprehension. Coloured photographs help to illustrate the subjects discussed. More material on the subject is available in 'Le chamanisme des Hmong' (The shamanism of the Hmong) by Guy Moréchand (*Bulletin de l'École Française d'Extrême-Orient*, vol. 54 [1968], p. 53-294). Moréchand was only able to present incomplete texts as he was not able to use a tape recorder when in Laos.

264 **Buddhism in Laos.**
Thao Nhouy Abhay. In: *Kingdom of Laos: the land of the million elephants and of the white parasol.* Compiled by René de Berval. Saigon, Vietnam: France Asie, 1959, p. 237-56.
A consideration of the way Buddhism was probably introduced into Laos, and the place it holds in the life of the Lao people. By means of an examination of the festivals as they occur throughout the year, he describes the festivals and celebrations; within

this, he considers the part Buddhism plays in home life. He concludes with an appeal for reforms in order to save and preserve Buddhism. This article is complemented by the neighbouring article in this volume by Kruong Pathoumxad, 'Organization of the Sangha' (p. 257-67). The Sangha, to which all Buddhist monks and novices belong, governs their activities and behaviour; in Laos it was governed by a regulation which had received the Royal Ordinance. Here the author describes the hierarchies of monks and temples which have been devised to enforce the regulation. The present government has made some efforts to reform Buddhism which are referred to in *Contemporary Laos*, edited by Martin Stuart-Fox (q.v.).

265 **The holy emerald jewel: some aspects of Buddhist symbolism and political legitimation in Thailand and Laos.**
Frank E. Reynolds. In: *Religion and legitimation of power in Thailand, Laos, and Burma.* Edited by Bardwell L. Smith. Chambersburg, Pennsylvania: Anima Books, 1978, p. 175-93.
The holy emerald jewel is more commonly known as the Emerald Buddha, presently enthroned in its own chapel in the grounds of the Grand Palace in Bangkok. Reynolds discusses it in its role as a Buddhist symbol of the legitimacy of royal power, and the myths and history surrounding it. The jewel was removed from Chiang Mai, in Lanna, modern north Thailand, in the sixteenth century by the Lao ruler, when he returned to Luang Prabang on his father's death. He moved it to Vientiane when he moved his capital there, and it remained in Vientiane until 1778 when a Thai general sent it to Thonburi, then capital of Thailand. It was installed in its present home by King Rama I, first ruler of the present Thai dynasty.

266 **Ritual and social hierarchy: an aspect of traditional religion in Buddhist Laos.**
Frank E. Reynolds. In: *Religion and legitimation of power in Thailand, Laos, and Burma.* Edited by Bardwell L. Smith. Chambersburg, Pennsylvania: Anima Books, 1978, p. 166-74.
Reynolds discusses the socio-religious ideal of Lao Buddhism as evinced in the ceremonies that endure in Luang Prabang. This essay is based on the more detailed studies of Archaimbault and Deydier but it provides a useful synthesis.

267 **Buddhism and society in Southeast Asia.**
Donald K. Swearer. Chambersburg, Pennsylvania: Anima, 1981. 82p. map. bibliog.
This essay looks at Theravada Buddhism in three social and political contexts: the village, the kingdom or nation state, and the modern city and town. Swearer examines in these three arenas the popular tradition; that is, the rituals, festivals and rites of passage which have evolved, the role of Buddhism as a source of political legitimation and national integration, and the changing roles of monks and laity in the modern, particularly urban, world. There is a useful glossary of Buddhist terminology at the end of the book.

268　**Rites et ceremonies en milieu bouddhiste lao.** (Buddhist rites and
ceremonies of Laos.)
Marcel Zago.　Rome: Università Gregoriana Editrice, 1972. 408p.
maps. bibliog. (Documenta Missionalia, no. 6).

A largely descriptive study of Buddhism as practised by the Lao ethnic group in Laos,
based mainly on the author's own observations and experience in Laos, where he was a
missionary from 1959 to 1965. In Laos he was in constant contact with Buddhists, and
later he continued a correspondence with his informants. Zago has also used the
available written sources in European languages, Pali, Thai and Lao. After a general
introduction, the work is arranged in three parts, the first on rites which are considered
genuinely Buddhist and were brought into the country with the religion itself. The
second part deals with rites and beliefs which have an indigenous element; the last
chapter of this second part on the festivals of the Buddhist year brings together aspects
of the first and second parts of the book. The third part analyses the symbiosis and
synthesis of the indigenous elements within Buddhism in order to indicate the past
development and the evolution of Buddhism in Laos. Zago has a useful article
'Buddhism in contemporary Laos' in *Buddhism in the modern world*, edited by
Heinrich Dumoulin, John C. Maraldo (New York: Macmillan, 1976).

Festivals and Games

269 **La course de pirogues au Laos: un complexe culturel.** (Dugout canoe racing in Laos: a cultural complex.)
Charles Archaimbault. Ascona, Switzerland: Artibus Asiae, 1972. 132p. maps.

Racing of canoes, or dugouts, is a phenomenon found throughout mainland South East Asia and in China. Archaimbault maintains that this is not merely a ceremony that is linked to the seasons and the rain, but that there are variations in meaning between countries, and within Laos itself variations in significance between regions. The races at Luang Prabang, Vientiane and Bassak, Champassak Province are examined. The races at Bassak are considered in detail. Maps and plates illustrate the text.

270 **La fête du T'at à Luong P'rabang.** (The *T'at* festival in Luang Prabang.)
Charles Archaimbault. In: *Essays offered to G. H. Luce by his colleagues and friends in honour of his seventy-fifth birthday.* Edited by Ba Shin, Jean Boisselier, A. B. Griswold. Ascona, Switzerland: Artibus Asiae, 1966, vol. 1, p. 5-47.

A detailed description of the annual, week-long festival of *T'at* which takes place at the beginning of the dry season. Archaimbault's description is based on the festival he witnessed in 1952; he also gives consideration to the significance of the festival, which enables the ruler's virtue to radiate throughout the kingdom.

271 **The New Year ceremony at Basak, South Laos.**
Charles Archaimbault, with an afterword by Prince Boun Oum. Ithaca, New York: Cornell University, Department of Asian Studies, Southeast Asia Program, 1971. 137p. (Data Paper Series, no. 78).

In Laos New Year ceremonies vary in the different regions; those of Bassak, formerly the capital of Champassak, seem to be related to local legend and history. The ceremony is connected with the purification of the city and its people, a renewal and an appeal for protection throughout the coming year. Archaimbault in this study reveals

86

the changes that have occurred in this ceremony since the writing of visitors' accounts in the previous century; he also refers to the differences in the ceremony in other parts of Laos. Prince Boun Oum, a descendant of the house of Champassak is the chief protagonist in the ceremonies and, unusually for an anthropological study, he provides his comments on this account of a ceremony which is linked with his family's history. This is a readable account of a ceremony that was already losing ground in the modern world, accompanied by photographs illustrating the event. Cornell have published an abridged English translation followed by the full text in French.

272 **The game of Phuy-tong.**
Katay Don Sasorith. In: *Kingdom of Laos: the land of the million elephants and of the white parasol.* Compiled by René de Berval. Saigon, Vietnam: France Asie, 1959, p. 198-205.

Phuy-tong is a card game popular all over Laos, played by up to six people. Here the cards, how they are dealt and the way they are played are described. This is a shortened version of the author's booklet *Comment joue-t'on le Phuy-tong* (Saigon, Vietnam: Imprimerie Nouvelle Albert Portail, 1931).

273 **Les fêtes profanes et religieuses au Laos.** (Religious and secular festivals in Laos.)
Pierre Somchine Nginn. Vientiane: Editions du Comité Littéraire, 1967. 2nd ed. 61p.

The description of the festivals is organized in chronological order as they occur during the year. Many celebrate events in the life of the Buddha, but even secular festivals, such as that for the New Year (held in April), have Buddhist elements linked with them. The book closes with a description of the rites and ceremonies linked with funerals. The descriptions are simple and include the stories that account for particular celebrations. The first edition of this book was published in 1961 (Compiègne, France: Imprimerie de Compiègne).

Society and Social Change

274 **Migrants and modernisation: a study of change in Lao society.**
Martin John Philip Barber.   Hull, England: University of Hull, 1979.
441p. maps. bibliog.

A doctoral thesis presented to the University of Hull in the Department of Sociology and Social Anthropology, and distributed by the author to major libraries. It is an important study of Lao society and the changes that have taken place. It is based on two years of fieldwork in Laos, after four years of residence and work there, and extensive reading. The detailed study is based on a rural community in Vientiane province and an urban community in the city of Vientiane. It is the impact of social, political and economic innovations on these communities which is analysed in detail. This was a period of rapid movement of people from rural to urban areas. It is an examination of the differences between urban and village life and the impact on each of the ideas and materials brought from the outside world. The first section is introductory and includes a bibliographical essay on previous studies on Lao society; this includes discussion of several important and unpublished theses produced in France and several works only produced in a semi-published form in Laos. An important observation is on the paucity of the work on Laos and the shallowness of much of it compared with that on Laos' neighbours. The major part of this work deals with economic relations in the two communities, political life in each, social relations, traditional and modern customs, and migration. There is a brief appendix assessing changes in Laos since 1974, the end of Barber's fieldwork, and the period of the changes in government. The work is very readable and not weighted down with jargon, as Barber came to social anthropology as a way of deepening his understanding of Laos rather than the reverse, although there is useful discussion of methodology and theories, including those of others which he rejects.

275 **The old man: a biographical account of a Lao villager.**
Fred Branfman, introduced and edited by Joel M. Halpern, James A. Hafner. Amherst, Massachusetts: International Area Studies Program, University of Massachusetts at Amherst, 1979. 49p. (Asian Studies Committee Occasional Paper Series, no. 4).

A further extract of Branfman's unpublished study of a Lao village; this work is complementary to his *The village of the Deep Pond, Ban Xa Phang Meuk, Laos* (q.v.). The old man is the son of one of the three founders of the village, and was born there in about 1900. In describing his life and the life of his five children, Branfman illustrates the way in which village life has changed and developed. This work challenges the picture of idyllic simplicity that village life described with broad strokes proposes. The old man has quarrelled with the monk and many of his neighbours, and is cared for by one daughter, although a son who is a soldier helps him financially.

276 **The village of the Deep Pond, Ban Xa Phang Meuk, Laos.**
Fred Branfman, introduced and edited by James A. Hafner, Joel M. Halpern. Amherst, Massachusetts: University of Massachusetts at Amherst, International Area Studies Program, 1978. 48p. map. bibliog. (Asian Studies Committee Occasional Papers Series, no. 3).

Based on Branfman's longer manuscript, this is a study of a farming village only nine kilometres north of Vientiane. Although only founded in 1890 by three migrants, Hafner describes it as representative of traditional Lao society. Branfman was not a trained sociologist, but his observations are based on a two-year residence in the village, 1967-69. The study discusses the village and its inhabitants and then concentrates on its economy; a subsistence economy that was becoming influenced and affected by the monetary economy of the encroaching town. Branfman concludes with a summary of the malaise which the changes of the past twenty years had brought to the village, and the sense of uncertainty which seemed to haunt the inhabitants.

277 **The Lao elite: a study of tradition and innovation.**
Joel M. Halpern. Santa Monica, California: Rand Corporation, 1960. 89p. (Rand Research Memorandum, RM-2636-RC).

A study of the Lao élite, particularly those in official positions, based on Halpern's field work in Laos and interviews with officials in 1959. He discusses the social background of the élite and kinship ties, traditional and colonial cultural influences, the extent of the élite, and relations with the rural population of Laos. Some of this research was incorporated into Halpern's *Government, politics, and social structure in Laos* (q.v.) where five members of the élite are profiled in the appendix 'Laos profiles'. Women receive only a brief mention.

278 **The role of the Chinese in Lao society.**
Joel M. Halpern. Santa Monica, California: Rand Corporation, 1961. 38p. bibliog. (Rand Paper, P-2161).

An outline of the notable characteristics of the Chinese as an urban ethnic group, and an assessment of their economic role in the Lao economy. The urban overseas Chinese community was a relatively recent arrival in Laos, the first migrants arriving about forty or fifty years before the publication of this paper. They had migrated from various areas of China and some had moved from Thailand and Vietnam to Laos.

Society and Social Change

Halpern provides interesting statistics about the Chinese community in 1959: the numbers in major urban centres; the size of the community as a percentage of the total population; their administrative structure; the number of businesses owned by the Chinese in the major towns; the percentage of the total number of businesses; a more detailed study of the types of businesses owned by the Chinese in the Vientiane area; and a demographic analysis of the Chinese population of Xieng Khouang province.

279 **Some reflections on the war in Laos, anthropological and otherwise.**
Joel M.Halpern. *Courrier de l'Extrême-Orient*, vol. 4, no. 44 (1970), p. 203-25. bibliog.

A somewhat meandering argument in which this anthropologist and sometime AID worker concludes that America's war effort in Laos is ultimately counter-productive both in Laos and at home. While considering that the United States could play a valid role in the economic development of Laos, as for example with projects on the Mekong River, he points out the overall negative effects aid has had on Lao society (although some projects such as those in education had been worthwhile and successful). He contrasts the effect of external aid on the areas controlled by the Royal Lao Government with the areas under Pathet Lao rule, and presumed to have received external aid from their neighbours.

280 **Yesterday and today in Laos: a girl's autobiographical notes.**
Nayen Phimmasone Lévy. In: *Women in the new Asia: the changing social roles of men and women in South and South-East Asia.* Edited by Barbara E. Ward. Paris: UNESCO, 1964, p. 244-65.

An account of the childhood and schooling of a young girl in Laos in the period between the two World Wars. Mme Lévy was the daughter of a Lao official who rose to the top rank of the administration. Though brief, this article conveys much of Lao traditional life and the changes that occurred during the French protectorate, and is enlivened by the personal nature of the story.

281 **The ethnic Chinese in the ASEAN states: bibliographical essays.**
Edited by Leo Suryadinata. Singapore: Institute of Southeast Asian Studies, 1989. 271p. bibliog.

A comprehensive survey and discussion of the published material on the Chinese in South East Asia. The first essay offers a regional perspective and a discussion of the Chinese language material on overseas migration. Laos is not covered, but this work is included because most of the Chinese in Laos reached there by a process of migration from the neighbouring South East Asian states.

282 Le dualisme urbain-rural au Laos et la récupération de l'ideologie traditionnelle. (Urban-rural dualism in Laos and the recovery of traditional ideology.)
Christian Taillard. *Asie du Sud-Est et Monde Insulindien: Bulletin du Centre de Documentation et de Recherche (CeDRASEMI)* (South East Asia and the Island World: Bulletin of the Centre for Documentation and Research (CeDRASEMI)), vol. 10, no. 1 (1979), p. 41-56.
Taillard argues that in Laos town and country operate in a symbiotic manner. He reviews the relationship before 1973 and examines developments up to 1976. In order to recover or restore traditional society and its values, Buddhist merit-making ceremonies and customary land tenure had been used for the interests of a powerful minority in high positions in order to reinforce their power. Taillard argues that the urban and rural are not separate spheres in Laos. Urban centres rely for both physical and spiritual support on the rural areas.

283 Families of the world: family life at the close of the twentieth century. Vol. 2: East Asia, Southeast Asia, and the Pacific.
Hélène Tremblay. New York: Farrar, Straus & Giroux, 1990. 283p. maps. bibliog.
The purpose of Tremblay's work is to introduce the families of the world to each other. In a few pages she sketches the daily life of a family from each country, describing the events of a particular day, and sketching in background information. Pictures of the family, the house and a family scene with a country map and statistical appendix complete each section. The families chosen, it is stated, accurately reflect the characteristics of that country. The family chosen to represent Laos is T'ai and the wife is recently widowed, so it is not perhaps as representative as one is led to believe. It is a sketch of life in a rural village outside Vientiane, where, as a pilot project, a new cash crop is being cultivated in place of rice, which is difficult to grow in that area. Tremblay has succeeded in presenting a portrait of a family and its life in Laos in the late 1980s which adds flesh to more scholarly accounts of rural life.

Refugees

284 **Resettlement of Indochinese refugees in the United States: a selective and annotated bibliography.**
Lawrence F. Ashmun. De Kalb, Illinois: Northern Illinois University, Center for Southeast Asian Studies, 1983. 207p. (Occasional Paper Series, no. 10).
This bibliography covers the period April 1975 to the end of 1981. It deals with most types of published work except newspaper articles, anonymous articles and commercial dictionaries and textbooks. There are extensive and helpful annotations to many of the items. This is particularly valuable where material deals with refugees from more than one of the Indochinese countries. Items with explicit titles have not been annotated. The arrangement is in alphabetical order by author, but there is a subject index where relevant references are grouped under the headings Hmong and Lao; there are other types of subject heading such as orphans and sponsors. A large part of the material listed was not published commercially.

285 **Les réfugiés originaires de l'Asie du Sud-Est: arrière plan historique et culturel, les motivations de départ. Rapport présenté au Président de la République . . .** (Refugees from South East Asia: historical and cultural background, the reasons for leaving.)
Georges Condominas, Richard Pottier. Paris: La Documentation Française, 1982. 227p. maps. bibliog.
Beginning with the historical and cultural background to the flights from Indo-China, the work continues with a study of the causes and phases of each exodus; a chapter is dedicated to each of the three countries . Laos is well covered in this section; there were several phases of refugee exodus and there were several social and ethnic groups involved. The reasons for their flight is set in the context of the economic and physical situation of Laos between 1975 and 1980. The work concludes with a section on the reasons for departure of each ethnic group, and their preferences for a future home.

286 **Southeast Asian Refugee Studies Newsletter.**
Minneapolis, Minnesota: Southeast Asian Refugee Studies Project,
Centre for Urban and Regional Affairs, University of Minnesotata,
1980- . quarterly.

The *Newsletter* serves to support the aims of the Southeast Asian Refugee Studies
Project; that is, to encourage, co-ordinate and support research related to refugees
from South East Asia, resettled in the United States. There are reviews of new
research, books and videos about the refugees. Material on refugees from Laos,
particularly the Hmong, represents a high proportion of the content of the *Newsletter*.

287 **The Indochinese refugee dilemma.**
Valerie O'Connor Sutter. Baton Rouge, Louisiana; London:
Louisiana State University Press, 1990. 256p. bibliog.

The refugee issue is considered from the perspective of the national interests of the
neighbouring states and the great powers, and discusses how these national interests
contribute to the problem and the search for solutions. It deals with the foreign policy
interests and how they affect, and are affected by, the Indochinese refugees; it
identifies the domestic concerns of the interested parties; it compares the United
States' involvement with Indochinese refugees with its involvement with Hungarian
refugees in 1956; it explores the role of the international humanitarian relief effort, and
in this context the relevance of international law; it considers the implications for the
outcome of the Indochinese refugee problem and the wider world context of the
problem of international refugees. Sutter's work is based on a field research, a
literature survey, a wide range of fugitive material, and interviews with officials
working with Indochinese refugees. Specific material on Laos is limited, but it covers
the reasons for departure, the treatment in first asylum camps, particularly in Thailand,
and the prospects of resettlement.

288 **Du Mékong à la Seine: le prix de la liberté.** (From the Mekong to the
Seine: the price of freedom.)
Trân Van Thêu. [Paris:] Fayard, 1990. 269p. map (Collection Les
Enfants du Fleuve).

Trân is a Vietnamese born in Laos; his parents, refugees from Vietnam. Aged eighteen
in 1975, he determined to leave Laos from the moment that the Republican
government came to power. He spent two years accumulating money to pay for a
passage across the Mekong. It is a portrait of the unofficial side of Lao life as he steals
and cheats to survive with no official papers. On more than one occasion he loses his
money just as he is ready to leave, and so finally he crosses the Mekong with two
friends using a petrol can as a float. In Thailand, however, the Vietnamese refugees
are treated as potential spies, and he is confined to closed camps run by the Thai
military for Vietnamese refugees, until finally he obtains a visa for France. Life in Laos
is described as one of hardship and nervous tension because of the lack of papers. Life
in the Thai camps is one of fear, deprivation and brutality, where financial help, used
for supplementary food, clothes and postage, is received from his family in Laos and
charitable French families. The book concludes with Trân's departure for France.

289 **Les naufragés de la liberté: le dernier exode des Méos**. (The castaways of freedom: the last exodus of the Hmong.)
Jean-Pierre Willem. Paris: Editions SOS, 1980. 286p. maps.

In 1977, Dr. Willem, with sponsorship from the organization Médecins sans Frontières, went to work in a refugee camp in northeast Thailand close to the border with Laos, adjacent to the Sayabouri region. The camp of Nam Yao had 13,500 refugees of whom nearly two-thirds were Hmong; more refugees entered while he was working there, as Laos was hit by drought and then floods, as well as political changes. This is not a chronological account, nor does it treat any subject in a scientific manner. It is a series of sketches, many lightly touched on, such as the financing of refugee camps, relations with the host country and the nutritional and medical problems of the refugees, and those which result from confining a large number of people in a small space. He records what he observed of the ethnic groups, especially the Hmong; the evolution of their customs; and the attempts to retain their customs. From some he records their experience of life in Laos since 1975; from others he records experiences of the use of chemicals called 'yellow rain'. There is an account of how five villages left in May 1975, led by a Christianized village, to be followed by a mass exodus. The most touching group whom he describes are the few families of Maabri in the camp, a hunter-gatherer group, whose numbers had dwindled to the extent that their survival in the long-term was most improbable. He also describes an expedition he joined with the refugee Hmong into Laos, but it tells us very little.

Public Health and Medicine

290 **Adventure in Viet-Nam: the story of Operation Brotherhood, 1954-1957.**
Miguel A. Bernad. Manila: OBI, 1974. 561p.

Operation Brotherhood was born from the Philippine Jaycee movement as a means of offering practical aid, largely medical, to a fellow Asian country. It was sponsored by the Philippine Jaycees (Junior Chamber of Commerce movement) and it was quickly adopted as a programme of the international movement. This volume is concerned with the launch of Operation Brotherhood and the work with the Vietnamese refugees in South Vietnam between 1954 and 1957; much of it has been drawn from Operation Brotherhood's own archives. In 1957 Operation Brotherhood set up clinics in Laos, and many accounts contain brief references to their doctors and nurses working there. This volume gives brief information on the beginnings of the programme in Laos, and refers to a history of the movement in Laos in preparation, but it has not yet been traced.

291 **Laos health survey: Mekong valley, 1968-1969.**
Gail F. Breakey, Emmanuel Voulgaropoulos. Honolulu, Hawaii: University Press of Hawaii, 1976. 129p. map.

Describes a project undertaken jointly by the Royal Government of Laos, the Thomas A. Dooley Foundation and the International Health Program, School of Public Health, University of Hawaii, the purpose of which was 'to establish baseline data on some of the health problems found among the people of the Mekong Valley in Laos'. Fifteen villages, representative of geographical areas and cultural groups both rural and urban, were surveyed. They looked at the environmental and sanitary conditions and analysed the incidence of specific types of disease and health conditions. In conclusion, they recommend specific action to be taken, including a large programme of education on health matters.

292 **Public health and the Mekong Project.**
Secretariat of the Committee for the Co-ordination of Investigations of
the Lower Mekong Basin. [Bangkok:] The Committee, 1972. 11p.
A survey of the public health concerns that are linked with the successful economic
development of the region. The key areas of concern are the eradication of malaria,
schistosomiasis and intestinal parasites, and the provision of clean drinking water.

293 **Promises to keep: the life of Doctor Thomas A. Dooley.**
Agnes W. Dooley. New York: Farrar, Straus & Cudahy, 1962. 272p.
The life story of Dr. Tom Dooley told by his mother. The second part of the book
deals with his plans for a medical mission to Laos. It describes how he set up his first
clinic at Vang Vieng, which he handed over to the Laos to manage, and then his
second at Muong Sing, close to the Chinese border. The account is based on his letters
and the accounts of others. Dr. Dooley also wrote books about each of these clinics, in
part to solicit further funds for MEDICO, the charitable organization for which he
worked and under which they were established. The first clinic is described in *The edge
of tomorrow* (New York: Farrar, Straus & Cudahy, 1958); the second in *The night they
burned the mountain* (New York: Farrar, Straus & Cudahy, 1960). Dr. Dooley's
accounts are impressionistic and intended to evoke a picture of the medical conditions
he encountered rather than a cool chronological account of events. The lack of medical
care available to those outside urban areas is made abundantly clear.

294 **Laotian health problems.**
Joel M. Halpern. Los Angeles: Department of Anthropology,
University of California, 1961. 38 leaves. bibliog. (Laos Project Paper,
no. 19).
Largely an assembly of material from other sources, nonetheless usefully summarized
here. It covers general health problems found in Laos, the role of traditional medicine
and modern medical facilities. It should be read with Halpern's *Laotian health statistics*
(Los Angeles: Department of Anthropology, University of California, 1960. 6p. (Laos
Project Paper, no. 10), which provides statistics basically for the period 1957 to 1959.

295 **A world geography of human diseases.**
Edited by G. Melvyn Howe. London: Academic Press, 1977. 621p.
maps. bibliog.
A collection of articles on diseases found world-wide, including tropical diseases such
as malaria, dengue fever and yaws found in Laos. Specific references to Laos can be
traced via the index.

296 **Some practices of traditional medecine [*sic*].**
Dr. Oudom Souvannavong. In: *Kingdom of Laos: the land of the
million elephants and of the white parasol.* Compiled by René de
Berval. Saigon, Vietnam: France Asie, 1959, p. 301-04.
Oudom Souvannavong, former Minister of Health, describes here four different types
of traditional medical practices. His viewpoint is clearly expressed in the names he
gives these practitioners; quack, magician and witch-doctor.

297 **Traditional and acculturative medical practices among the ethnic Lao: a study in Rockford and Elgin, Illinois.**
Mary Lou Robertson. *South East Asian Review*, vol. 9, no. 1-2 (1984), p. 1–97. bibliog.

Written within the anthropological discipline of acculturation, the author seeks to give a better understanding of the medical background and beliefs of the Lao settled in Illinois. The major part of the study is concerned with a description of traditional Lao medical practice based on the experience of her informants in Illinois and a survey of the literature in English. She examines theories of illness, traditional healers, home treatments and childbirth practices, preventive measures (that is amulets and tattoos), and ceremonies related to health care.

298 **Global epidemiology: a geography of disease and sanitation.**
James Stevens Simmons, Tom F. Whayne, Gaylord West Anderson, Harold MacLachlan Horack et al. Philadelphia: J. B. Lippincott, 1944. 504p. maps. bibliog.

An encyclopaedic study, country by country of the geography and climate, public health, medical facilities and diseases to be found in the countries of South, South East and East Asia. Prepared by US army surgeons in preparation for the needs of war, it offers the modern reader a useful portrait of medical conditions in French Indo-China on the eve of the struggle for independence. Malaria was then, as it is now, responsible for most of the recorded illness in the region.

299 **Les Laotiens: coutumes, hygiène, pratiques médicales.** (The Laotians: their medical and hygienic practices and customs.)
C. Spire. Paris: Challamel, 1907. 64p. bibliog.

Spire travelled in Laos on a botanical mission in 1901-02 that was researching the medicinal plants used by the peoples of Laos. Here he documents the concepts of medical care, anatomy and physiology of the inhabitants. Their treatments and the drugs used are dicussed, and there is a guide to medicinal plants and their uses based on Lao manuscripts.

300 **Poppies, pipes and people: opium and its use in Laos.**
Joseph Westermeyer. Berkeley, California: University of California Press, 1982. 336p. maps. bibliog.

Based on the author's experience in Laos between 1965 and 1975 as a medical practitioner, this work looks at opium and its place in Laos. Opium was used as part of folk medicine, as a painkiller and as an intoxicant. The major part of this study looks at addiction and its treatment. The social effects of the anti-narcotics law and the disruption of opium farming by the war, which had helped to introduce the use of heroin in Laos, concludes the work.

Politics and
Administration

301 **Apprentice revolutionaries: the communist movement in Laos, 1930-
1985.**
MacAlister Brown, Joseph J. Zasloff. Stanford, California: Hoover
Institution Press, 1986. 463p. bibliog. (Histories of Ruling Communist
Parties.)

The first part of this book is a history of the evolution of the Communist Party of Laos
(Phak Phasason Patavit Lao) up to the establishment of the Lao People's Democratic
Republic. The title used here refers to the authors' thesis that the success of the
communists in Laos was a result of the guidance they received from the Vietnamese,
combined with external material aid. The second part of the book deals with the first
ten years of government of the Lao People's Democratic Republic under the
leadership of those who had fought for the revolution over the previous thirty years.
They consider the political institutions and policies on political, economic, social and
foreign relations matters. Brown and Zasloff have not been in Laos since 1975, but
base their research on the accounts of those journalists and scholars who have visited
Laos since that date. They have also used information gathered from interviews held in
Thailand with Lao refugees and the monitored broadcasts from Laos. There is an
extensive section of appendices which provide basic documents of the Lao communist
movement in English, a chronology of events from April 1974 to the end of
1975, information on the communist leadership, correspondence between Prince
Souphanouvong and the Lao government in exile in 1949, and important treaties.
There is an extensive bibliography. A clear summary of the history of Laos since 1945
and the growth of what is now the Lao People's Revolutionary Party is given in 'Lao
People's Democratic Republic' by Laura J. Summers (In: *Marxist governments: a
world survey.* Edited by Bogdan Szajkowski. London: Macmillan, 1981, vol. 2, p. 468-
92. map. bibliog.).

302 **Lao People's Democratic Republic government structure: a reference aid.**

Central Intelligence Agency, Directorate of Intelligence.
[Washington, DC:] The Author, 1990. 1 fold. sheet (LDA 90-13920).

The most recently published history, this chart lists the main organs of government, justice and the military, with the names of the key officials and their posts. Brief explanatory information is appended.

303 **Lao People's Revolutionary Party: a reference aid.**

Central Intelligence Agency, Directorate of Intelligence.
[Washington, DC:] The Author, 1990. 1 fold. sheet. map. (LDA 90-13921).

In chart format this sets out the names of the members of the Central Committee of the Lao People's Revolutionary Party and its main organs, the Politburo and Secretariat. The names of its mass organizations and their leaders are given, as are the names of the Standing Committees of the Central Committee and their Chairpersons. Photographs and brief statements are provided about the three men identified as the key players of the Politburo. Brief explanatory information is appended on the Party Congress. It can be anticipated that further issues of this chart will be made as updates become necessary.

304 **The training of Vietnamese communist cadres in Laos: the notes of Do Xuan Tao, Vietnamese economic specialist assigned to the Pathet Lao in Xieng Khouang, Laos, 1968.**

Do Xuan Tao, edited by Joel M. Halpern, William S. Turley.
Brussels: Centre d'Études du Sud-Est Asiatique et de l'Extrême-Orient, 1977. 116 leaves. (Courrier de l'Extrême-Orient, no. 66).

These appear to be the notes made by Do Xuan Tao during a course in Hanoi to prepare him for a three-year tour of duty in Laos. The significance of these notes is that they provide substantive information on the Vietnamese role in the Laotian revolution. They also present the insider's view of the Vietnamese and Laotian revolutions, and the views of the Vietnamese on the Lao and the ethnic minorities in Indo-China. The editors have provided an introduction which sets the work in its historical context. These notes tell us something of the economic life in the liberated zone of Laos, but the majority of the notes are concerned with the model of a socialist revolution which Vietnam offers Laos.

305 **The Pathet Lao: a 'liberation' party.**

Bernard B. Fall. In: *The communist revolution in Asia: tactics, goals, and achievements.* Edited by Robert A. Scalapino. Englewood Cliffs, New Jersey: Prentice-Hall, 1965, p. 173-97. bibliog.

A broad survey of the Pathet Lao, beginning with an account of the establishment of the Pathet Lao as a political party, from the political education and experience of its leader Prince Souphanouvong, through the period of anti-colonial and anti-Japanese resistance of the Lao Issara movement, to the foundation of Pathet Lao in 1950 as a resistance government. Fall then considers the political structure of the Pathet Lao and their political and military activities from 1957 to 1965. In his pamphlet *Comments on Bernard Fall's 'The Pathet Lao: a "liberation party"'* (Santa Monica, California: Rand,

1968. 6p.) Paul F. Langer offers some refinements on Fall's paper based on more recent data. Langer challenges the importance of the ethnic minorities in the Pathet Lao; he also identifies the communist element in Laos, not as the Neo Lao Haksat but as the Lao People's Party (Phak Pasason Lao), whose Secretary-General was Kaysone Phomvihane.

306 Revolution in Laos: the 'fourth generation' of people's war?
Don Fletcher, Geoffrey C. Gunn. Townsville, Australia: James Cook University of North Queensland, 1981. 83p. bibliog. (Southeast Asia Monograph Series, no. 8).

An analysis of the revolution in Laos in the light of the general propositions of Chalmers Johnson's theories as expressed in his *Revolutionary change* (Boston; Massachusetts: Little, Brown, 1966). Fletcher and Gunn present a statement on Lao social structure and the international aspects of the conflict. They follow this with the major part of the study: a discussion of the revolutionary strategy of the people's war in Laos. In this chapter they try to integrate the perspectives of the studies of the Rand Corporation research and the contrary views of the Committee of Concerned Asian Scholars. The work is a thumbnail sketch of the development and eventual success of a people's revolution in Laos, charted through and measured against established views of what revolution entails.

307 Les administrations et les services publics indochinois. (The administration and public services in Indo-China.)
J. de Galembert. Hanoi: Le-Van-Tan, 1931. 2nd ed. 1023p.

A descriptive work, linked to the relevant legal provisions, which outlines the administrative divisions and management of French Indo-China and its public services from the judiciary to the forest service, from medical services to taxation. In addition to detailed chapter schemes there is also a subject index to the volume.

308 Organisation administrative au Laos. (Administrative organization in Laos.)
Dominique Guerrini. [Vientiane:] IRDA, 1967. 79p. map.

Guerrini, an expert in public administration, compiled this text as a basis for a course in public administration within Laos. She sets out the actual way in which central, provincial and district administration was organized in Laos. She produced a shorter statement on administration in *Organigrammes: organisation politique et administration du Laos* (Organigrams: political and administrative organization in Laos) (Vientiane: USAID Mission to Laos, 1973. 20p.). She assembled a collection of texts, laws and regulations on public powers, legislation, regulation and territorial organization in *Recueil méthodique de législation et réglementation lao* (Systematic collection of Lao legislation and regulations) (Bangkok: Siva Phorn, 1968. 2nd ed. 180p.).

309 **Laos.**
  Geoffrey C. Gunn. In: *Military-civilian relations in South-East Asia.*
  Edited by Zakaria Haji Ahmad, Harold Crouch. Singapore: Oxford
  University Press, 1985, p. 197-233.
A study of the nature of Party-army and army-civilian relations, examined in three
stages. In the first, on the Forces Armées Royaume, Gunn seeks a sociological
explanation for the transformation of its officer corps from professionalism to quasi-
warlordism. In the second, he gives a historical overview of the relations between the
military and the governing power in Laos, and the political consequences of the
phenomenon described in the first section. In the third and final section, he discusses
whether or not the military has risen as a new class in Laos in the post-revolutionary
regime; it is an examination of the Lao People's Liberation Army, or Lao People's
Army as it became known from 1982, in the political development of Laos. This
article, based largely on secondary sources, is rife with the undigested jargon of
political science, but underneath that there is a useful survey of the military role in Lao
politics.

310 **Political struggles in Laos, 1930-1954: Vietnamese communist power and
  the Lao struggle for national independence.**
  Geoffrey C. Gunn. Bangkok: Editions Duang Kamol, 1988. 325p.
  maps. bibliog.
A revised version of the author's doctoral thesis, it is based on French archival and
published sources. Gunn notes that the pre-1945 communist activities in Laos were
largely among the Vietnamese minority resident in Laos. The inner cadre of the
present Lao communist leadership were the victors in the power struggle in the Lao
Issara guerilla movement. It is valuable for the detailed way in which it traces the
development of events from 1930 to 1954, including the period of the Japanese
occupation of Laos. These are events only covered briefly elsewhere. There is also a
historical introduction to the main part of the work and comments on events since
1975. The original title of the thesis was *Road through the mountains: the origins of
nationalism and communism in Laos, 1930-1945* (Ann Arbor, Michigan: University
Microfilms International, 1987).

311 **Les aspirations du peuple lao ou, Les revendications des Lao-Issara.**
  (The aspirations of the Lao people, or The claims of the Lao-Issara.)
  Katay Don Sasorith. Bangkok: Editions Lao-Issara, 1949. 22p.
  (Collection Bang-Faï Lao-Issara).
One of a number of publications of the *Lao-Issara* movement in exile in Bangkok,
written by Katay Don Sasorith under his pseudonyms, Arsène Lapin, Don Sasorith,
William Rabbit. This work collects three of his articles from the *Lao-Issara* journal
Bang-Faï. They voice the objections to the French-imposed government in Laos, and
claim the independence of Laos in all matters, not merely the areas permitted under
the French Union. Another collection of his articles, which takes its title from the
words of Phoui Sannanikone (*Depuis le retour de la domination française le Laos
n'avance pas* [Since the return of French domination, Laos makes no progress.].
Bangkok: Editions Lao-Issara, 1949. 23p. [Collection Bang-Faï Lao-Issara]), blames
the backwardness of Laos on the continuance of French colonialism, now disguised as
a form of independence. In addition to Katay's own writings, this series included
pamphlets by others, such as Singha Soukhaseum's *Faudra-t-il evacuer l'Indochine?*
(Will it be necessary to evacuate Indo-China?) (Bangkok: Editions Lao-Issara, 1949.

29p. [Collection Bang-Faï Lao-Issara]): starting from the views of Jean Dorsenne in 1932, the author argues that the aspirations of the peoples of Indo-China for independence demand that the French withdraw.

312 **Le Laos: son évolution politique, sa place dans l'Union française.** (Laos: its political development and its place in the French Union.) Katay Don Sasorith. Paris: Éditions Berger-Levrault, 1953. Reprinted, New York: AMS Press, 1975. 155p. map.

Written by one of the senior officers in the *Lao Issara* movement, who at the time of writing this work was employed as in the *Haut Conseil de l'Union française* (the Directorate of the French Union, which was a grouping of metropolitan France, Algeria, overseas territories and the free association of the independent states of Indo-China). Katay became head of government in 1955. The book is intended as an introduction to the newly independent Laos for the general public. There is a brief historical account that outlines the development of governments in Laos from monarchy, French annexation and protection to the newly independent status. What is of particular interest is the account of events from the Japanese *coup de force* (seizure of power) in March 1945 to the agreement in 1949 of Laos' independence and entry into the *Union française* by an active participant and fighter for independence. The second part of the book is composed of appendices: the text of the Constitution in French as promulgated in 1947, and revised in 1949 and 1952; documents relating to the recognition of the independence of Laos by France; the decree dissolving the provisional government of Free Laos and the *Lao Issara* movement; and finally, an analysis and summary of François Iché's book on the international and political status of Laos. This last document by Katay was written in 1938 and discusses *Le statut politique et international du Laos français: sa condition juridique dans la communauté du droit des gens* (The political and international status of French Laos: its legal state in the law of nations) (Toulouse, France: Moderne, 1935. 219p. map.). Iché's thesis was that those Lao within the frontiers of Thailand were free citizens, those in the kingdom of Luang Prabang lived under a French protectorate, and those in the rest of French Laos lived in a colony.

313 **Revolution in Laos: practice and prospects.** Kaysone Phomvihane. Moscow: Progress, 1981. 255p.

The author is the General Secretary of the Central Committee of the Lao People's Revolutionary Party and Prime Minister of the People's Democratic Republic of Laos. As an active participant in the revolution, he covers the history of events up to the communist victory; the lessons which are to be learned from the strategy adopted; and the hopes and plans to be adopted for the development of a socialist Laos.

314 **Revolution in Laos: the North Vietnamese and the Pathet Lao.** P. F. Langer, Joseph J.Zasloff. Santa Monica, California: Rand Corporation, 1969. 233p. maps. (Rand Memorandum, RM-5935-ARPA).

The second in a series of studies on the nature of the Lao communist movement, it 'seeks to integrate and analyze the hitherto scattered information on the presence and activities of the Vietnamese Communists in Laos since the Second World War'. The focus of this study is the military and advisory support of the North Vietnamese to the Pathet Lao and its significance in sustaining the Lao communist movement. Part 1 is a historical survey of relations up to the Geneva Conference 1961-62. Part 2 analyses

North Vietnamese advice and military support in the 1960s. There is a useful chronology of the Lao communist movement from 1945 to 1968 in an appendix. Their conclusion is of contemporary relevance, as it discusses whether the Democratic Republic of Vietnam has plans to take over some or all of Laos, and the relations between the two partners. They do not favour the takeover view, although they consider that the political situation in this frontier region will always be of great concern to the Vietnamese.

315 **Documents sur le 25e anniversaire de la fondation du Parti Populaire Revolutionnaire Lao.** (Documents for the 25th anniversary of the foundation of the Lao People's Revolutionary Party.)
Vientiane: Editions en Langues Étrangères, 1980. 31p.

A brief history of the Party and its successes, with particular emphasis on the years 1975 to 1980. In the second part there is a statement of the Party's programmes and objectives. In the same vein is *Pages historiques de la lutte heroique du peuple lao* (Historic pages from the heroic struggle of the Lao people) (Vientiane: Editions en Langues Étrangères, 1980. 35p.).

316 **The third congress of the Lao People's Revolutionary Party: documents and materials, April 27-30, 1982.**
Moscow: Progress Publishers, 1984. 117p.

Translated from the Russian, this work includes the political report of the Central Committee of the Lao People's Revolutionary Party to the third congress, given by Kaysone Phomvihane, and the objectives and tasks of the first five-year plan for the country's socio-economic development, by Nouhak Phoumsavanh.

317 **The role of North Vietnamese cadres in the Pathet Lao administration of Xieng Khouang province.**
Edwin T. McKeithen. [Vientiane:] USAID Mission to Laos, 1970. 13p.

Based on interviews with refugees from the Plain of Jars and Xieng Khouang city, and on documents left behind there by the North Vietnamese, McKeithen's thesis is that the North Vietnamese ran the administration but preserved the illusion that decisions were made by Pathet Lao officials. The North Vietnamese mission was to revolutionize the society, but at a pace that would not alienate the Lao, hence the need to work through the Pathet Lao. McKeithen believed that the object of the North Vietnamese was both to spread the doctrines of Marxism-Leninism, but also to develop the agricultural lands of Laos for ultimate Vietnamese use and even possibly annexation. He details the apparent organization of the North Vietnamese cadres based on documents and reports, and the organization, such as taxation and food distribution, which they set up in the Pathet Lao area. He has written further on these matters in his *Life under the P.L. in the Xieng Khouang Ville area* ([Vientiane:] USAID Mission to Laos, 1969. 31p.).

Politics and Administration

318 **Les débuts du socialisme au Laos.** (The beginnings of socialism in Laos.)
Youri Mikhéev. Moscow: Novosti, 1985. 71p.
Written for the tenth anniversary of the People's Democratic Republic of Laos, and here translated from the Russian original. About half the work is concerned with the history of Laos between 1945 and the end of 1975. The second part looks at the efforts to rebuild Laos economically, socially and as an international power. It records the achievements of the first ten years of the new government; this is illustrated with sixteen pages of photographs.

319 **Political program of the Neo Lao Haksat: Lao Patriotic Front.**
Neo Lao Haksat. [n.p.]: Neo Lao Haksat Publications, 1968. 21p.
English-language text of the twelve-point political programme adopted at the Extraordinary Congress of October 31, 1968.

320 **Laos.**
Roger M. Smith. In: *Governments and politics of Southeast Asia.* Edited by George McT. Kahin. Ithaca, New York; London: Cornell University Press, 1964. 2nd ed, p. 527-92. map. bibliog.
Following the common format of this work, the section on Laos deals with the historical background, the contemporary economy and society, the political process and its elements, the monarchy, the executive, the legislature, the judiciary, the administration, political parties and elections. It concludes with a survey of current economic and social problems. A useful summary for the period up to 1964.

321 **Communism in South-east Asia.**
Justus M. van der Kroef. London: Macmillan, 1981. 342p. bibliog.
The first chapter deals with the rise of communism in South East Asia and refers to the development of the Lao Communist Party (Phak Phasason Lao), the Lao Issara, and the Neo Lao Haksat and their opposition to the French-supported monarchy up to the events of 1976. The second chapter covers the contemporary political scene, that is the period 1976 to 1978. The third chapter deals with the programmes and tactics of particular communist parties, and the fourth with the appeal they hold for the population of each country. The book concludes with a look at international relations within the region and with China and the USSR, and a look at possible future developments. Laos only occupies a fraction of the coverage of this volume but the writing is succinct and precise, and Laos is set within the context of Indo-China in particular and South East Asia in general.

322 **Laos.**
Joseph J. Zasloff, Lewis M. Stern. In: *Political parties of Asia and the Pacific.* Edited by Haruhiro Fukui. Westport, Connecticut: Greenwood Press, 1985, vol. 2, p. 679-99. bibliog.
A brief survey of Lao political history from 1950 to 1975 is followed by encyclopaedia-style entries for the political parties that existed in Laos during that period. There are cross-references from different forms of names and initials used. It is a useful rapid reference work, but it is not totally consistent on the romanization of names.

323 **The Pathet Lao: leadership and organization.**
Joseph J. Zasloff.   Lexington, Massachusetts: Lexington Books, 1973.
174p. map.

A study of the Pathet Lao, or Lao Revolutionary Movement, as a political movement, rather than a study of its military actions. The work considers the social and ethnic origins of the leadership of the People's Party of Laos (the Phak Phasason Lao), its politics, administration and fighting forces. This is accompanied by appendices which give some Neo Lao Haksat (Lao Patriotic Front) documents and profiles of leaders. A useful work for its documentation, it is based on a series of interviews conducted in Laos in 1967 with Lao who had participated in the Lao Issara movement with Pathet Lao leaders, with others who had known or worked with Pathet Lao leaders, and interviews with Pathet Lao defectors and prisoners. Pathet Lao documents and broadcasts were also used. This material was updated with more recent documents and interviews with defectors and refugees.

Law and Constitution

324 **Lao People's Democratic Republic (formerly Laos).**
Dana Blaustein, Joseph J. Zasloff, Patricia E. Larkin. In:
Constitutions of countries of the world. Edited by P. Blaustein,
Gisbert H. Flanz. Dobbs Ferry, New York: Oceana Publications,
1985, 128p. bibliog.

The text of the new Lao constitution is in the last stages of preparation. The present entry for Laos in this loose-leaf publication, which is regularly updated, fills the gap with the constitutional material that exists for Laos. A chronology of historical events, basically from 1945 to 1984, with a sentence or short paragraph on each entry introduces the text. Zasloff contributes an article on the 'Fundamental institutions of the Lao People's Democratic Republic' (p. 27-30). This is followed by documents relating to the present constitutional position. There is the text of the law of 1982 which established the Council of Ministers (p. 50-66). In the Prime Minister's report for 1984, given here, he announces that a constitutional drafting commission has been set up. All the texts are in English, several of them have been taken from monitored broadcasts.

325 **Indochine.** (Indo-China).
Yvonne Bongert. In: *Introduction bibliographique à l'histoire du droit et à l'ethnologie juridique – Bibliographical introduction to legal history and ethnology.* Edited by John Gilissen. Brussels: Les Editions de l'Institut de Sociologie, Université Libre de Bruxelles, 1963- , Section E/11, 1967, 102p. map.

Provides bibliographical information on the law of the different ethnic groups of former French Indo-China. The work is divided into three divisions: French Indo-China, subdivided under Indo-China as a whole and its five administrative divisions; the independent Indochinese states; and finally a briefer section on the ethnic minorities of Indo-China. The section on French Indo-China as a whole is wide-ranging and should be consulted for all aspects of French colonial law and administration. The sections on Laos cover both ancient Lao legal traditions as well as contemporary codes of law and customary practice.

326 **Agreement on the re-establishment of peace and realisation of national concord in Laos.**
     Central Joint Commission for Implementation of the Agreements on the Re-establishment of Peace and Realisation of National Concord in Laos. Vientiane: The Author, 1974. 125 leaves.

Here is presented the text of the Vientiane peace accord of 21 February 1973; the protocol provided for in the peace accord, for the detailed arrangements, 14 September 1973; and the provisions agreed for the implementation of the agreements, 19 March 1974. The peace accord and protocol are given in both the Vientiane Government version and the Neo Lao Haksat version. They were then forwarded in this compilation to the President of the International Commission for Supervision and Control in Laos. It is a collection of twelve stencilled documents; in each case there is the French text and the unofficial English translation of it. The agreements were originally written in Lao.

327 **A concise legal history of South-East Asia.**
     M. B. Hooker. Oxford: Clarendon Press, 1978. 289p. bibliog.

Laos is covered in the chapter on the French legal world; that is, the legal inheritance of French Indo-China. Hooker outlines (p. 161-66) the specific details as they related to Laos. The problem of the conflict of laws is dealt with in a further section of the chapter.

328 **L'action des pouvoirs publics dans la répartition et l'affectation du sol en vue de l'aménagement et du développement au Laos.** (The function of the authorities on the division and assignment of land with reference to their management and development in Laos.)
     Inpèng Suryadhay. *Revue Juridique et Politique, Indépendance et Co-opération*, vol. 4 (1970), p. 1319-20.

Inpèng outlines the 1953, 1957, 1960 and 1963 laws on land in Laos. He focuses on unused land. This is one of several articles contributed to this issue of the journal. There is also 'La domaine national au Laos' (National property in Laos) (*Revue Juridique et Politique, Indépendance et Coopération*, vol. 4 (1970), p. 937-38, which deals with the 1953 law on public and private property. He discusses and surveys the change from the 1927 code to the 1958 law, which provided unassailable titles to land, in 'La propriété foncière selon des pratiques coutoumières lao' (Real property according to the Lao customary practice) (*Revue Juridique et Politique, Indépendance et Coopération*, vol. 4 (1970), p. 747-50).

329 **The Thai Thammasat (with a note on the Lao texts).**
Yoneo Ishii. In: *The laws of South-East Asia*. Vol. 1: *The pre-modern texts*. Edited by M. B. Hooker. Singapore: Butterworth (Asia), 1986, p. 143-201.

The note on the Lao texts is indeed brief (p. 198-200). Ishii notes that it is still an area for study, and lists the known texts with brief notes on them and details of where they have been published. It should be noted that his definition of Laos includes Lanna or northern Thailand.

330 **Aviation laws of Bulgaria, the People's Republic of China, the CSSR, the German Democratic Republic, Hungary, the Democratic People's Republic of Korea, Laos, Poland, Romania, the USSR, Yugoslavia and the Republic of Vietnam.**
Edited by J. L. Kneifel. [Munich: The Editor, 1985.] 6 vols.

The collection of laws was assembled for the author's book on the air law of socialist states. Laos is covered briefly in volume three (p. 1550-74). There are two exchanges of notes in 1954 and 1955, between Thailand and the Royal Government of Laos, establishing an air link between Vientiane and Bangkok. The text of these is in French. The other document is the agreement made between Laos and Singapore in 1974 for an air service between the two countries.

331 **Journal Judiciaire.** (Legal journal.)
Vientiane: Ministère de la Justice, 1963- .

Articles may be published in Lao or French. There are articles on general subjects such as jurisprudence, and on specific subjects such as the organization of the courts. It also publishes the texts of particular laws, ordinances and court judgements.

332 **L'Indochine et ses traités, 1946.** (Indo-China and its treaties, 1946.)
Roger Lévy. Paris: Hartmann, 1947. 105p. (Centre d'Études de Politique Étrangère, Publication, no. 19).

A collection of the treaties signed by France and the governments of Indo-China, Laos, Cambodia and Vietnam, and the treaties signed with other countries such as China and Thailand, concerning Indo-China. The last document is the French constitution of September 1946 which includes the clauses on the formation of the French Union. In his introduction Lévy provides the historical background to these treaties.

333 **La conception du droit dans l'Indochine hinayaniste.** (The idea of law in Theravada Buddhist Indo-China.)
Robert Lingat. *Bulletin de l'École Française de l'Extrême-Orient*, vol. 44, no. 1 (1947-50), p. 163-87.

Lingat suggests that the Buddhists of South East Asia rejected the Hindu Dharmasastra, and looked solely to Buddhism for a source of law and civilizing forces. This need was met by the Mons who produced the works of interpretation preserved in the Dharmasastra. He outlines how this Pali juridical literature was developed and influenced the different Buddhist countries of mainland South East Asia. Lingat comments that its influence on Laos is still to be studied, and this remains the case.

334 Land problems in Laos.
A. N. Seth. Bangkok: Food and Agriculture Organization, Regional
Office for Asia and the Far East, 1968. rev. ed. 18 leaves.
Seth describes the administration, tenure and allotment of land in Laos, as well as the
resettlement of evacuees from the areas which had been inundated by the Nam Ngum
dam. He notes the lack of a land tax, land records and effective land administration.

335 Labor law and practice in the Kingdom of Laos.
United States: Office of Economic and Social Research, Bureau of
Labor Statistics. Washington, DC: United States, Department of
Labor, Bureau of Labor Statistics, 1970. 50p. map. bibliog. (BLS
report, no. 381).
One of a series of reports aimed at providing information for those in the United States
employing local workers abroad, and other interested parties. It is based on material
gathered in the field by the Department of Labor representative. This report, prepared
by Theodore Bleecker and Donald Bell, provides a summary of the economic, social,
and governmental background to employment, with information on the legislation
affecting employment. It summarizes the 1967 labour code for Laos which replaced the
French Indo-China labour code, and gives examples of current practice throughout.
The principal legislation prior to 1967 is listed in the 1965 edition of this work.

**336 Code civil et commercial lao modifié. (Modified Lao civil and
commercial code of law.)**
Va Bouapha. Vientiane: Imprimerie Nationale, 1973? 2nd ed. 228p.
A bilingual French and Lao text of the Civil and Commercial code of Laos, which
deals with family law property law, and contract law. This edition was issued with an
18-page appendix of a law on the registration of legal matters such as births, deaths
and marriages. This code had been substantially revised in 1965. The Lao People's
Democratic Republic began issuing the new codes in Lao in 1990.

**337 Code Penal: code penal modifié. (The penal code: the modified penal
code.)**
Va Bouapha. Vientiane: Imprimerie Nationale, 1969. 198p.
A bilingual French and Lao text of the penal code which was almost totally revised in
1965 from the original, first promulgated in 1928. The new penal code for Laos was
published in Lao in 1990.

338 Traditional and constitutional law: a study of change in Laos.
Joseph J. Westermeyer. *Asian Survey*, vol. 11, no. 6 (1971), p. 562-
69.
Based on the author's observation, this is a study of problem-solving within the
coexistent systems of customary and codified law in Laos. There are interesting
parallels in that even in the formal system few cases reach the courts but are dealt with
by officials, and so like the traditional system which seeks consensus on the solution,
both parties are brought to agree the justice of the solution. Codified law is used when

Law and Constitution

village matters cannot be solved by customary measures, in an urban setting, and when the matter refers to foreigners. It is noted that in both systems insoluble cases may be dealt with by assassination outside the official cognisance of the authorities.

Foreign Relations

339 **A l'école des diplomates: la perte et le retour d'Angkor.** (At the school
of diplomats: the loss and return of Angkor.)
F. Bernard. Paris: Les Oeuvres Representatives, 1933. 240p. map.
Written by the President of the Commission for the delimitation of the French-Siamese
frontier, 1904-07, it recounts the history of relations between France and Thailand
(Siam). Beginning with the first treaties in the seventeenth century, it concludes with
the treaty of 1907. The definition of the frontier between Laos and Thailand,
established as a result of the later treaties, is interwoven in this text. The revision of
the frontier that occurred between 1904 and 1907 was not great for Laos, but for
Cambodia it restored the province of Battambang, a section of the Mekong and the
complex of monuments at Angkor.

340 **SEATO: the failure of an alliance strategy.**
Leszek Buszynski. Singapore: Singapore University Press, 1983. 263p.
bibliog.
SEATO (the South-East Asia Treaty Organisation) was formed under the auspices of
the South-East Asia Collective Defence Treaty, 8 September, 1954. The signatories
undertook to protect the sovereign rights of nations within the treaty area, and agreed
to meet aggression by armed attack on nations within the treaty area. The protocol to
the treaty specified that Laos and Cambodia fell within these provisions of the treaty.
The Laotian crises of 1959 and 1960-61 are dealt with in a chapter of this book, and
Buszynski makes clear that they exposed SEATO's inability to deal with the problem
of communist subversion. SEATO's presence exacerbated hostilities, and it became
clear that the members had different views on the best way to act in the situation. The
acceptance of the neutralization of Laos in 1962 led directly to the downgrading of
SEATO operations, and led to the Thai seeking assurances from the United States
which went beyond the provisions of the treaty. Buszynski offers an important analysis
of a particular set of external forces which influenced the foreign powers who
endeavoured to resolve the Laotian crises.

341 **Brother enemy: the war after the war.**
Nayan Chanda. San Diego, California; New York; London: Harcourt
Brace Jovanovich, 1986. 479p. maps.

A journalist's view of the situation in Indo-China in the ten years after the fall of
Saigon, April 29 1975, that some have called the Third Indochinese War. Much of it is
based on the events Chanda witnessed personally, as well as his interviews with the
national leaders of the region, and it is written in a very readable and immediate style.
Chanda chronicles the growing conflicts and rivalries between the three Indochinese
states and their relations with the superpowers. Laos is a minor player in this account,
but Chanda keeps a very complex story moving in a very clear way.

342 **Conventions et traités entre la France et le Siam sur le Laos, 1893-1947.**
(Conventions and treaties between France and Siam (Thailand)
concerning Laos, 1893-1947.)
Péninsule, no. 16/17 (1988), p. 9-180. map.

The text of sixteen agreements from 1893 to 1947 is given here in French. Apart from
those of 1893, 1904 and 1907 which fixed the boundaries of Laos during the French
protectorate, there are several for 1926 and 1937 governing commerce and navigation
on the Mekong, the peace treaty of 1941 when Thailand seized territory from Laos and
Cambodia, and the treaties and agreements of 1946 and 1947 to regulate the frontier to
its present position.

343 **Red brotherhood at war: Vietnam, Cambodia and Laos since 1975.**
Grant Evans, Kelvin Rowley. London: Verso, 1990. 2nd ed. 322p.
maps. bibliog.

A study of the relations between the three states of Indo-China since the departure of
United States forces in 1975. Evans and Rowley unravel the conflicts that have beset
the region, that have been called the Third Indochinese War. Their discussion revolves
around the strength of nationalism as a motive force for events both before and after
1975, and the role of the political ideology of communism. They argue that nationalism
is a stronger force in events in the region. They contest the view that Laos is a colony
of Vietnam, but point out that its foreign policy must by force of its size, its population
and its position as a buffer state be linked with that of Vietnam, and Laos must opt for
a protective alliance. This second edition takes into account the improvements in
international relations in the region over the six years since the first edition.

344 **The 1940 Franco-Thai border dispute and Phibuun Songkhraam's
commitment to Japan.**
E. Thadeus Flood. *Journal of Southeast Asian History*, vol. 10, no. 2
(1969), p. 304-25.

The border between Siam or Thailand and Laos and Cambodia had been established
by treaty with France, most recently in 1904 and 1926. It was not acceptable to the
Thai, and they used the opportunity of the Japanese presence in French Indo-China
and Thailand to adjust the border in their favour. Flood examines the history of the
problem of the border from 1893 to 1941, and uses recently available Japanese and
Thai sources.

345 **For peace and stability in Southeast Asia.**

Hanoi: Foreign Languages Publishing House, 1983. 69p.

A series of documents issued by the governments of the three Indochinese states, published to present their analysis of the situation in South East Asia and the proposals they have put forward with a view to ending the tensions in the region. The relevant documents are 'Communiqué of the sixth conference of Foreign Ministers of Laos, Kampuchea and Vietnam (July 6-7, 1982), (p. 9-18); 'Note of the Foreign Minister of the Lao People's Democratic Republic to the Foreign Ministers of ASEAN countries (September 15, 1982) (p. 19-25); 'Statement of the summit conference of Laos, Kampuchea and Vietnam (March 3, 1983) (p. 26-34); 'Statement on the presence in Kampuchea of volunteers from the Vietnamese army, February 23, 1983' [a statement from Laos] (p. 35-41); 'Communiqué of the extraordinary meeting of Foreign Ministers of Laos, Kampuchea and Vietnam in Phnom Penh (April 12, 1983) (p. 54-60); 'Appendix. Solidarity between Laos, Kampuchea and Vietnam: chronology' (p. 61-69). These statements are all directed against the world powers and ASEAN, but particularly against the government of China for their continuing support for the Khmer Rouge and Democratic Kampuchea as the legitimate government of Cambodia. It provides a view of the concerted action in foreign affairs of the three Indochinese states.

346 **Bibliography on landlocked states.**

Martin Ira Glassner. Dordrecht, Netherlands: Nijhoff, 1986. 2nd ed. 210p.

A comprehensive bibliography of material relating to access to and from the sea, and access to the resources of the sea, for land-locked states published since 1945. From the subject index one can trace all the articles relating to Laos.

347 **Franco-British rivalry over Siam, 1896-1904.**

Minton F. Goldman. *Journal of Southeast Asian Studies*, vol. 3, no. 2 (1972), p. 210-28. map.

An examination of the negotiations between Britain and France to establish a secure boundary between their territories in Burma and Tonkin, and to define the extent of the French presence on the eastern boundary between Siam and Laos. Secret treaties between Britain and France underlay the terms of the treaty the Siamese were forced to accept from the French in 1904.

348 **Indochina in North Vietnamese strategy.**

Melvin Gurtov. Santa Monica, California: Rand Corporation, 1971. 28p. map. bibliog. (Rand Paper, P4605).

An attempt to assess North Vietnam's policies in Indochina in 1971. The author looks back over the policies of the Vietnamese communists in the previous forty years, from the founding of the Indochinese Communist Party in 1929. This paper is in the school of thought that sees Laos as essentially a puppet of the North Vietnamese strategy and long-term planning. Its focus sharpens on the events of 1968 to the time of writing, and it concludes with an effort to assess what possible future outcomes there may be for Laos and Cambodia.

349 **The Soviet Union, China, and the Pathet Lao: analysis and chronology.**
Paul F. Langer. Santa Monica, California: Rand Corporation, 1972.
121p. map. (Rand Paper, P-4765).
A study of Soviet and Chinese policies towards Laos, and their objectives. Langer sees
this in terms of China's objective of national security, which required the removal of all
hostile powers and their influence from its borders, and the Sino-Soviet conflict, which
prevented the Soviet Union from withdrawing from a region of no security interest to
it. The Chinese strategy he sees as promoting a 'people's war', whereas the Soviet
Union sought a political solution that would ensure a government that was friendly to
the Soviet Union. More than half of this book is a detailed chronolgy of Chinese and
Russian relations with Laos between 1961 and 1971.

350 **White book: the truth about Thai-Lao relations.**
[Vientiane:] Ministry of Foreign Affairs, Lao People's Democratic
Republic, 1984. 48p. map.
The subject of this book is evidence to support the allegation that the Thais, as a result
of their ultra-rightist rulers, 'have colluded with external forces in pursuing a
hegemonist and expansionist policy against Laos'. More than half the book deals with
Thailand's activities before 1975. The second part chronicles Thai-Lao relations from
1975 to 1984, beginning with the Thai offer of asylum to political refugees from Laos,
to the occupation of three Lao villages by Thailand in 1984. It also deals with the Thai
closure of the frontier and control of goods for transit to third countries. More specific
material on the incidents in 1984 are found in *The question of the Thai aggression on
June 6, 1984 against Lao territory before the Security Council of the United Nations,
New York, October 9, 1984* (Vientiane: Ministry of Foreign Affairs, Lao People's
Democratic Republic, 1984. 64p.) and *Memorandum on the attack and occupation of
three Lao villages, Bane May, Bane Kang and Bane Savang by the troops of ultra-
rightist reactionaries among Thai ruling circles* (Vientiane: Ministry of Foreign Affairs,
Lao People's Democratic Republic, 1984. 16p. map.).

351 **Southeast Asia and the law of the sea: some preliminary observations on
the political geography of Southeast Asian seas.**
Lee Yong Leng. Singapore: Singapore University Press, 1980. rev.
ed. 75p. maps, bibliog.
Examines from a geographical standpoint the main contentious issues debated at the
United Nations Law of the Sea Conference as they apply to the waters of South East
Asia. Chapter 8 deals with the land-locked states, including Laos. Although, as he
describes, there are projects in both China and Vietnam to upgrade the routes linking
Laos with Da Nang, Ho Chi Minh City and Yunnan to all weather roads, his
conclusion is that Laos, with some of the other states, is not well placed in relation to
the sea and will be a loser in the scramble for ocean resources.

352   U.S. intervention in Laos and its impact on Laotian relations with
Thailand and Vietnam.
Usha Mahajani.   In: *Conflict and stability in Southeast Asia*.   Edited
by Mark W. Zacher, R. Stephen Milne.   Garden City, New York:
Doubleday/Anchor, 1974, p. 237-74.
Professor Mahajani argues that intervention by the United States has changed the
position of Laos from the traditional one of a buffer zone to a major battleground. She
first examines the traditional relations of Laos with Vietnam and Thailand. She
continues by examining the nature and depth of American intervention and its
maintenance and support of the Lao government of Prince Souvanna Phouma. It is
argued that this intervention has changed the relationship of Laos with her neighbours
Thailand and Vietnam, and Thai-Vietnamese competition has led to direct conflict, a
new phenomenon. There is a clear and succinct summary of the political history of
Laos, particularly after 1945, and a clear statement of the American role in Laos.

353   **Auguste Pavie diplomate: la question franco-siamoise des états laotiens,**
1884-96. (Auguste Pavie diplomat: The Franco-Siamese question of the
Lao states, 1884-96.)
Petithuguenin.   *Revue d'Histoire des Colonies*, vol. 35, nos. 3-4
(1948), p. 200-30.
Written on the occasion of the hundredth anniversary of Pavie's birth, Petithuguenin
recalls the ideal which inspired the founders of the French colonial empire. This is an
admiring portrait of Pavie and his work in establishing the frontier between Laos and
Siam (modern Thailand), which he sets in the historical context of the region. It is
written in an accessible style for the general reader.

354   **Map of mainland Asia by treaty.**
J. R. V. Prescott.   Melbourne, Australia: Melbourne University Press,
1975. 518p. maps. bibliog.
Prescott examines each of the mainland Asian boundaries; there is a chapter devoted
to each. Five chapters relate to Laos: these are, the boundary between Burma and
Laos; the boundary of Thailand with Cambodia and Laos; the Cambodia-Laos
boundary, 1893-1905; the boundary of Laos with North and South Vietnam; and the
boundary of China with North Vietnam and Laos. Each chapter begins with the
sources of the documents on which it is based. There is brief history of the
circumstances in which the boundary has been determined in modern times, with
extracts from documents. Each concludes with the key clauses of the relevant treaty
and bibliographical references are given. In this work he does not appear to consider
the frontier problems which arose between Thailand and French Indo-China in the
1940s, when Thailand reclaimed territories in Laos and Cambodia with the support of
the Japanese, who had occupied French Indo-China, but which were restored at the
end of the Second World War. Prescott has worked on this subject over many years,
and for a systematic treatise on frontiers and boundaries one should read his *Political*
frontiers and boundaries (London: Allen & Unwin, 1987. 315p. maps.).

355 **Indian foreign policy in Cambodia, Laos and Vietnam, 1947-1964.**
   D. R. SarDesai.   Berkeley, California: University of California Press,
   1968. 336p. bibliog.

A study of the history of the first seventeen years of the foreign policy of independent
India. This experience of emerging from colonial rule affected India's view of the
nationalist aspirations of the three Indochinese states. Apart from coverage in the
more general chapters, SarDesai devotes two chapters to Laos. The first, covering the
period of 1954 to 1958, deals with India's role in the International Control
Commission. The second deals with the Laotian crisis of 1959 to 1962, and examines
India's view of the neutralist coup and her role in the achievement of the second
Geneva Convention, and the policy of neutrality.

356 **The end of nowhere: American policy toward Laos since 1954.**
   Charles A. Stevenson.   Boston, Massachusetts: Beacon Press, 1972.
   367p. map. bibliog.

A case study of the evolution of United States' policy toward Laos since 1954. It draws
on the literature of decision-making; much of this was still classified. Stevenson has
relied on material available in the public record, as well as interviews with eighty-six
participants in decision-making. The study is arranged chronologically. In an appendix
he has given a chronology of major events relating to Laos, 1954-71.

357 **Lao foreign policy.**
   Martin Stuart-Fox.   In: *The political economy of foreign policy in
   Southeast Asia.*   Edited by David Wurfel, Bruce Barton.   London:
   Macmillan, 1990, p. 272-87. bibliog.

An analysis of the foreign policy of the Lao People's Democratic Republic, which saw
a drastic restructuring from the neutralist but pro-western position of the Royal Lao
Government. Laos still faced the severe constraints in formulating foreign policy posed
by its position as a land-locked state. Stuart-Fox sees the main tasks of their foreign
policy as maintaining Lao interests; that is, the preservation of the national state and
the development of a national identity, while undertaking the maximization of
international links to provide the resources needed for economic development. He
outlines the scope of Lao foreign policy within the constraints such as the small size of
its army, the difficult terrain, the need for both economic and political reasons to
remain on reasonable terms with Thailand, and the limits imposed by the treaty of
friendship with Vietnam. He judges that they have been reasonably successful in their
basic aims of securing the state, establishing a national identity and obtaining foreign
aid.

358 **Le Laos: stratégies d'un état-tampon.** (Laos: strategies of a buffer
   state.)
   Christian Taillard.   Montpellier, France: Groupement d'Intérêt Public
   RECLUS, 1989. 200p. maps. bibliog. (Collection Territoires).

Laos has been a buffer state since the fourteenth century and the author considers its
present state, while keeping in mind its past experience. He looks at the political and
economic steps taken by the present government both for internal development and
international survival. He backs up his arguments with useful and previously
unpublished evidence in maps and statistics. He offers a confident prediction for the
continued future of Laos as a buffer state.

359 **Vietnam and Laos: master and apprentice.**
Joseph J. Zasloff.   In: *Postwar Indochina: old enemies and new allies*.   Edited by Joseph J. Zasloff.   Arlington, Virginia: Center for the Study of Foreign Affairs, 1988, p. 37-62. (Study of Foreign Affairs Series).

A study of the special relationship between Vietnam and Laos in its historical and contemporary aspects. This relationship, which enables Vietnam to feel more secure on it western border, provides Laos with political, military and economic assistance. The text of the 1977 treaty of friendship and co-operation between the Lao People's Democratic Republic and the Socialist Republic of Vietnam is given on p. 280-83 of this volume.

Economy and Economic Development

360 **Les rites d'ouverture de la mine de fer de Bàn Bo Mon (Laos).** (Rituals on the opening of the iron mine of Bàn Bo Mon in Laos.)
Charles Archaimbault. *Bulletin de l'École Française d'Extrême-Orient*, vol. 75 (1985), p. 369-401.

An account of a ceremony witnessed by the author in December 1955 at the village of Bo Mon, seventy kilometres north-west of Xieng Khouang; an area inhabited by the mountain-dwelling Tai-speaking group Archaimbault calls *p'uon*, referred to elsewhere as Phuan. The name of the village ('mine of the mulberry trees') refers to one of the other principal resources of the village, the cultivation of silk worms for weaving silk textiles. Archaimbault recounts the legend of the village, of a giant, one of the original residents, who revealed the site of the seams of iron ore and introduced the cultivation of mulberry trees. He describes briefly the opencast mining, the communal smelting of the ore and the forging done by each household in the context of the description of the ceremonies, which occurred at the beginning of the mining season, and lasted four months between the end of harvest and the beginning of the new season of cultivation. Archaimabult links what he observed with other studies of traditional mining elsewhere in the world, and observes that these rites, beliefs and taboos are found in mining folklore worldwide; he draws out the similarities.

361 **Asian Development Bank annual report.**
Manila: Asian Development Bank, 1967- . annual.

The annual report of the Asian Development Bank provides useful information on development projects in Laos. It provides country reports on operational strategy, loans and technical assistance, and project implementation. In the statistical annex the economic data on the member countries is found; in the case of Laos it is usually in reference to loans and grant-financed technical assistance (twenty projects were financed in 1989). The *ADB Quarterly Review*, also published by the Asian Development Bank, provides details of policy statements by the Bank's governors and regular updates on programmes approved for technical assistance. There is a profile of a member country in each issue.

362 **The complete guide to countertrade and offset in South East Asia, China and the Far East.**
Jonathan Bell. London: COI Publications, 1988. 399p. bibliog.
After an initial section on the nature of countertrade and offset, Bell presents a country-by-country analysis of the situation in South East Asia and the Far East. Laos is covered very briefly, but it is a useful summary of what is traded and what prospects there are for trade with Laos. In a separate section he gives the names and addresses of all the relevant government departments, banks and agencies to contact for those interested in trading with Laos.

363 **Thai-Laos economic relations: a new perspective.**
Bunyaraks Ninsananda et al. Bangkok: 1977. 2nd ed. 100p. bibliog.
A study of past, present and future economic relations between Laos and Thailand. The authors conclude that whereas past trade relations have been based on the principle of comparative cost, they anticipate that the new government of Laos will tend towards a centrally planned economy which may be less flexible, may affect the exchange rates, and may stress foreign trade at the expense of cost advantages. An appendix (p. 52-91) provides statistics on trade between Thailand and Laos between 1970 and 1975.

364 **An introduction to the *Report on indicative basin plan: a proposed framework for the development of water and related sources of the Lower Mekong Basin, 1970*.**
Committee for Co-ordination of Investigations of the Lower Mekong Basin. Bangkok: The Committee, [1972]. 37p. map.
The *Report on indicative basin plan: a proposed framework for the development of water and related sources of the Lower Mekong Basin, 1970* (Committee for Co-ordination of Investigations of the Lower Mekong Basin. Bangkok: 1971. 705p. maps.) was released to the press in 1972. It described a framework for the Lower Mekong Basin development for the next thirty years. This booklet is an introduction and brief summary of the plan. The five photographic plates illustrate some of the projects which have been achieved under the first years of the development plan, including the Nam Ngum dam in Laos, which provides hydroelectric power for the Vientiane region and northeast Thailand. In P. Lafont's *Bibliographie du Laos* (q.v.) (vol. 2, p. 253-55) many of the documents associated with the Mekong development are listed.

365 **Economic and social survey of Asia and the Pacific.**
Bangkok: United Nations, Economic and Social Commission for Asia and the Pacific, 1974- . annual.
Each annual survey highlights recent developments in the economic and social spheres as they affect the countries of Asia and the Pacific. Laos figures in the chapters devoted to the least developed economies. The title of this work for 1946-73 was *Economic and social survey of Asia and the Far East*, (Bankok: UN Economic Commission for Asia and the Far East). Since 1957 each issue in the second part has also focused on a major aspect or problem of the economies of Asia and the Pacific.

366 **Economy and society of Laos: brief survey.**
Joel M. Halpern. New Haven, Connecticut: Southeast Asia Studies, Yale University, 1964. 180p. maps. bibliog. (Monograph Series, no. 5).
Based on data collected in 1957 and 1959 in Laos, as well as the publications of others, this work presents a socio-economic picture of northern and central Laos. The urban economy formed a very small part of the Lao economy, and the major part of the work is devoted to the agricultural sector and the rural economy. The relation of the participants to both subsistence and cash economies is considered in detail. The concluding section of tables supports the preceding chapters and gives details of the prices and use of foodstuffs and household necessities.

367 **Laos and Mekong Basin development.**
Joel M. Halpern, James A. Hafner. In: *Mekong Basin development: Laos and Thailand: selected bibliographies*. Joel M. Halpern, James A. Hafner, Walter Haney. Bruxelles: Centre d'Étude du Sud-Est Asiatique et de l'Extrême-Orient, 1974, p. 31-141. (Courrier de l'Extrême-Orient, vol. 8, no. 59).
Intended as a working bibliography, and to indicate the range of material available, it concentrates mainly on English-language material, and in particular on the publications of the United States and the international agencies involved with work on the development of the Mekong Basin. The work is arranged under broad subject divisions; unfortunately there is no contents page. The subjects covered are agriculture (p. 32-40), community development (p. 41-45), economy (p. 45-64), education (p. 65-77), general (p. 78-112), geography and natural resources (p. 112-27), medicine and health (p. 127-30), and social science (p. 130-41). The general section is 'devoted exclusively to sample listings from the JPRS', mainly its title *Translations on South and East Asia* (which has since become *East Asia: Southeast Asia* [q.v.]).

368 **Laos: Marxism in a subsistence rural economy.**
W. Randall Ireson, Carol J. Ireson. *Bulletin of Concerned Asian Scholars*, vol. 21, nos. 2-4 (1989), p. 59-75. maps.
A survey article on the present situation in Laos. The authors offer a view of Laos in the current climate of relaxing economic controls, one in which the Lao are optimistic about the future.

369 **Aspects socio-économiques du Laos médiéval.** (Some socio-economic aspects of mediaeval Laos.)
Keo Manivanna. In: *Sur le 'mode de production asiatique'*. (On the Asiatic mode of production). Centre d'Études et de Recherches Marxistes. Paris: Éditions Sociales, 1969, p. 311-25.
Keo Manivanna makes it clear at the outset that most of the research on Lao history remains to be done. The collection of oral traditions is in its infancy, and most of the Lao manuscripts and archives remain to be studied. Most of the published work on Lao history has been written by Western historians. Her essay concentrates on the Lan Xang period of Lao history from the fourteenth to the seventeenth century. She describes the formation of Lan Xang, the imposition of the late Khmer model of kingship, Buddhism and government on the populations. The study of the Thai of Son La in Vietnam, she suggests, can furnish some idea of the social structure before the

creation of Lan Xang. She provides a fluent description of a society with an economy based on exchange: the forest products collected by the proto-Indochinese ethnic groups and their dry rice exchanged for the production of the lowland Lao, who in their turn traded it with neighbouring countries for their products. At village level, subsistence agricultural production persisted. There is little documentation to support this argument, some of which is extrapolated backwards from knowledge of life in the recent past. She concludes that Lan Xang can be said to conform to the 'asiatic mode of production' inasmuch as the economy rested still on the rural communities; that there was a form of state in which the King acted as mediator of the interests of the community and where free men were subject to corvée labour and taxes which were revenues for the King and the aristocracy. While written within the context of a particular historical approach, this work is very readable and not weighted down with jargon.

370 **Plan cadre de développement économique et social, 1969-1974: priorité au secteur productif.** (Outline plan for economic and social development, 1969-1974: priority to the productive sector.)
Laos: Ministère du Plan et de la Coopération, Commissariat General au Plan. Vientiane: Ministère du Plan, 1969. 260p. maps.

The plan sets out the economic objectives, which were to achieve economic and social development and to remove certain serious inequalities in the society. It then proposed the means of achieving them during the next five years. The projects proposed included the building of the Nam Ngum dam and the associated electricity power supply, housing for refugees, an internal airport for Vientiane, slaughterhouses, cement works, a north-south telecommunications link, a bridge across the Mekong, medical centres and a dam at Pa Mong. This document was republished in microfiche by IDC. (Inter Documentation Co.), Leiden, Netherlands.

371 **Plan de développement économique et social du Laos: période de 5 ans du 1er juillet 1959 au 30 juin 1964.** (Economic and social development plan for Laos: for the five years 1 July 1959 to 30 June 1964.)
Laos: Commissariat au Plan, Ministère du Plan. Vientiane: The Author, 1960. 162 leaves.

Originally devised in 1952 and approved in 1953, the implementation of this five-year plan was delayed by the political troubles. Its value now lies in providing a base line for the economy of independent Laos. Some retrospective statistics provide the background to the plan. It expresses the awareness of the need to improve agricultural production, particularly of livestock; the need to improve air and road services in face of the lack of rail or river transport; the need to improve educational facilities; the need to improve the physical health of the population; and the need to find sources of electricity and other raw materials to replace expensive imports. Each field of government activity is analysed and improvements are budgeted for. Although some local input of funding was expected, the main success of the plan was seen to lie in the maintenance of the value of the kip and the ability to attract substantial sources of foreign aid to finance it. This work has been republished in a microfiche edition by IDC (Inter Documentation Co.), Leiden, Netherlands. A report on the first year of working of the plan was published in 1960: *Plan de développement économique et social: premier rapport annuel. État des réalisations effectuées au cours de la première année 1959-1960, et programme pour la deuxième année 1960-1961.* (Economic and social development plan: first annual report. Work realized in the first year, 1959-1960 and programme for the second year 1960-1961) (Commissariat au Plan. Vientiane: Ministère du Plan, 1960. 98p.). This was also republished in a microfiche edition by IDC (Inter Documentation Co.), Leiden, Netherlands.

372 **Socialism in a subsistence economy: the Laotian way. An analysis of development patterns in Laos after 1975.**
Hans U. Luther. Bangkok: Chulalongkorn University Social Research Institute, 1983. 65 leaves, map. bibliog.

After a brief socio-economic profile of Laos, Luther describes the efforts to transform the economy of Laos from its state in 1975 of a partially feudal and partially colonial structure into grass-roots socialism. He acknowledges the difficulties for foreign scholars in attempting to study contemporary Laos because of the travel restrictions in force. He concludes by trying to evaluate the post-war development policies. 'The main point this paper attempts to illustrate is that a landlocked and extremely poor country like Laos has great and specific difficulties and problems to extricate itself from the legacy of colonial deformation and thus to redress its political *and* economic independence' (f. 3). Two speeches by Kaysone Phomvihane on the transition to socialism are appended, as they give evidence of the leaders' views of the Lao path to socialism.

373 **A behavioral research project for the Sedone Valley Program, southern Laos: preliminary presentation of interviews and questionnaire data from Lao villagers.**
Kenneth G. Orr. Vientiane: USAID Mission to Laos, 1966. 201p.

A collection of basic social and economic data, by Lao research assistants, in villages in southern Laos undergoing development. The purpose of the research was to judge the effectiveness of the joint USAID, Royal Lao Government development programme. The bulk of this study is the tabulated responses to the questionnaire from the eight villages surveyed, but there are also fieldnotes of interviews and discussions held during the research project.

374 **Patterns of consumption in the Lao household: a preliminary presentation of data.**
Kenneth G. Orr. Vientiane: USAID Mission to Laos, 1967. 110p.

Based on a questionnaire survey, this paper endeavours to present a quantitative and qualitative assessment of consumption patterns in a rural Lao household. A discussion of the consumption of foodstuffs is followed by consideration of the use of fuel, water, household implements, stimulants, medicines, clothing and adornment, and expenditure for ceremonies and religious rites. This discussion is linked to the tabulated statment of findings from the village survey, and illustrations of the items themselves. This study was a continuation of the previous work on southern Laos, published as *A behavioral research project for the Sedone Valley Program, southern Laos: preliminary presentation of interviews and questionnaire data from Lao villagers* (q.v.).

375 **Evolution économique du Laos depuis son accession à l'indépendance, période 1955-1962.** (The economic development of Laos since independence, with particular reference to 1955-1962.)
Pane Rassavong. Bordeaux, France: Université de Bordeaux, Faculté de Droit et des Sciences Economiques, 1962. 111p. maps. bibliog.
Beginning with the end of the Indochinese Economic Union, this study examines the Lao economy in the first seven years of independence. Based on official statistics, United Nations statistics and interviews with key officials, this work presents a view of the precariousness of the Lao economy before the effects of war had distorted it further. Rassavong signals the dangers inherent in foreign aid, and the need to discourage imported products which ended local production, for example of silk thread. His hope is for economic independence to match political independence, but in its land-locked state Laos is dependent on its neighbours for access to the sea, and the larger foreign powers for economic aid and military assistance.

376 **Quarterly Economic Review of Indochina: Vietnam, Laos, Cambodia.**
London: Economist Intelligence Unit, 1976- . quarterly (and annual supplement).
The major part of this journal is the review by country with statistical tables. The review covers both the political scene and the economy; the statistics are economic indicators for the quarter and information on foreign trade. Each issue begins with a section called 'Outlook' which summarizes the economic and political prospects for each of the three states. The annual supplement brings together general information on the government and economy of each of the countries, and statistical summaries. Before 1976 the title of this publication was *Quarterly Economic Review of Indochina: South Vietnam, North Vietnam, Cambodia, Laos.*

377 **The economic development of French Indo-China.**
Charles Robequain. Reprinted, New York: AMS Press, 1974. 400p.
First published in French in 1939, an English translation was published in 1944 by Oxford University Press and a supplement was added ('Recent developments in Indo-China, 1939-1943' by John R. Andrus, Katrine R. C. Greene); that is the text reprinted in this edition. The author states in his preface, 'My wish has been to show the change effected in the economy of Indo-China as a result of the French occupation'. A fairly optimistic picture of the economic development and future of Indo-China is drawn here. It covers the roots of economic development, its resources, people, communications and capital, and then assesses the new economic developments in industry, plantations, changes in indigenous agriculture, and foreign trade. Laos was little developed economically under French rule, and so plays a smaller part in this book. The index is not complete and one needs to check topics such as tin for example, as well as the entries under Laos. The work was intended to complement Pierre Gourou's *Land utilization in French Indo-China* (q.v.) and so does not deal with land in any detail.

378 **The Lower Mekong: challenge to cooperation in Southeast Asia.**
C. Hart Schaaf, Russell H. Fifield. Princeton, New Jersey: Van
Nostrand, 1963. 136p. maps. bibliog. (Van Nostrand Searchlight Book,
no. 12).

Two distinct contributions on the Lower Mekong. Fifield presents a historical,
geographic and political picture of Cambodia, Laos, Thailand and Vietnam, in which
he discusses the complicated relations between them and their relations with the
outside world. Schaaf, executive agent of the Committee for the Coordination of
Investigations of the Lower Mekong Basin (a United Nations project), describes the
project to unlock the potential of the Mekong for the economic development of the
four countries with foreign economic assistance. He traces how a great engineering
project came into being. This is a most readable account of the genesis of the Lower
Mekong Project, much of which remains to be done. The United Nations statute
establishing the Committee is given as an appendix.

379 **Report on development assistance for 1975.**
Resident Representative of the United Nations Development
Programme in the Lao Peoples' Democratic Republic. Vientiane:
UNDP, 1976. [24]p.

During the year in question the political situation in Laos altered radically as the
government changed from a monarchy to a republic. During the year many aid
projects withdrew their personnel, particularly those of the United States. The needs
of Laos are seen to be greater self-sufficiency in foodstuffs and the ability to make
better use of foreign assistance offered. It is reported that the World Health
Organization had negotiated its first health country programme for Laos: rural hygiene
and sanitation, in which eradication of malaria and the training of personnel would
receive the first priority. It is clear that the economic and health problems of Laos of
the previous fifteen years remained to be tackled. The major part of the document is a
tabulated statement of the 'Externally financed pre-investment and technical assistance
projects and activities', arranged by sector such as agriculture or health. There have
been subsequent United Nations Development Programme (UNDP) reports on Laos,
but they are internal documents and not published for general use.

380 **Facts on foreign aid to Laos.**
United States Agency for International Development, Mission to Laos.
[Vientiane:] USAID Mission to Laos, 1971. 202p. map.

Intended to provide information for visitors and to answer enquiries, this work
provides a guide to the politics, government and economy of Laos as a background to
the information on United States economic and administrative assistance programmes,
other foreign assistance to Laos, and the work of the Foreign Exchange Operations
Fund for Laos. A useful source of information on the foreign aid programmes and
statistics relating to various aspects of economic, administrative and social performance
in the 1960s. The first section provides a text of the Geneva Conference on the
agreement on the cessation of hostilites in Laos, the declaration of neutrality (1962),
and the protocol to the declaration of neutrality (1962). The section on the Lao
government provides a summary of the Constitution in English, lists of the members of
the Provisional Government of National Union (1962), members of the Government of
National Union (1970) and the ministries of the Royal Lao Government. At least one
supplement was produced to this guide, published by USAID in June 1971 and entitled
Facts on foreign aid to Laos: Supplement 1, Refugees. USAID also published a series of

information sheets called *Facts, photographs*, unnumbered and often undated, those seen deal with the aspects of relief to refugees and with education, and date from the period 1972-73. They are usually four pages long, and contain photographs and statistics relating to the topic.

381 **U.S. economic assistance to the Royal Lao Government 1962-1972.**
United States Agency for International Development, Mission to Laos.   Vientiane: USAID Mission to Laos, 1972. 32p.
A statistical summary of the use to which money provided under the foreign aid programme had been put. Over sixty per cent of the more than five hundred million dollars provided over ten years was used in refugee relief programmes. Thirty-eight per cent was provided under the heading of economic stabilization, which covered the activities of the Foreign Exchange Operations Fund, the US Import Program and direct grants. The statistical data provided illustrate the uses of economic assistance funds and the results that can be expressed in quantitative terms.

382 **Economic and social aspects of Lower Mekong development: a report.**
Gilbert F. White, Egbert de Vries, Harold B. Dunkerley, John V. Krutilla.   Bangkok: Committee for Co-ordination of Investigations of the Lower Mekong Basin, 1962. 106p. maps.
The groundwork study to establish the work needed to exploit the Lower Mekong to the greatest benefit of the four neighbouring countries: Laos, Thailand, Cambodia and Vietnam. It bears in mind the economic position of those countries, which could not afford to undertake expensive capital projects with low prospect of financial return for many years, when making its recommendations. The principal areas of their recommendations were for hydroelectric power schemes, water storage for irrigation, the reduction of floods and the provision of navigable waterways. The political tensions in the area impeded progress, and these projects are beginning to be taken up again.

383 **Economic reform and structural change in Laos.**
William Worner.   *Southeast Asian Affairs*, (1989), p. 187-208.
This essay on Laos in 1988 has been highlighted because it summarizes the important developments in that year. New initiatives were launched in economic policy, international relations and domestic politics. Worner reviews these changes concisely, giving the background to the situation as well as the details of the new policies. In the economic field these were a new foreign investment code, a move away from collectivization of agriculture, the encouragement of private business and greater independence of state enterprises. 1988 saw the first elections both for local and national government since 1975. Relations with Thailand improved and there was progress in diplomatic and aid links with other countries. Worner's paper 'Money, prices and policies in Laos: 1969-1980' in *Proceedings of the International Conference on Thai Studies, Canberra, 3-6 July 1987* (compiled by Ann Buller. [Canberra: Australian National University, 1987], vol. 3, pt. 2, p. 477-503) provides relevant background information on the recent history of inflation and monetary policy in Laos.

384   **A comparative study of refugee and non-refugee villages: part 1, a survey of long-established villages of the Vientiane Plain.**
Robert M. Wulff.   Vientiane: USAID Mission to Laos, 1972. [44]p. maps.

A study based on a questionnaire administered in six long-established villages in the Vientiane Plain. The purpose was to determine what constituted the average economic situation in villages in order to measure the success of assistance to the refugee villages. It provides a concise summary of a wide range of variables in the economic life of peasant agriculturalists and village tradesmen such as blacksmiths. Although in its illustrations it shows different types of housing according to varying economic success, the figures provided are averaged for all households across the six villages. The statistics collected must be treated with some caution as they relied on the memories of the respondents and undoubtedly what was thought to be the appropriate answer. Nonetheless in describing each village we are provided with information on the number of households, provision of schools, wells, transport services, temples, and illustrations of housing, granaries and public buildings. The study of refugee resettlement villages was published as *A comparative study of refugee and non-refugee villages; part 2, a survey of refugee resettlement villages in Laos* (Vientiane: USAID Mission to Laos, 1974).

Far Eastern Economic Review.
See item no. 519.

Banking and Finance

385 **Compte rendu des operations: exercice . . .** (Statement of accounts: for
   the financial year . . . .)
   Vientiane: Banque Nationale du Laos, [1957]- . annual or biannual.
The annual statement of accounts of the operations of the National Bank of Laos. It
provides an analysis of the monetary and economic situation in Laos for the year in
question. This is complemented by statistical appendices.

386 **Money and banking in China and Southeast Asia during the Japanese
   military occupation 1937-1945.**
   Richard A. Banyai.   Taipei, Taiwan: Tai Wan Enterprises, 1974.
   150p. maps. bibliog.
The coverage of French Indo-China is brief and outlines events from 1939 to 1945. The
recognition by the Vichy Government of Japan's right to discuss economic conventions
and grant military facilities to Japan in Indo-China, had a profound impact on the
economy and the value of the French piastre during the occupation. Prices rose sharply
as imported goods became scarce. After the Japanese *coup de force* (March 1945),
Japan appointed a manager to control the French banks. The Japanese did not issue
any bank notes in Indo-China and their troops were paid in Indochinese piastres.

387 **Capital, savings and credit among Lao peasants.**
   Joel M. Halpern.   In: *Capital, savings and credit in peasant societies:
   studies from Asia, Oceania, the Caribbean and Middle America:
   essays.*   Edited by Raymond Firth, B. S. Yamey.   London: Allen &
   Unwin, 1964, p. 82-103. bibliog.
A study based on the Lao peasants of the lowland areas around Vientiane and Luang
Prabang in the late 1950s. Halpern discusses the categories of cultivated land, gardens,
irrigated rice fields and *swidden* areas still available to most peasants. Apart from land
which may be owned or rented, the other major capital resource of the peasant is
livestock. Cash income may be earned from market gardening and handicrafts, petty

trading or daily labour. Halpern compares those considered wealthy in Laos with a successful rice farmer in the Central Plain of Thailand, whose income and rice harvests would be almost twice as great. The use of money and the values of the peasantry are discussed. Halpern comments, as have others, on the importance for the Lao of expenditure on Buddhist matters and the use of aid money for the repair of *vats*. There seems to have been little change in peasant behaviour and attitudes over the last thirty years: see G. Evans' *Lao peasants under socialism* (q.v.).

388 **Ébauche d'une comptabilité nationale lao: comptes économiques provisoires pour 1964.** (An outline of a national accounting system for Laos: provisional accounts for 1964.)

Laos: Ministère du Plan et de la Coopération, Commissariat au Plan. [Vientiane:] The Author, 1967. 96 leaves, fold. sheet.

This was the first attempt at producing national accounts for Laos, and in effect offers a baseline for such studies on Laos. It appears to have been the only volume published. It should be read with the two national development plans, *Plan de développement économique et social du Laos: période de 5 ans du 1er juillet 1959 au 30 juin 1964* (Economic and social development plan for Laos: for the five years 1 July 1959 to 30 June 1964) (q.v.) and *Plan cadre de développement économique et social, 1969-1974* (Outline plan for economic and social development, 1969-1974) (q.v.).

389 **Des pionniers en Extrême-Orient: histoire de la Banque de l'Indochine, 1875-1975.** (Pioneers in the Far East: a history of the Banque de l'Indochine, 1875-1975.)

Marc Meuleau. Paris: Fayard, 1990. 647p. maps.

To mark the centenary of the Banque de l'Indochine, Meuleau has used the unpublished papers of the Bank's archives to record its history up to its merger with the Banque de Suez et de l'Union des Mines, to form the Banque Indosuez. In time it took on some of the role of a Central Bank for French Indo-China, and was responsible for the issue of currency. There is very little on this aspect of its work, or on Laos. Its two principal branches in Laos were opened after independence, in Vientiane in 1953, and in Paksé in 1958. Two examples of banknotes are given on the cover of the book.

390 **The development of capitalism in colonial Indochina, 1870-1940.**

Martin J. Murray. Berkeley, California: University of California Press, 1980. 685p. bibliog.

Capitalism is dealt with in this book mainly from the point of view of the whole of colonial French Indo-China, as for example in its study of the role of banks and banking. Laos is dealt with specifically as regards tin and coal mining. Murray deals extensively with forms of labour including corvée, which was a significantly burdensome introduction of the colonial rulers in Laos.

Agriculture, Fishing, Forestry

391 **Agricultural development in the Mekong Basin: goals, priorities, and strategies.**

Washington, DC: Resources for the Future, 1971. 106p. map.

This report was prepared by the staff of Resources for the Future at the request of the International Bank for Reconstruction and Development; it was published for a wider audience. It is a study by experts in their subjects but, with one exception, with no experience of Laos. Thus it is based on extensive reading of the available material and not by analysis on the spot, although an anthropologist with knowledge of the area was attached to the team. The area affected by the course of the Lower Mekong and its tributaries is most of Laos and Cambodia, a sizeable area of southern Vietnam and about one-third of Thailand. The study considers the benefits that can be derived for agriculture and the potential for hydroelectric power if schemes for one or more dams were undertaken. This report highlights the problems with the broadest brush strokes, not least the need for administrative reform and an end to the war to enable development projects to proceed. Although based on published work, this book does not provide a guide to that literature as footnotes are few. The main emphasis of the work is on the value and feasibility of the Pa Mong dam project. The interest for Laos is that surplus electricity is currently an important export.

392 **Les techniques rituelles de la pêche du palo'm au Laos.** (Rituals practised in association with fishing for palo'm in Laos.)

Charles Archaimbault. *Bulletin de l'Ecole Française d'Extrême-Orient*, vol. 49, no. 1 (1958), p. 297-335.

Archaimbault studied the rituals associated with fishing for palo'm, a member of the *siluridae* family of fish which grow to two metres in length in the rivers of Laos. It is based on his ethnographic studies between 1953 and 1955 in Luang Prabang, Vientiane and Bassak. He describes the rituals employed at the beginning of the season. It is illustrated with nineteen photographs.

393 **The traditional use of forests in mainland Southeast Asia.**
James L. Cobban. Athens, Ohio: Ohio University, Center for
International Studies, 1968. 23 leaves. map. (Papers in International
Studies: Southeast Asia Series, no. 5).

Cobban's paper highlights the importance of forest products in supplementing the
income and diet of peoples living at subsistence level. The study is divided into the
three categories of forest, evergreen, deciduous and littoral, and subdivided by studies
of the products derived from them. Indigenous use, he argues, was not prejudicial to
the forest habitat, unlike the larger projects funded by external capital. Cobban uses
the botanical names for the trees and it is necessary to have a good botanical dictionary
to hand when reading the work. There is unfortunately no index.

394 **Agrarian change in communist Laos.**
Grant Evans. Singapore: Institute of Southeast Asian Studies, 1988.
88p. (ISEAS Occasional Paper, no. 85).

An analysis of the evolution of agrarian policy in Laos since 1975. The author
examines the attempts to bring about a socialist transformation of agriculture in Laos.
Early efforts to force the pace on collectivization were relaxed after 1979. The whole is
set in the context of the economic situation inherited and prevailing in Laos.

395 **Land reform in the Lao revolution.**
Grant Evans. In: *Proceedings of the International Conference on Thai
Studies, Canberra, 3-6 July 1987*. Compiled by Ann Buller. [Canberra:
Australian National University, 1987], vol. 3, pt. 2, p. 457-65.

'The aims of this paper are simple. They are to question some claims made about land
tenure in Laos by writers in the post-1975 period'. Evans briefly surveys the historical
background of land tenure and peasant society to determine the basis of the position in
1975. A largely subsistence economy until the large inflow of US economic aid created
a market for wage labour in cities like Vientiane, this in turn created conditions for
wage labour in agriculture. Migration of the population to the Vientiane Plain,
attracted by this work (some of it from northeast Thailand, some of it resettled refugee
villages), resulted in pressure on the land available for cultivation. This has lessened to
some extent as some of the migrants and other Lao have dispersed, either to Thailand
or back to the Plain of Jars. His thesis is that there were not large holdings of land by
absentee landlords in Laos, and that larger peasant landholdings of about five hectares
have tended to be broken up again both by natural dispersal to heirs and by sale.
Evans concludes that the new Lao government was wise not to embark on a
programme of land reform; that 'simplistic computations of landholding or rates of
tenancy are poor indicators of class differentiation and therefore a poor basis for policy
decisions'; the Lao government has tried by collectivization to transcend the natural
economy, and a social compromise between the state and the peasantry is still being
worked out.

396 **Lao peasants under socialism.**
Grant Evans. New Haven, Connecticut: Yale University Press, 1990.
268p. map.

The first major study of rural Laos since the installation of a socialist government in
1975. Evans examines the efforts of the new government at collectivization of
agriculture, the peasants' response and its apparent failure. It is based on research

visits to Laos between 1979 and 1987, and more detailed research on the development of co-operatives in a number of villages in the Vientiane region. Evans, while considering the broad perspective of the challenge to socialist ideals which a peasant society poses, provides the detail which enables the reader to come to an understanding of the economic life of the peasant in Laos today.

397 **FAO production yearbook.**
Rome: Food and Agriculture Organization, 1946- . annual.

This is a collection of worldwide statistics focused on agricultural activity. There are statistics on land use, population, agricultural production, crop production by crop, livestock production by category, food supply, pesticide use and prices. Many of the statistics for Laos are FAO estimates.

398 **Land utilization in French Indochina.**
Pierre Gourou.   New York: Institute of Pacific Relations, 1945. 588p. maps.

A study of indigenous land use that examines the subject under three broad headings: the physical background, the distribution of population and the factors governing the economic exploitation of the land and its resources. Gourou's main area of research had been in Vietnam and his coverage of Laos is limited; this was partly because he relied on official reports and statistics which were very limited in the case of Laos, and partly because his particular concern was with the intensive cultivation of land for food in heavily populated areas which was not a problem for Laos. In his chapter on forestry he shows that Laos had half the forested area of Indo-China, which in turn was two-thirds of the surface of Laos, but the Forestry Service had provided no statistics for Laos. One of the factors which was holding back the population of the region, and to which he devotes a chapter (malaria), still plays a significant part in handicapping progress in Laos. The work was first published in French as *L'utilisation du sol en Indochine Française* (Paris: Hartmann, 1940. 466p. maps.). It was intended as a companion work to Robequain's *The economic development of French Indo-China* (q.v.).

399 **La forêt et l'oeuvre du Service Forestier au Laos.** (The forest and the work of the Forestry Department in Laos.)
H. Guibier. *Bulletin des Amis du Vieux Hué*, (1941), p. 101-99.

A description of the forest cover of Laos and the work of the Forestry Department. It is estimated that sixty per cent of the country is still covered by forest.

400 **The Kammu year: its lore and music.**
Kristina Lindell, Håkan Lundström, Jan Olof Svantesson, Damrong Tayanin.   London: Curzon Press, 1982. 191p. map. bibliog. (Scandinavian Institute of Asian Studies. Studies on Asian Topics, no. 4).

A composite work by members of the University of Lund, it deals with the Kammu or Khmu-speaking ethnic group of Laos. They are *swidden* (slash and burn) cultivators of the uplands, and they grow glutinous rice as well as cash crops such as cotton, tobacco and tea. Their language belongs to the Mon-Khmer group of languages. They are distributed all over northern Laos, which would appear to be their homeland, but Khmu speakers are also found in the neighbouring areas of Thailand, Vietnam and

China. The subject of this book is the Khmu farming year, presented through studies of the people and their calendar in relation to the agricultural cycle and the folk beliefs and music which accompany it. There is also some consideration given to the place of music in Khmu culture through the study of this special case. The Khmu have received little attention from scholars, and this study forms part of a wider study of their society.

401 **Introducing the Lao: toward an understanding of the lowland farmers in Laos.**
Kenneth G. Orr. Vientiane: USAID/Laos, 1967. 206p.

A working paper which it was intended to develop into a handbook, this work is a useful compendium of information on the life and work of the lowland farmer, his wife and family. Farming and traditional festivals are the main topics of this work, as well as some consideration of the role of the American development technician in this milieu. Much of the information is presented in the form of translated conversations and interviews, and the work is illustrated with helpful sketches and diagrams.

402 **Laos.**
C. L. Pierson. In: *World atlas of agriculture. Vol. 2: Asia and Oceania.* Edited by the Committee for the World Atlas of Agriculture. Novara, Italy: Istituto Geografico De Agostini, 1973, p. 342-49. maps. bibliog.

This article covers physical environment and communications, population, exploitation of resources, ownership and land tenure, land utilization, agricultural economy, crops, and animal husbandry. It is illustrated with statistics mainly from the 1960s.

403 **Rapport au gouvernement du Laos sur l'établissement d'un programme phytosanitaire.** (Report to the government of Laos on the establishment of a programme of plant protection.)
Based on the work of George H. Plumb. Rome: Organisation des Nations Unies pour l'Alimentation et l'Agriculture (FAO), 1966. 14p. (Programme des Nations Unies pour le Développement, no. AT2194).

A brief report that tells us much about agricultural problems in Laos and the problems of introducing projects of technical assistance. Despite the importance of agriculture to the economy of Laos, there had been no study of the plant diseases or insect pests common to Laos. The project on which Dr. Plumb was sent was intended to do field research, set up a laboratory and prepare local staff to continue the work. One can only admire Dr. Plumb for what he achieved, but his work could not progress until there were adequate resources to finance the necessary laboratory work and sufficient staff trained to the appropriate level. The problems caused by the war only added to the difficulties. With the assistance of a Colombo Plan radio expert Plumb did produce a series of radio broadcasts aimed at the small farmer, to encourage him to contact the agricultural extension officers; others on insect pests, to be linked to exhibitons in market towns, were prepared before his departure. At the root of the problem was the lack of staff with a sufficient level of education, so that the foreign expert could not transmit his knowledge. A report on insect pests in northeast Thailand gives some indication of what might be expected in the Vientiane Plain:*Survey of insect pests: part B: vegetable insect pests* (Jutharat Attajarusit, edited by Mekong Secretariat.

Bangkok: Mekong Secretariat, 1979. 54p. [Nam Pong Environmental Management Research Project, Working Document, no. 6]).

404 **Les Hmong du Laos face au développement.** (The Hmong of Laos facing development.)

Yang Dao. Vientiane: Editions Siaosavath, 1975. 202p. maps. bibliog.

Based on the author's doctoral thesis, it is a study of Hmong society, its current socio-economic position and the prospects for both economic and social development for the Hmong. The author is himself a Hmong, and in 1974 became a member of the National Mixed Political Council. One particular feature of Yang Dao's research was to investigate the possibilities for large-scale cultivation of cash crops, poultry and cattle to replace the reliance on opium as a source of income. This work was also reported to be published in English as *The Hmong of Laos in the vanguard of development* (Vientiane, 1976), but it has not been seen.

Transport and Communications

405 L'aeronautique militaire de l'Indochine. (Military air services of Indochina.)
Hanoi: Imprimerie d'Extrême-Orient, 1931. 208p. maps. (Exposition Coloniale Internationale, Paris, 1931. Indochine Française: Section Générale: Troupes de l'Indochine).

A survey of the state of the air service, its development over the eleven years from 1919 to 1930, and outlines for future developments. There is technical information on the aircraft used and photographs of the aeroplanes. There are aerial photographs of many of the landing areas and other features of the region such as mines and rice fields. There is an examination of medical, postal and economic air services; in the case of the postal service these were experimental explorations to assess the justification for the establishment of regular postal and passenger services; the findings are set out here. The difficulty of communications in Laos and with Laos from the other parts of Indo-China is explored; the potential of air transport for unlocking the wealth of Laos is suggested.

406 Southeast Asian regional transport survey.
Asian Development Bank. Singapore: Straits Times Press, 1972-73. 5 vols. maps. bibliog.

This survey was prepared at the behest of the Asian Development Bank by Arthur D. Little Inc. and associated consultants, and under the Bank's supervision. The purpose of the survey was to identify regional transport needs and projects to meet them. It is primarily concerned with internationally-oriented transport. The report proposes a recommended investment programme, and places special emphasis on institutional and policy changes which must accompany this programme. Laos was one of the seven countries included in the survey. The first book provides an overall survey of the transport needs and problems of the region, and summarizes the existing situation and the recommendations for each country. Book two, published in two parts, presents the basic analyses of the survey, and looks at the prospects for economic growth and the region's maritime and air transport systems. The supporting material for this is in the two volumes of Book Three. The recommendations for Laos are relatively modest and take into account the low level of economic activity and the persistence of military operations. They see a need for improved road communication to reduce the cost of imports and exports, but recognize that the cost of installing and maintaining a new road cannot be met from current economic activity. The survey provides a very good picture of the transportation situation in Laos in 1970, and apart from the upgrading of some international roads there has been little change.

407 **Transit problems of three Asian land-locked countries: Afghanistan, Nepal and Laos.**
Martin Ira Glassner. Baltimore, Maryland: University of Maryland, School of Law, 1983. 52p. maps. (Occasional Papers/Reprints Series in Contemporary Asian studies, no. 4 – 1983 [57]).
The problem of access to the sea for countries with no coast is examined from the perspective of international law. Glassner sets out the general problems and the international agreements which have been reached before discussing each of his three case-studies in detail. All three are countries which are economically poor, and the need to send imports and exports via a third country exaggerates the economic difficulties they face. In the study of Laos (p. 34-44) he considers the general economic background as well as the history of the agreements with both South Vietnam (prior to 1975) and Thailand for transit traffic. There is a detailed consideration of the transit routes through Thailand and Vietnam and an account of the transport and warehousing facilities available, as well as projected improvements such as improving the roads established in the colonial period to Vietnam and the construction of a road and rail bridge across the Mekong. The main period under discussion in this work is 1978-82.

408 **Transport development and planning in Southeast Asia: a selected bibliography.**
James A. Hafner, David Janes. Monticello, Illinois: Council of Planning Librarians, 1974. 40p. (Council of Planning Librarians Exchange Bibliography, no. 653).
This bibliography is arranged in country groupings; unfortunately there is no contents page to indicate this. Vietnam, Cambodia and Laos are grouped in one block of references. A number of the items listed are planning studies and generally uncirculated documents, often prepared by contract research organizations and official United States government aid missions. There are also references to articles published in conventional journals.

409 **Transport and communications bulletin for Asia and the Pacific.**
New York; Bangkok: United Nations, Economic and Social Commission for Asia and the Pacific, 1976- . annual.
A newsy journal, issued approximately annually, which reports on transport and communications developments in the Asia Pacific region, but includes articles on developments elsewhere in the world that seem relevant to the Asian situation. Laos has not figured largely in its pages until recently, but in view of efforts to improve roads and links to the sea for Laos, it will be likely to grow in relevance. Issue no. 57 (1985) was a special issue entitled *Launching of the transport and communications decade for Asia and the Pacific, 1985-1994.* It covers the ESCAP mandate for action,

the ministerial report and recommendations, and the technical studies that backed up the programme. In an appendix, phases 1 and 2 of the regional action programme are outlined. These set the context for developments in the region.

Employment and Labour

410 **Labour conditions in Indo-China.**
International Labour Office. Geneva: International Labour Office,
1938. 331p.

Now of historical interest, this study provides a picture of employment in colonial
Indo-China. After providing a general background it examines forced or compulsory
labour, which was of particular significance in Laos, waged labour (both contract and
non-contract), handicraftsmen, peasants and immigrant workers. A statistical appendix
provides summaries of relevant statistics from the official statistics. Statements are well
supported by the footnotes.

411 **Rapport intérimaire au gouvernement du Laos sur le développement de
l'artisanat et des petites industries.** (Interim report to the government of
Laos in the development of craft and small-scale industries.)
International Labour Organization. Geneva: BIT, 1961. 88p.

The report of expert M. Paulin on a six-month enquiry prior to a larger project of
United Nations technical assistance. There is a survey of the economic and technical
background to the craft and small-scale industries of Laos, a programme of
recommendations, and a list of suggestions for areas which should be developed to
enable local products to replace expensive imports and even provide products which
could be sold in neighbouring Thailand. His picture of what could and needed to be
done provides a clear picture of the economy of Laos in 1961. Technical assistance
work was hampered by the outbreaks of fighting. The final report was published the
following year: *Rapport final au gouvernement du Laos sur le développement de
l'artisanat et des petites industries* (Final report to the government of Laos on the
development of craft and small-scale industries) (Geneva: BIT, 1962. 46p.); as were
M. Paulin's final recommendations, *Programme élargi d'assistance technique: rapport
final au gouvernement du Laos sur le développement de l'artisanat et des petites
industries* (Enlarged programme of technical assistance: final report to the government

of Laos in the development of craft and small-scale industries) (Geneva: BIT, 1962. 46p.).

412 **Employment and development in Laos: some problems and policies.**
Azizur Rahman Khan, Eddy Lee. Bangkok: Asian Employment Programme, Asian Regional Team for Employment Promotion, 1980. 66p. map.
A preliminary report and the assessment by the writers of the problems and possible solutions for employment planning in Laos. They attempt to compile a picture of the state of the economy in the face of a lack of statistics, in a country that experienced twenty years of civil war. They cover labour force and employment; employment, production and consumption in agriculture; the socialist transformation of agriculture; and the non-agricultural sectors. They endeavour to indicate some statistical data for each. They conclude with some priorities for employment policy, which include the development of an effective statistical service.

413 **Human bondage in Southeast Asia.**
Bruno Lasker. Chapel Hill, North Carolina: University of North Carolina Press, 1950. 406p.
A study of what is loosely called slavery in the South East Asian region, both in historical times and up to the time of writing. The types of restriction of freedom which are discussed are slavery, serfdom, peonage, debt bondage, corvée labour, indentured and other contract labour, and forced labour during the Japanese occupation. This work is largely based on published sources which are only referred to in the notes, and which do not appear conveniently in a bibliography.

414 **Report of a survey of rural households in the Hat Xai Fong district in Vientiane Province of the Lao People's Democratic Republic.**
Chandan Mukherjee, A. V. Jose. Bangkok: Asian Employment Programme (ILO-ARTEP), 1982. 47p.
This survey was initially intended to form part of a training programme on the scientific collection of statistical data on the economy. There is a complete lack of such data in Laos, and thus no firm empirical data base for the economy. The major part of this booklet presents the results of the sample survey in two hundred households. It was published because of the absence of reliable data for Laos, although it represents information on a small part of the country. The objectives of the survey were to obtain information on the size and composition of households, on the distribution in various industrial and occupational categories, on estimates of income and employment from agriculture, to quantify non-farm activities, to ascertain assets particularly of livestock, to quantify use of labour in crop cultivation, to estimate the extent of unemployment and underemployment, and to assess the size of the consumption basket of rural households. As the editors conclude, the survey reveals a predominantly agrarian economy, and while scope exists for using labour in other capacities, consumption of basic food requisites was adequate.

Labor law and practice in the Kingdom of Laos.
See item no. 335.

Statistics

415 **Annuaire statistique du Laos**. (Statistical yearbook of Laos.)
Laos: Direction de la Statistique. Vientiane: The Author, 1951- .
annual.

This was the first statistical series produced for Laos, which had not previously had its own statistical service. It took over from the general series for Indo-China. It maintains the principal series of the Indo-China statistics and provides more detail by province. It covers the subject areas of climate, territory, population, public health, teaching, religion, justice, prisons, agriculture, forestry, industry, transport, communications, finance, commerce, customs, civil service personnel, revenue, domestic consumption and index of prices. The responsible department from volume 4 (1953-57) onwards is the Service de la Statistique du Laos. Statistics for earlier years will be found in the *Annuaire statistique de l'Indochine* (Statistical yearbook for Indo-China) of the Service de la Statistique Générale, volumes 1 to 11 (1927-48), and the transitional volumes of the government of the French Union.

416 **Bibliography of statistical sources on Southeast Asia, c. 1750-1990.**
Compiled by Jennifer Brewster, Anne Booth. Canberra: Australian
National University, Economic History of Southeast Asia Project,
1990. 120p. (Data Paper Series/Sources of the Economic History of
Southeast Asia, no. 1).

A bibliography designed to offer a historical perspective to statistical series. It deals with statistics on population, agriculture, industry, mining, energy and commerce, transport and communications, trade and balance of payments, money, banking and public finance, national income, wages and the labour force, prices and household expenditure, as well as social and general statistical series. Where available, specific titles are given for Laos, but the supranational and Indo-China sections offer useful sources when there is a gap and provide details on titles for the pre-independence period.

417 **Bulletin statistique du Laos.** (Statistical bulletin of Laos.)
Service de la Statistique du Laos. Vientiane: The Author, 1950- .
biannual.

Originally a quarterly statement of statistics, cumulated in the final volume for each
year. It follows the same categories as the *Annuaire statistique du Laos* (q.v.). From
1969 onwards it has been published at six-monthly intervals. The title of the series
varies and appears as *Bulletin de statistiques du Laos* (Statistics bulletin of Laos) and
the name of the responsible department also changes to the Service National de la
Statistique.

418 **Statistical yearbook for Asia and the Pacific.**
Bangkok: Economic and Social Commission for Asia and the Pacific,
1974- . annual.

A range of national statistics is presented for each country covered by the programme
of the Economic and Social Commission. Laos is represented, with statistics ranging
from population figures to social statistics and including figures on imports and exports,
agriculture, industry and transport. The statistics are presented to give comparative
figures for the previous ten years in each volume.

419 **Statistiques essentielles pour l'année.** (Essential statistics for the year.)
Service National de la Statistique. Vientiane: The Author, 1969- .
annual.

A summary of statistics on a national basis of the eleven principal categories
established in the *Annuaire statistique du Laos* (q.v.). The issue for 1969 includes a
section of textual commentary on the statistics.

Education

420 **The education system in Laos during the French protectorate, 1893-1945.**
Marjorie Elaine Emling.   Ithaca, New York: Cornell University, 1969. 82 leaves. bibliog.
Produced as an MA thesis for Cornell University, this work presents a historical survey of education in Laos both chronologically and by level of education. There is a consideration of the traditional education given by the Buddhist monks in the *vats* and the efforts of the French to harness this to provide education for a wider population. The other chapters consider primary and secondary, professional and higher education. Secondary education was restricted to one school in Vientiane, the Collège Pavie, and any further studies were pursued in other parts of Indo-China or Europe. Prince Phetsarath's biography illustrates the education available to members of the élite; *Iron man of Laos Prince Phetsarath Ratanavongsa* (q.v.).

421 **Education in the Kingdom of Laos.**
Walter Haney.   In: *Mekong Basin development: Laos and Thailand: selected bibliographies.*   Joel M.Halpern, James A.Hafner, Walter Haney.   Brussels: Centre d'Etude du Sud-Est Asiatique et de l'Extrême-Orient, 1974, p. 1-30. (Courrier de l'Extrême-Orient, vol. 8, no. 59).
A bibliography of over 120 items, most of them extensively annotated, presented as an initial effort in this subject area. Many of the items listed were produced under the auspices of the international agencies working on the Mekong Basin development projects.

Education

422 Education in the communist zone of Laos.
Paul F. Langer. Santa Monica, California: Rand Corporation, 1971. 39p. (Rand Paper, P-4726).

Operating in the area of Laos which had had the least benefit from the limited colonial education system, the Neo Lao Haksat established a programme to eradicate a high illiteracy rate both in children and adults. Langer's work is based on an examination of monitored broadcasts, the reports of sympathetic outside observers and the accounts of Lao who had left the area. He also considers the text books that were developed for what perforce remained elementary level education. Further education had to be pursued abroad.

423 Statistique de l'education pour l'année . . . (Educational statistics for the year.)
Laos: Ministère de l'Education Nationale. [Vientiane:] The Author, 1962- . annual.

Published annually from 1962, this work gives statistics on the budget available, the number of schools, teachers and pupils at each level of education, the number of students studying abroad and the broad subject areas of their studies. The most recent year examined (1971-72) had expanded to 203 stencilled pages.

424 Report on the activities of the Ministry of Education, Vientiane, Laos, 1972.
Leuam Insisienmay. [Vientiane: USAID/Laos, 1972.] 28p.

An unofficial English translation of the Minister's report presented to the Lao National Assembly. It can be seen as a final statement of the educational policy and achievements of the Royal Lao Government. The Minister reminds his audience that 1972 was the tenth anniversary of the implementation of the Education Reform Act of 1962. After an historical introduction, the Minister outlines the objectives and achievements in all the spheres of education; he includes the work of the National Library and the Royal Lao Academy. The second part of the work is devoted to a discussion of the problems and difficulties faced in education, and the future perspectives for education in Laos.

425 Higher education and development in South-East Asia. Vol. 3, part 2: Language policy and higher education.
Richard Noss. Paris: UNESCO & International Association of Universities, 1967. 216p.

For the first third of the book there is a general consideration of language policies and education. This is followed by a series of country studies including one on Laos (p. 123-32). It surveys the present educational system and the effects of past policies. The picture drawn is not one of great promise. The lack of material written in Lao, and the need for many students to study abroad, the writer acknowledges, produces the need for instruction in a second language for all those progressing beyond elementary education. This was catered for in the 1962 Royal Ordinance on education.

426 **Compulsory education in Laos.**
Somlith Patthamavong. In: *Compulsory education in Cambodia, Laos, and Viet-Nam.* By Charles Bilodeau, Somlith Pathammavong, Le Quang Hong. Paris: UNESCO, 1955. p. 71-111. bibliog. (Studies on Compulsory Education, no. 14).
Written in 1952, this study provides a baseline for the history of primary education in Laos, particularly the developments over the previous sixty years from the establishment of the French protectorate in 1893. It deals essentially with primary education, as this was the only level which was compulsory. Somlith cites the key features of the law of 1951 on compulsory, free, primary education. He notes that the government did not intend it to be strictly applied in view of the poverty and conservatism of the population. He concludes with a survey of the problems that remain to be tackled: to establish an appropriate curriculum, to prepare sufficient textboooks in Lao, to train an adequate number of teachers, and to provide adequate buildings for the pupils and homes for the teachers.

427 **Higher education in Laos with special reference to the Royal Institute of Law and Administration.**
Tenh Teso. In: *Development of higher education in Southeast Asia: problems and issues.* Edited by Yip Yat Hoong. Singapore: Regional Institute of Higher Education and Development, 1973. p. 79-85.
Written by its Director, this is an account of the Royal Institute, its programmes and organization. Its courses in law and economics were primarily intended for training civil servants and magistrates. With the Faculty of Medicine it formed part of the embryonic Sisavang Vong University, founded in 1958.

Literature

General

428 Laos.
Pierre-Bernard Lafont.   In: *South-East Asia languages and literatures: a select guide*.   Edited by Patricia Herbert, Anthony Milner.   Whiting Bay, Arran, Scotland: Kiscadale; Honolulu, Hawaii: University Press of Hawaii, 1989, p. 67-76. bibliog.

This essay provides a brief introduction to Laos, particularly for those interested in its language and literature, and provides the necessary bibliographical guidance to enable each topic to be pursued further. The topics covered are the dating systems, language, script, manuscripts, printing and publishing and literature. The author has written a similar, more broadly focused essay, 'Le Laos' in *Introduction à la connaissance de la Péninsule Indochinoise* (Paris: Centre d'Histoire et Civilisations de la Péninsule Indochinoise, 1983, p. 61-81). This same work includes two other useful essays, 'Les Hmong' by B. Gay and 'Les Proto Indochinois' by Pham Cao Duong.

429 Versification.
Thao Nhouy Abhay.   In: *Kingdom of Laos: the land of the million elephants and of the white parasol*.   Compiled by René de Berval.   Saigon, Vietnam: France Asie, 1959, p. 345-58.

A brief article on prosody and other techniques used in Lao poetry; a poetry which was intended mainly to be read aloud. Examples of some of the points are given in quotations of Lao poetry in romanized Lao.

430 **Tai literatures: a bibliography of works in foreign languages.**
E. H. S. Simmonds. *Bulletin of the Association of British Orientalists*,
n.s. 3 (1965), p. 5-60.

About a third of this bibliography is devoted to the Lao and other Tai ethnic groups of
Laos and northern Thailand. Various genres of literature are covered as well as
inscriptions and related ethnographic material. There are annotations where necessary.
Several of the items listed also contain translations or extracts from the literature
discussed.

Classical literature

431 **A Lao epic poem: Thao Hung or Cheuang.**
James R. Chamberlain. *Péninsule*, no. 11-12 (1985-86), p. 189-214.

A translation of work by Maha Sila Viravong on Thao Hung, a historical epic and one
of the three poems he considered a Lao literary masterpiece. It is a translation of his
synopsis of the poem, produced to accompany a Thai transliteration and material
extracted from an article he wrote about the poem in Lao.

432 **Recherches sur la littérature laotienne.** (Research on Lao literature.)
Louis Finot. *Bulletin de l'École Française d'Extrême-Orient*, vol. 17
(1917), p. 1-218.

Based on a study of manuscripts from the Buddhist monasteries and pagodas of Luang
Prabang that had been collected in the Royal Library and the Library of the École
Française d'Extrême-Orient. Finot's task was to sample the material in order to give
some idea of the nature of Lao literature, rather than just a listing of titles, although he
does provide a list of the 1,163 titles. He examines each of the classes of literature and
provides a detailed survey of them, and he includes synopses of the folktales. Peltier,
in *Le roman classique lao* (q.v.) is critical of this work both because Finot knew no Lao
and relied on Lao informants, and because this work is based on a study of the
manuscripts of one region and so does not reflect regional variations. Others still see
this as a fundamental article, still unsurpassed, on Lao literature and it certainly
remains the most comprehensive survey. Peltier's work, for example, is a study of only
one of the classes of literature. The study of the manuscripts led Finot to include a
study of the scripts used in the manuscripts.

433 **P'ra Lak-P'ra Lam: version lao du Ramayana. P'ommachak: version
'Tay Lu du Ramayana.** (P'ra Lak-Prá Lam: Lao version of Ramayana.
P'ommachak: Tai Lu version of Ramayana.)
Pierre-Bernard Lafont. Vientiane: École Française d'Extrême-Orient,
1957. 34 leaves. (École Française d'Extrême-Orient, Bibliothèque de
Diffusion, no. 6).

A summary of the two versions of the Indian Ramayana story as found in Laos: the
one from Vientiane, the Lao version; the other from Muong Sing, in the Upper
Mekong province, the Tai Lu (or Tay Lu) version. The Lao version is no mere
translation, but an original Lao retelling of the story, which is still extremely popular.

Literature. Classical literature

The Tai Lu version on the other hand seems to have been an adaptation of this foreign work for local religious needs; this may explain its short form and lack of evolutionary development. In this booklet Lafont sets both versions in their local context, and he provides brief summaries of the stories as they are recounted in two particular manuscripts.

434 **La reine exilée et son fils: *Nang Tèng One*: poème épique laotien narrant une des vies du Bouddha.** (The exiled queen and her son or, Nang Teng On: epic Lao poem narrating one of the lives of the Buddha.) Translated by Jean Lichtenstein. *Péninsule*, no. 18-19 (1989), p. 3-274.

A translation of the Lao text published in 1967 by the Comité Littéraire Lao, based on manuscripts conserved in the Royal Library of Luang Prabang. Lichtenstein suggests that the original Lao version dates from somewhere between the fifteenth and seventeenth centuries by an unknown author, and may have existed prior to that in another Tai language. The story of Lady Teng On recounts one of the early lives or incarnations of the Buddha and his near relations, but it is not part of the canonical Jataka tales but one of the extra-canonical Jataka stories popular in South East Asia. In this version, while theoretically set in India, the customs and details of daily life are all Lao. Lichtenstein has provided a prose translation and omitted all the repetition which is part of Lao literary style. He has also divided the work into chapters to bring out the major events and to cater for Western logic. He has provided an extensive glossary of unfamiliar terms.

435 **Chanthakhat: oeuvre littéraire lao.** (Chanthakhat: a Lao literary work.) Translated by Pierre Somchine Nginn. Vientiane: Comité Littéraire Lao, 1966. 29p.

An abridged translation of a work of classical Lao literature. The story concerns two brothers from Champa, Sourignakhat and Chanthakhat. They have a series of adventures and each one, despite being a commoner, marries a foreign princess. They have each revived a princess after death by virtue of the magical powers of some tree bark, which was revealed to them during their travels and adventures.

436 **Sinsay: chef-d'oeuvre de la littérature lao.** (Sinsay: masterpiece of Lao literature.) Pangkham, translated by Thao Nhouy Abhay, Pierre Somchine Nginn. Bangkok: Tiew-chuy Sae Tiew, 1965. 80p.

A prose translation into French of the poem, Sinsay (or Sinxay), a Jataka tale in its Lao version. The translation is prefaced by a summary of the poem and a discussion of the Lao tradition of the story. Thao Nhouy Abhay has published a shorter version in English as 'Sin Xay' in *Kingdom of Laos: the land of the million elephants and of the white parasol* (q.v.) (p. 359-73).

437 **Le roman classique lao.** (Classical Lao fiction.)
Anatole-Roger Peltier. Paris: École Française d'Extrême-Orient,
1988. 676p. maps. bibliog. (Publications de l'École Française
d'Extrême-Orient, vol. 152).

Presented in three sections, the first is a study of classical Lao fiction under various
headings (verse and language, the characters, daily life, the magical, and Buddhism
and other beliefs). As the author reminds us this genre of traditional written folk
literature was very popular in Laos until the 1960s. The second part provides a
summary of thirty-seven works considered by literate Lao as most characteristic of
their literature. The third part is a translation of a whole work, entitled 'The white
nightjar', which illustrates how the Lao storytellers developed a story. The author
suggests that the whole of Lao literature is a virgin field for study, and this is the first in
a proposed series on Lao literary genres.

438 **Un texte classique lao: le Syvsvat.** (A classical Lao text: the syvsvat.)
Anatole-Roger Peltier. Paris: École Française d'Extrême-Orient,
1971. 191p. bibliog. (Textes et Documents sur l'Indochine; no. 10).

A translation of the Lao text published in 1963 by Maha Sila Viravong in Vientiane,
which was transcribed from a Lao manuscript. The Syvsvat is a series of edifying tales,
which develop themes from the Jatakas, the Panchatantra, Suphasit or words of
wisdom of the Buddha. Their origin has not been established, but the manuscript
evidence suggests that they were known in the north, south and central regions of
Laos. Their object is to provide a moral code to educate ignorant princes, and give
them the necessary guidelines for the future when they would govern in their turn.
Towards the end of the book, the king's officials and the population as a whole are
seen as the recipients of this moral education. Peltier describes this work as not only a
great Lao literary text but also a mine of information on the way of life and thought of
the Lao in former times.

439 **Initiation à la littérature laotienne.** (Introduction to Lao literature.)
Phouvong Phimmasone. Hanoi: Publications de l'École Française
d'Extrême-Orient, 1948. 85 leaves. (Cours et Conférences de l'École
Française d'Extrême-Orient, 1948-49).

The author goes through the various written sources available for the study of Lao
writing. He covers inscriptions, palm-leaf manuscripts and folding paper manuscript
books. He then discusses the various genres of Lao literature and gives brief
descriptions of contents and translations of extracts.

440 **La littérature bouddhique lao.** (Lao Buddhist literature.)
Phouvong Phimmasone. In: *Présence du Bouddhisme* (The presence
of Buddhism), special issue of *France-Asie*, vol. 16 (1959), p. 893-904.

Phouvong sets out in a systematic way the types of Buddhist literature, which he
describes as the richest of all the branches of Lao literature, and which constitute an
important source of inspiration for all Lao literature. He describes the Buddhist canon,
the Tipitaka, and the Lao versions extant, then the extra-canonical texts, which include
hagiographic legends, lives of saints, stories of Buddhist relics, and treatises of doctrine
and piety. The third category of literature he describes as 'technical treatises', which
include grammatical, metrical, lexicographical, astrological and political works. The
last sets out the precepts for a good ruler and the symbols of kingship. A further study

of the Jataka stories is found in another article in this volume by Ginette Terral-Martini entitled 'Les Jataka et la littérature de l'Indochine bouddhique' (The Jataka stories and Indochinese Buddhist literature) (p. 483-96).

441 The Krsna saga in Laos: a study in the Brah Ku'td Brah Ban or the story of Banasura.
Sachchidanand Sahai.   Delhi: BR Publishing, 1978. 124p. bibliog.

An interesting study of a Laotian adaptation of the legend of Banasura or Usa-Aniruddha. In this version from Laos the four-armed Krsna-Narayana is the king of Brah Go (Ban Pha Kho) in present-day Thailand, and Bana the king of Lan Xang in Laos. The story is set in a Lao background, but it includes story elements from both early and later Indian sources. Sahai used three manuscripts from Laos to prepare this study. In his first chapter he analyses the Indian versions of the story of Banasura or Usa-Aniruddha. In the second he gives the main episodes of the Lao version and notes features which are common to the Indian and Lao versions. In the third chapter he examines the material contained in the last two sections of the manuscript which contain a description of the divinities of Laos and legends regarding place-names. The fourth chapter gives an English translation of one of the manuscripts, with variant readings from the others. The text of the manuscript is reproduced photographically at the end of the book.

442 Ramayana in Laos: a study of Gvay Dvorabhi.
Sachchidanand Sahai.   Delhi: BR Publishing, 1976. 148p.

One of the lesser versions of the Rama story, translated by Dr. Sahai, and also reproduced in Lao script here; it is preceded by an introduction. This translation is based on the text of manuscript housed in the Royal Palace, Luang Prabang, and written in the Yuan script, prevalent in northern Laos and Chiang Mai (Thailand). The introduction to the work concludes with a comparison of this version of the Rama story with the Lao version of Valmiki's Ramayana, the *Phra Lak Phra Lam*. The English translation is linked to the pagination of the Lao text. The work is illustrated with photographs of the murals in Vat Oup-Moung in Vientiane, which depict the story.

443 The Nang Tan Tay, or, The Lao Arabian nights. Vol. 1: Nanthapakone.
Abridged and translated by Vo Thu Tinh.   Vientiane: Cultural Survey of Laos, 1972. 116p.

The Nang Tan Tay is the Lao version of the Indian Panchatantra, a collection of fables. The Lao version is believed to have been composed of five volumes, but only four have been discovered among surviving Lao manuscripts. The stories, or fables, were intended to present political principles in an attractive form to the sons of King Mihilaropya in ancient India. In each volume there is a key story which provides a framework into which the other tales are inserted. Each tale usually concludes with a verse in which political ideas or ethics are encapsulated. In this volume, which appears to have been the only one published, Vo Thu Tinh presents a free and abridged translation of the first volume which is concerned with the bull Nantha, in Lao the *Nanthapakone*. It begins with the story of how the tales came to be told, the events which lead up to King Vimala killing a virgin every day after she has passed the night with him. Wily Tang Tay begins her cycle of stories, which cause the king to reverse his decision. The protagonists of the tales are largely animal, and the point of the tales in this volume is that the wise ruler exercises his power with justice and mercy, and uses his intelligence to discriminate between flattery and wise counsel.

444   **Phra Lak Phra Lam: le Ramayana lao.** (Phra Lak Phra Lam: the lao
Ramayana story.)
Vo Thu Tinh.   Vientiane: Vithagna, 1972. 94p. bibliog. (Littérature
Lao, no. 1).
Vo Thu Tinh discusses the Vientiane text of the Lao version of the Ramayana, that is
the *Phra Lak Phra Lam*. He makes a comparison with the version of Luang Prabang
that the National Library published in Lao in 1971. The work begins with an
introduction, then an explanatory cast list of the principal characters of the story. The
broad outlines of the epic are recounted, and four episodes are retold in a free
translation. In appendices he summarizes the Luang Prabang and Muong Sing versions
of the Ramayana story. The book is illustrated with photographs of the murals of the
story from Vat Oup Moung in Vientiane.

Modern Lao literature

445   **Mes poèmes.** (My poems.)
Khamchan Pradith.   Vientiane: Editions Pitouphoum, 1970. 2nd ed.
33p.
A collection of poetry in Lao, French and English. Khamchan has been a career
diplomat and held high office in Laos; he is also a journalist and poet.

446   **La littérature politique lao.** (Lao political literature.)
Pierre-Bernard Lafont.   In: *Littératures contemporaines de l'Asie du
Sud-Est* (Contemporary literatures of South East Asia).   Edited by
Pierre-Bernard Lafont, D. Lombard.   Paris: Asiathèque, 1974, p. 41-
55.
The birth of political literature in Laos can be traced to the attack by the Japanese on
the French troops in Indo-China, 9th March 1945. This literature, which is not widely
known, is discussed here. Written in both Lao and French, the use of Lao was a new
departure. The work is strongly political; some is in the form of manifestos and
statements about the fighting and role of foreign powers in Laos. The other main genre
is patriotic literature published by the Neo Lao Haksat, which recounts the heroic
struggle of the people against the Americans and the Royal Government forces. In this
article Lafont considers a selection of titles in some detail.

447   **Pearls of great price: Southeast Asian writings.**
Edited by Gail Lando, Grace Sandness.   Maple Grove, Minnesota:
Mini World Publications, 1986. 82p.
Just over half the contributions in this volume are by writers from Laos. These are
biographical incidents recounted by young people who have made a new home in the
United States of America. They tell of incidents from daily life, the day-to-day reality
of living with war before 1975, then the hardships when the war was over and, in some
cases, the escape to a new life.

448 **Rains in the jungle: Lao short stories.**
[n.p.]: Neo Lao Haksat Publications, 1967. 77p.
Five stories by writers in the Neo Lao Haksat with themes from the lives of those
caught up in the fight against the United States in Laos.

449 **The wood grouse.**
[n.p.]: Neo Lao Haksat Publications, 1968. 112p.
A collection of nine short stories by four Lao writers involved in the fight against the
United States. Each story has some aspect of the resistance for its theme.

450 **Worthy daughters and sons of the Lao people.**
[n.p.]: Neo Lao Haksat Publications, 1966. 90p.
Seven stories which capture the exploits of seven members of the Neo Lao Haksat in
their fight to free Laos from the American and French presence.

451 **Les gars du 97.** (The lads of the 97th.)
Phou Louang. [n.p.]: Editions du Neo Lao Haksat, 1971. 97p.
The story of a unit of the Pathet Lao in action, presented in a fictionalized account. As
the publishers state in their preface, it is intended to round out the bald details of
official communiqués.

452 **La littérature lao contemporaine.** (Contemporary Lao literature.)
Saveng Phinith. In: *Littératures contemporaines de l'Asie du Sud-Est*
(Contemporary literatures of South East Asia). Edited by Pierre-
Bernard Lafont, D. Lombard. Paris: Asiathèque, 1974. p. 29-39.
Modern Lao literature has its beginnings in 1941 with the publications of the *Lao Nhay*
movement of young Lao writers, that is the Movement for Lao Renovation, and this
article traces its development. The new literature was largely francophone until 1963,
except in Pathet Lao areas, but by the time of writing of this article (1972) ninety per
cent of publications were written in Lao. The author considers the problem for writers
of an educated population that did not have a taste for reading, and the more insidious
problem of Thai television which can be received in Laos; influenced by it. Lao
language and literature were becoming despised by the Lao people as second-rate
compared with Thai language and literature.

Oral literature

453 **Les chansons de Sao Van Di: moeurs du Laos.**
Jean Ajalbert. Paris: Editions Sudestasie, 1988. 101p.
An adaptation and translation of Lao songs by the author. He links the songs of a
young girl, Sao Van Di, with a narrative of the love story, which they punctuate. The
work is illustrated with line drawings and coloured plates, commissioned from a Lao
artist. This a new edition of a work that was first published in 1905 by Fasquelle, Paris.

454 **La destinée de l'homme: traduction d'un *lam long kong* du Sud Laos.**
(The destiny of man: the translation of a *lam long kong* from southern
Laos.)
Catherine Choron-Baix. *ASEMI: Asie du Sud-Est et Monde
Insulindien* (ASEMI: South East Asia and the Island World), vol. 11,
no. 1-4 (1980), p. 311-16.
The *lam long kong* originates from the banks of the Mekong in southern Laos. It is a
poem or *lam* sung at major ceremonies, particularly communal agricultural festivals, by
the *lam* masters of competing villages. Choron-Baix gives here an extensive extract in
French from such a poem recorded in Paris in 1980.

455 **Littérature orale: le *lam* du Laos.** (Oral literature: the *lam* of Laos.)
Catherine Choron-Baix. *ASEMI: Asie du Sud-Est et Monde
Insulindien* (ASEMI: South East Asia and the Island World), vol. 14,
nos. 1-4 (1985), p. 85-101.
Lam is one of the most popular forms of oral literature found among the Lao. Choron-
Baix records here new forms of *lam* which have developed among the Lao refugees in
camps in Thailand. These poems carry the traditional themes of love and Buddhist
morals but some also tell about the grief of exile, they are reproduced in extensive
extracts in French and Lao.

456 **Courting poetry in Laos: a textual and linguistic analysis.**
Carol J. Compton. De Kalb, Illinois: Northern Illinois University,
Center for Southeast Asian Studies, 1979. 252p. map. bibliog. (Special
Report, no. 18).
A description of one form of Lao oral literature, *lam*, specifically *lam sithandone*,
poetry usually performed musically by two singers, generally a man and a woman.
Compton describes the performance and provides a full English translation of the Lao
text. In the study which follows she discusses aspects of the transmission and learning
of *lam*, and analyses the interaction of thematic, musical, poetic, grammatical and
phonological structures in performance.

457 **Littérature orale et migration chez les Hmong refugiés du Laos.** (Oral
literature and migration among Hmong refugees from Laos.)
Jean-Pierre Hassoun. *ASEMI: Asie du Sud-Est et Monde Insulindien*
(ASEMI: South East Asia and the Island World), vol. 14, nos. 1-4
(1985), p. 103-38. bibliog.
Hassoun recorded seven Hmong songs in the refugee camp of Ban Vinai in Thailand.
In these the Hmong, with no tradition of writing, recorded their experience of
departure from Laos and dispersal to other parts of the world. The availability of
cassette recorders enabled the Hmong to preserve these songs, and Hassoun notes that
Hmong refugees in France listened to them in the first year of their arrival. The text of
the songs is given in French and two levels of reading the texts are offered.

458 **Songs of the love nights of the Lao.**
English version by E. Powys Mather. *Eastern love*, vol. 10, p. 79-106.
A selection of Lao folk-songs in the form of love poetry, in English translation. Thirty-nine examples are given here. They are sung largely on *wan-pak* nights. The author refers to a study of the literature of Indo-China, possibly in volume 12 of this work, but it has not been traced.

459 **À propos du *Sinxay* légende nationale lao et de son traitement oral en période révolutionnaire.** (The *Sinxay* story and its oral treatment during the revolutionary period.)
Jean-François Papet. *Asie du Sud-Est et Monde Insulindien: Bulletin du Centre de Documentation et de Recherche (CeDRASEMI)* (South East Asia and the Island World: Bulletin of the Centre for Documentation and Research [CeDRASEMI]), vol. 10, nos. 2-4 (1979), p. 247-69.
A retelling of the Sinsay legend in 1975, in the region of Savannakhet-Kengkok. In retelling the tale the story-teller makes clear the parallels between the experience of the Pathet Lao in the forest fighting the 'magical' powers of Western armaments, and Sinsay's fight against the ogres and their magic powers. Papet has provided an almost complete translation of this retelling of the story he recorded, with some explanatory material.

Folk literature, legends and proverbs

460 **Le récit Khamou de Chuang et ses implications historiques pour le Nord-Laos.** (The Khmu story of Chuang and its historical implications for north Laos.)
Michel Ferlus. *Asie du Sud-Est et Monde Insulindien: Bulletin du Centre de Documentation et de Recherche (CeDRASEMI)* (South East Asia and the Island World: Bulletin of the Centre for Documentation and Research [CeDRASEMI]), vol. 7, no. 1 (1976), p. 21-29.
This story of the Khmu, some of the Mon-Khmer inhabitants of the area of Laos prior to the arrival of the Lao, is given in translation, transcription and literal translation. Ferlus recorded it in Laos in 1970. There are, he comments, two types of themes, the historic and the mythic. They can be read as a history of the peopling of the region by T'ai and Vietnamese. He argues that the Lao epic poem of Chuang or Thao Hung is a retelling in which the ethnic roles are reversed and the Khmu myth is adopted by the Lao invaders.

461 Contes laotiens et contes cambodgiens. (Lao and Cambodian tales.)
Adhémard Leclère. Reprinted, New York: AMS Press, 1975. 272p.
The Lao tales form about two-thirds of this work. They are grouped according to theme, legal tales, tales of the Visayamatya, tales of the Kapila-yaksa and tales of the princess. Leclère indicates, in notes, the variations between the Lao and Cambodian versions. This was first published in 1903.

462 Sieng Hmieng.
Translated by Jean Lichtenstein. *Péninsule*, nos. 6-7 (1983), 231p.
An important group of folk-tales in Laos is that known as the legend of Sieng Hmieng, known as Si Thananchai in Thailand, and under other names in other South East Asian countries. Here they are presented in a translation of the text published by the Comité Littéraire Lao in 1968, based on sixteenth- and seventeenth-century manuscripts. The translator has endeavoured to retain the original style as closely as possible; any necessary additions are indicated. The thirty tales here recount how Sii Thanonsay, a poor boy, is adopted by the King of Dvaravati. While a novice monk, he acquires the name Sieng Hmieng, which records a trick he played on some poor men taking leaf tea to the king. He regularly outwits others with his tricks with words. In this cycle of tales Sieng Hmieng plays the fool and challenges the authority of the king. In the last tale of this set Sieng Hmieng is bested by a young monk. The translator in a brief introduction sets these tales in their context and suggests their significance in Lao tradition. He provides a thorough glossary to terms in the text.

463 Folk tales from Kammu II: a story-teller's tales.
Kristina Lindell, Jan-Öjvind Swahn, Damrong Tayanin. London: Curzon Press, 1980. 185p. map. bibliog. (Scandinavian Institute of Asian Studies Monograph Series, no. 40).
A second collection of eighteen stories collected from a Khmu story-teller formerly living in northern Laos. There are brief notes on the context of the telling of the tales. The stories are translated very literally and word-for-word. Attractive line drawings by a Khmu illustrate points in the stories.

464 Folk tales from Kammu III: pearls of Kammu literature.
Kristina Lindell, Jan Öjvind Swahn, Damrong Tayanin. London: Curzon Press, 1984. 325p. bibliog. (Scandinavian Institute of Asian Studies Monograph Series, no. 51).
A large collection of tales from one Khmu story-teller. The compilers have endeavoured to establish what might constitute the repertoire of a story-teller. The narrator of these stories is more unusual in that he is aware of different cultural traditions and was very eager to work with the project to preserve the culture of his ethnic group. More than 150 tales and rhymes are translated in this collection, some illustrated with line drawings. The compilers have provided more information on the Khmu that complements the information in their other works (q.v.).

Literature. Folk literature, legends and proverbs

465 **A Kammu story-listener's tales.**
Kristina Lindell, Jan-Öjvind Swahn, Damrong Tayanin. London:
Curzon Press, 1977. 113p. bibliog. (Scandinavian Institute of Asian
Studies Monograph Series, no. 33).
A collection of twenty stories from a Khmu story-teller, who left Laos in his youth and
has lived in Thailand for many years. The compilers provide a brief introduction to the
Khmu and their literature as a preface to the tales.

466 **Grandmother's path, grandfather's way: Hmong preservation project,
oral lore, generation to generation.**
Lue Vang, Judy Lewis. Rancho Cordova, California: Zellerbach
Family Fund, 1984. 197p. bibliog.
A compilation of Hmong folklore intended to help preserve the culture among the
refugee community in the United States. The whole text is in English and Hmong; it
covers folk tales, proverbs, oral literary techniques, poetry and traditional needlework,
and concludes with an account of a typical Hmong day and the daily life of each month
of the year.

467 **Lao proverbs.**
Russell Marcus. Bangkok: Craftsman Press, 1969. 56p.
This book is largely translated from *Supasit buran* (Traditional proverbs), published by
the Lao Comité Littéraire in 1961. The most well-known and most typically Lao
proverbs have been selected. The entries are given in Lao, in transcription, in a literal
translation and an equivalent meaning. The compiler has prefaced his selection by a
few remarks on the differences between Lao and American social behaviour, the
context from which proverbial sayings arise. The proverbs are grouped under the
terms, which form the key point of the proverb, such as knowledge, luck, time and
wealth. Some of the proverbs are illustrated through the text.

468 **Contes et legendes Hmong Blanc.** (Tales and legends of the White
Hmong.)
Jean Mottin. Bangkok: Don Bosco Press, c.1982. 387p.
These tales and legends, recorded between 1974 and 1975, are transcribed in White
Hmong and translated into French. They have been grouped under themes: the
creation of the world, historical, customs and beliefs, and those for entertainment.

469 **Indochinese folk tales.**
Tran My-van. [Darwin, Australia:] Northern Territory Multicultural
Education Co-ordinating Committee, [1985]. 57p. map.
A selection of twenty folk-tales from Indo-China, of which six are specifically from
Laos. They are told in a simple style suitable for young people and illustrated with line
drawings.

Western fiction set in Laos

470   **Tam-tam sur le Mékong.** (Tom-tom on the Mekong.)
Alain Aymard.   Paris: France Empire, 1985. 346p.

A fictionalized account of a French commando parachuted into Thailand to organize guerilla resistance in mid-Laos against the Chinese and Vietnamese, after the Japanese capitulation in August 1945. The events of the novel include the love story of a Laotian princess and encounters with the whole gamut of Lao society. The author was himself sent into Laos in this way.

471   **The ugly American.**
William J. Lederer, Eugene Burdick.   New York: W. W. Norton, 1958. 285p.

A political novel set in the imaginary country of Sarkhan. This work was a critique of US policy and activities in Indo-China and elsewhere in Asia, which the authors in their 'Factual epilogue' point out is based on real events and real officials. The ugliness of the title refers to the inability or unwillingness to know and understand the peoples and cultures of Asia on their own terms by American officials who do not learn the local language, never leave their own circle and import inappropriate technology. The point is made by contrasting them with a minority of Americans who develop a real understanding, but whose views and expertise are constantly ignored or bypassed.

472   **L'exotisme indochinois dans la littérature française depuis 1860.**
(Indochinese exoticism in French literature since 1860.)
Louis Malleret.   Paris: Larose, 1934. 372p. bibliog.

Intended to provide an explanation of a literary movement and mark its stages of development, this work is not a literary history of Indo-China. Beginning in the mid-nineteenth century it traces the appearance of Indo-China in French literature, and includes the accounts of conquest which helped fire the imaginations of the French and established the nostalgic and sinister themes that have obscured the image of Indo-China. The work is divided into four parts: *L'Indochine et la tradition exotique* (Indo-China and the exotic tradition); *Le cycle européen* (The European cycle); *Préliminaires à l'interprétation asiatiques* (Preliminary steps towards an asian interpretation); and *Le cycle asiatique* (The Asian cycle). This is essentially a study of literature written by French authors, although the emerging phenomenon of translations of indigenous literature is touched upon. The work is illustrated with extensive quotations from the publications considered. It is written within an older tradition so that bibliographical references are given in the footnotes and there are no indexes, although there are detailed Contents notes.

473   **The brinkman.**
Desmond Meiring.   London: Hodder & Stoughton, 1964. 251p. map.

A novel set in Laos in the period 1959 to 1960. It offers a fictionalized and somewhat simplified version of Lao political history in that period. It gives an idea of the manoeuvrings of the various groups of foreigners resident in Laos at the time.

474 **Opium rouge.** (Red opium.)
Bernard Moinet. Paris: France-Empire, 1966. 377p. maps.

A fictionalized account of the counter-revolutionary war of the French-Lao forces during the First Indochinese War in the area of Houa Phans.

475 **The Laotian fragments.**
John Clark Pratt. New York: Viking Press, 1974. 245p. map.

A fictional account dealing with aerial operations and the situation in Laos in the second half of the 1960s. It is presented as fragments of the journal, letters and tape recordings of a Major William Blake, United States Air Force. He was shot down on a mission while employed on Project 404, approved in 1966 by the Department of Defense to provide help and logistic support for the Army and Air Attachés to Laos. Administratively, he was assigned to the Joint United States Military Assistance Group. Also included are extracts from contemporary printed documents with Blake's annotations. The whole is presented by the 'editor' Professor Harding as if he were presenting documents for an archive.

476 **Kham la laotienne: l'or et les filles du Laos.** (Kham the young Lao girl: gold and the girls of Laos.)
Louis-Charles Royer. Paris: Editions de France, 1935. 283p.

A novel based on the search for a gold mine, which goes from Paris, via Singapore and Bangkok, to Laos. Enigmatic Kham leads the Frenchman Morgat away from the Western obsession with material wealth to Laotian values.

Art and Architecture

General

477 **Arts of Asia**.
Hong Kong: Arts of Asia Publications, 1970- . bi-monthly

A glossy, illustrated magazine aimed at art collectors. The articles are brief but well-illustrated, and it provides accessible articles in English. Articles on Laos include: 'Laotian silver' by Jackie Passmore (vol. 3, no. 6 (1973), p. 46-9) on antique jewellery and tribal artefacts; 'Wat Phra Keo' by Helene Cooke, Alexandra Smith (vol. 1, no. 6 (1971), p. 63-67), a brief survey of the museum, its range of exhibits and illustrations of a few of its holdings; 'Luang Prabang: wood carving and decorative arts' by Charles F. B. Wilding-White (vol. 7, no. 2 (1977), p. 57-61), a study of traditional wood carving, materials and motifs, and the work on preservation and restoration; 'Luang Prabang and its temples' by Charles F. B. Wilding-White (vol. 6, no. 1 (1976), p. 50-57. map.), a brief survey of architectural themes, and an attempt to suggest a framework for the study of Lao architecture.

478 **L'image du Buddha dans l'art lao.** (The image of the Buddha in Lao art.)
Thao Boun Souk (i.e. Pierre-Marie Gagneux). Vientiane: Henry M.Demain, 1971. 42p. bibliog.

Buddha images vary in style within each Buddhist country, and this brief study is a preliminary attempt to identify and explore the Lao image. It is preliminary, since work on Lao art is in its infancy apart from the studies of Parmentier (1988) (q.v.) and Marchal (1964) (q.v.). As Boun Souk states, the study of Lao art is a neglected field, and it has tended to be overshadowed by studies of the art of its more politically and culturally powerful neighbours. In this work the author looks at the non-personified images such as the wheel of law and the footprints of the Buddha, as well as the representations of the Buddha in human form. It is largely an illustrated catalogue of surviving works of Buddhist art in Laos, with a brief connecting text. The illustrations would make the work useful to an iconographer. Most of the items were held in museums or important *Vats* in Vientiane and Luang Prabang. Where known, the name of the craftsman is recorded.

479 **Louang Phrabang: 600 ans d'art bouddhique lao.** (Luang Prabang: 600 years of Lao Buddhist art.)
Thao Boun Souk (i.e. Pierre-Marie Gagneux). Paris: Quartz International, 1974. 160p. maps. bibliog.

A descriptive guide to the Buddhist monasteries of Luang Prabang. There are some introductory notes on the principal architectural features and styles of the monasteries or *vats*.

480 **Indochina: art in the melting-pot of races.**
Bernard Philippe Groslier. London: Methuen, 1962. 261p. maps. bibliog.

A translation of the work first published in German, and also translated into French. Laos is treated very briefly in this work, but there are four coloured plates illustrating Lao statues and temples and a couple of figures. This work was published in the United States under the title *The art of Indochina* (New York: Crown, 1962).

481 **Yao ceremonial paintings.**
Jacques Lemoine, with the assistance of Donald Gibson. Bangkok: White Lotus, 1982. 168p. maps. bibliog.

The Yao, an ethnic group which now extends from China, through northern Vietnam, Laos and northeastern Thailand, are *swidden* cultivators. From the centuries that they lived in China, the religion they have developed is a borrowing from the Chinese Taoist tradition. This book is concerned with the Mien Yao and their paintings, which illustrate the Yao Taoist pantheon. The event which provoked the publication of this work was the large-scale sale of these paintings to foreign collectors by Yao refugees, although the author notes a slowing down in the trade. Lavishly illustrated, largely in colour, this work is both a guide to the paintings and Mien Yao Taoism. It is to a lesser extent a sketch of Yao history and society. A short note on this subject with substantial illustration has been published as 'Yao Taoist paintings' by Jacques Lemoine (*Arts of Asia*, vol. 11, no. 1 (1981), p. 61-71).

482 **L'art decoratif au Laos.** (Decorative art in Laos.)
Henri Marchal. *Arts Asiatiques*, vol. 10, no. 2 (1964).

A special issue of the journal devoted to decorative art in Laos. Marchal's aim is to preserve the detail of Lao decorative motifs, either in drawings made of them, or in photographs. He fears they are on the point of disappearing, as they are made in perishable materials and are vulnerable to damage by climate and insects, or even insensitive restoration. He believes they have a quality and individuality which is worth recognizing. He discusses particular aspects of decoration with references to the extensive group of illustrations, and concludes with a study of the iconography of Lao Buddha images. He provides a glossary for the terminology he uses. The article is illustrated with fifty-six photographs and forty-eight figures of decorative motifs, architectural details or Buddha images.

483 **Decorative art.**
Henri Marchal. In: *Kingdom of Laos: the land of the million elephants and of the white parasol.* Compiled by René de Berval. Saigon, Vietnam: France Asie, 1959, p. 71-80.

A summary of the key features of ornament and design in Lao art, illustrated by six pages of plates and sketches. The decoration of Buddhist temple doors and roofs is discussed; these are largely made in perishable material. The intrusion of motifs from Western art receives a mention.

484 **Le temple de Vat Phou, province de Champassak.** (The temple of Vat Phu in Champassak Province.)
Henri Marchal. [Vientiane:] Département des Cultes, [1957]. 37p. bibliog.

An architectural description of the monument, a Khmer temple in the outer reaches of the Khmer empire. Marchal continues with the history of the region and of the temple's construction. He concludes with an account of the festivals still celebrated at the temple. There are several photographs of the temple and the surrounding countryside.

485 **L'art du Laos.** (The art of Laos.)
Henri Parmentier. Paris: École Française d'Extrême-Orient, 1988. rev. ed. 2 vols. (Publications de l'École Française d'Extrême-Orient, no. 35).

This is in effect an inventory of the Buddhist temples (*vats*) of Laos. Parmentier offers an analysis of the architectural and artistic styles which developed in Laos, and has chronicled them region by region. This is a new edition of the work first published posthumously in 1954, prepared by Madeleine Giteau who has been able to add from her more recent research in Laos. The original research was conducted between 1911 and 1927 and, even when first published, many of the Buddhist temples no longer existed. Giteau has retained Parmentier's text and augmented it with notes. She has made particularly important additions to the work on sculpture and the iconography of Buddha images, where there has been much work since Parmentier's studies. She has added some more recent photographs to the volume of photographs and sketches, and she has updated the information on the reconstruction and restoration of temples in Luang Prabang and Vientiane.

486 **Le temple de Vat Phu.** (The temple of Vat Phou.)
Henri Parmentier. *Bulletin de l'École Française d'Extrême-Orient*, vol. 14, no. 2 (1914), p. 1-31.

A study of Vat Phu, that is the Pagoda of the Mountain. It is the most northerly Khmer monument situated in Champassak in modern Laos. Parmentier gives a detailed description of the monument, and there are seven plates of plans and eighteen photographs.

487 The That Luang of Vientiane.
Phouvong Phimmasone. *Asia*, vol. 3, no. 9 (1953), p. 91-101.
A historical and archaeological study of the most venerated Buddhist shrine in Laos. The That Luang is a stupa, or reliquary mount, built over a relic of the Buddha in the village of That Luang outside Vientiane.

488 The art of Southeast Asia: Cambodia Vietnam Thailand Laos Burma Java Bali.
Philip Rawson. London: Thames & Hudson, 1967. Reprinted, 1990. 288p. maps. bibliog. (World of Art).
Rawson offers a survey of art from the beginning of the Christian era to the modern period. Laos is covered in the chapter on Siam and Laos. There is relevant material on the cultures of the area, before the arrival of the Lao, in the chapters on early Indo-China and Khmer art. The work contains a good range of illustrations.

489 A guide to the wats of Vientiane.
Anna-Brita Rosell. Bangkok: Louis Printing Co., 1989. 64p. bibliog.
Designed as a guide for those new to Laos, Rosell gives some general information on Buddhism in Laos, on the significance of the different styles of Buddha images, and on visiting a *vat* for a foreigner. There is a description of the three *vats* which are now museums: the That Luang, the Wat Phra Keo and the Wat Sisaket (Wat Phra Keo is the museum of religious art). The third section is devoted to a representative collection of the *vats* in Vientiane. The whole work is complemented by numerous colour photographs, by Nils Andersson, of features of the *vats* and Buddha images, the daily practice of Buddhism and the festivals in Vientiane.

Textiles, pottery and metalworking

490 The kettledrums of Southeast Asia: a Bronze Age world and its aftermath.
A. J. Bernet Kempers. Rotterdam, Netherlands: A. A. Balkema, 1988. 599p. maps. bibliog. (Modern Quaternary Research in Southeast Asia, vol. 10 [1986/87]).
In this comprehensive survey of the kettledrums of South East Asia, Bernet Kempers ranges from the Bronze Age, or as he suggests the Bronze-Iron age, to the continued use and manufacture of these drums in the modern era amongst the hill tribes of Laos and other countries. He outlines the discovery and research on the drums, establishes a typology of form and structure, function and use as musical instruments. About a quarter of the text is devoted to the decoration found on the drums. He discusses their distribution and chronology and concludes with a consideration of the aftermath, that is, more modern use. The volume concludes with inventories of known drums and over a hundred and twenty photographic plates of drums and particular features. The material on Laos is less than for some of the other countries, but it is nonetheless important. A more popular treatment of the subject will be found in Roxanna M. Brown 'Bronze drums of Laos' (*Arts of Asia*, vol. 5, no. 1 (1975), p. 48-55).

491 **The ceramics of South-East Asia: their dating and identification.**
Roxanna M. Brown. Singapore; Oxford: Oxford University Press,
1988. 2nd ed. 130p. maps. bibliog.

Laos figures in the chapter 'Northern and other Thai kilns'. The origins of the potters and their kilns have not been established, and earlier theories are cast into doubt by the discovery of more and more kiln sites. The kiln sites in this area date mainly from the late thirteenth century to the second half of the sixteenth century. The lack of any significant archaeological work in Laos means that very little has yet been discovered. The two sites discussed here are at Vientiane and Pnu Lao, Phuka. Brown gives details of the only confirmed kiln site in Laos, just outside Vientiane at Ban Mae Tao Hai, or Jar Kilns Village, where seven kilns and 350 nearly intact ceramics were excavated; she also includes a map of the site and outlines of the various ceramics found. Based on associated Chinese sherds found at the site, and given the date of the removal of the capital of Lan Xang to Vientiane, it is surmised that the kilns could not date from a period much earlier than 1563 and not later than the sack of Vientiane in 1828. Information on the second site in Laos is based on reports; some details are given here, but the crucial text of a letter about it is found in *Northern Thai ceramics* by J. C. Shaw. (Kuala Lumpur; Oxford: Oxford University Press, 1981. 270p. maps. bibliog. [Oxford in Asia Studies in Ceramics] p. 67-68). Both Brown and Shaw imply that the two sites in Laos were set up by potters fleeing from Thailand.

492 **Lao textiles: ancient symbols – living art.**
Patricia Cheeseman. Bangkok: White Lotus, 1988. 140p. maps.
bibliog.

A detailed description of the textile traditions of the Lao peoples, with many coloured photographs of the textiles. The author was based in Laos from 1973 to 1981. It is concerned with the textiles of the Tai peoples of Laos and not the other ethnic groups. The author discusses the materials, silk, the dyes, the weaving techniques and the traditions of each region; these are all amply illustrated with the author's own photographs. A useful glossary completes the work. Cheeseman has published a brief illustrated extract of this work as 'The antique weavings of the Lao Neua' (*Arts of Asia*, vol. 12, no. 4 [1982], p. 120-25).

493 **Michigan Hmong arts: textiles in transition.**
Edited by C. Kurt Dewhurst, Marsha McDowell. East Lansing,
Michigan: Museum, Michigan State University, 1984. 74p. map.
bibliog. (Publications of the Museum, Michigan State University, Folk
Culture Series, vol. 3, no. 2).

A catalogue produced in conjunction with an exhibition at the Kresge Art Gallery, Michigan State University, of Hmong textiles that have evolved since their departure from Laos. The experience of preparing textiles in the refugee camps for international sale and the experience of life in foreign countries has influenced the evolution of traditional designs and techniques. The work shown is based largely on patchwork and embroidery techniques. Chapters of text introduce the background of the Hmong textiles and the progress to the new styles. The bulk of the book is devoted to the photographs of the exhibits and their creators.

Art and Architecture. Textiles, pottery and metalworking

494 **Handwoven textiles of South-East Asia.**
Sylvia Fraser-Lu.   Singapore; Oxford: Oxford University Press, 1988.
229p. maps. bibliog.
The 'primary purpose of this work is to make known to the general public the beauty
and scope of South-East Asian handwoven textiles, both past and present'. It
concentrates on loom-woven fabrics, and the first part is a general introduction to
weaving. The second part discusses textiles by country. Laos forms part of the chapter
on Indo-China. Fraser-Lu covers the types of fabrics woven, the materials and the way
they are used as dress. Some aspects of the textiles are shown in illustrations.

495 **Silverware of South-East Asia.**
Sylvia Fraser-Lu.   Singapore: Oxford University Press, 1989. 124p.
maps. bibliog. (Images of Asia).
Written for the general reader, this work offers a broad view of the tradition of
silversmithing in South East Asia, which dates back over three thousand years.
Chapters on historical background and the techniques of silversmithing are followed by
chapters on each geographic region. Laos is covered in the chapter on Indo-China; the
text is accompanied by appropriate illustrations of silver objects.

496 **Hmong batik: a textile technique from Laos.**
Jane Mallinson, Nancy Donnelly, Ly Hang.   Seattle, Washington:
Mallinson/Information Services, 1988. 87p. map. bibliog.
A celebration of the batik of the Blue Hmong women, used in making their
characteristic skirts. The book covers all aspects of the batik: both its manufacture, and
the techniques and the social role textiles, and specifically the skirts, play in Hmong
life. These are set in context by a brief history of the Hmong, the story of the origin of
batik and some notes on recent developments, which had begun in Laos and continue
in the United States.

497 **Folk pottery in South-East Asia.**
Dawn F. Rooney.   Singapore: Oxford University Press, 1987. 73p.
maps. bibliog. (Images of Asia).
Aimed at non-specialist readers, this work surveys the folk pottery of South East Asia,
the pottery used in daily life. It looks at South East Asian glazed wares, imported
pottery and the contemporary production. References to Laos are sprinkled through
the text, but they must be sought out as there is no index.

Houses

498 **Elements comparatifs sur les habitations des ethnies de langues thai.** (A comparison of aspects of the houses of Thai-speaking ethnic groups). Sophie Charpentier, Pierre Clément. Paris: CERA-CeDRASEMI, 1978. 259p. maps. bibliog.

This study examines traditional styles of rural houses currently being built in Thailand and Laos and the ways in which they are grouped, the choice of position and the patterns of occupation. The effect this has had on the evolution of architectural features is assessed. The major emphasis of this work is on the Tai groups in Thailand, but the Lao are also considered. The whole work is complemented by extensive illustration with photographs and sketches.

499 **L'habitation lao dans les régions de Vientiane et de Louang Prabang.** (Lao houses in the regions of Vientiane and Luang Prabang.) Sophie Charpentier, Pierre Clément. Paris: Editions Peeters, 1990. 2 vols. bibliog.

A meticulous and pioneering work of ethno-architecture. The work is divided into three parts: the first considers historical reports of Lao houses; and offers a typology of the Lao house, the second part looks at the composition of the Lao house, its use, its placing and the village; the third part examines the construction of the house in detail. The whole work is well provided with sketches and illustrations.

500 **The Lao house: Vientiane and Luang Prabang.** Sophie Charpentier. In: *The house in East and Southeast Asia: anthropological and architectural aspects.* Edited by K. G. Izikowitz, P. Sorensen. London: Curzon Press, 1982, (Scandinavian Institute of Asian Studies. Monograph Series, no. 30). p. 49-61. bibliog.

A study of the house in the Lao village context. Charpentier considers both the temporary shelters built in the paddy-fields on the model of houses, and the two patterns of houses found around Vientiane and Luang Prabang. She considers the building of houses under various aspects, social and economic, ritual and technical. Line drawings illustrate the points made about shape and layout.

501 **The spatial organization of the Lao house.** Pierre Clément. In: *The house in East and Southeast Asia: anthropological and architectural aspects.* Edited by K. G. Izikowitz, P. Sorensen. London: Curzon Press, 1982, (Scandinavian Institute of Asian Studies. Monograph Series, no. 30). p. 62-70. bibliog.

This paper analyses the plan of the Lao house and endeavours to analyse the significance of the positioning of villages and houses, and the use of space in houses. These details have both an astrological and a spiritual significance for the Lao. Clément extends this study in a more speculative way by comparing the rules for the spatial organization of Lao houses with what is known of other Tai groups in his paper 'The Lao house among the Thai houses: a comparative survey and a preliminary classification' (In: *The house in East and Southeast Asia: anthropological and*

Art and Architecture. Houses

architectural aspects. Edited by K. G. Izikowitz, P. Sorensen.   London: Curzon Press, 1982, p. 71–80. map. bibliog. [Scandinavian Institute of Asian Studies. Monograph Series, no. 30]).

Music

General

502 **Music of the Hmong: singing voices and talking reeds.**
Amy Catlin. Providence, Rhode Island: Rhode Island College Office
of Publications, 1981? 16p. bibliog.
Produced to explain the refugee Hmong to the Americans, this work explains briefly
the Hmong tradition of improvised songs and the musical instruments which produce
the music which accompanies it. Much is conveyed in such a brief work, and there are
excellent photographs illustrating the text. The typographical layout is irritating. There
is some general information on the Hmong language and use of names.

503 **La musique du Cambodge et du Laos.** (The music of Cambodia and
Laos.)
Alain Daniélou. Pondichery, India: Institut Français d'Indologie,
1957. 37p. bibliog. (Publications de l'Institut Français d'Indologie,
no. 9).
Daniélou claims that, apart from minor differences, the orchestra used for serious
music for orchestra in Thailand, Cambodia and Laos is practically identical, and it is in
this framework that he discusses the subject. He considers the various groups of
instruments and their musical scales, and the different orchestral groupings formed
with the instruments. He discusses each instrument in detail; this is illustrated by
sketches and photographs. He is interested in the links with India, the historical
evidence about musical instruments to be seen in the bas-reliefs of Angkor, in
Cambodia, and in the distribution of the instruments seen in those carvings in modern
South East Asia.

504 **Apprenez le khène: essai d'une méthode moderne. Learn to play the khene: essay on a modern method.**
Kham-Ouane Ratanavong. Vientiane: Editions Bulletin des Amis du Royaume Lao, 1973. 73p.
In a bilingual French-English text this work describes the *khene* and how it is to be played. The *khene*, also spelt *kaen*, is a musical instrument, a mouth-organ, based on pairs of pipes that look like a miniature raft with a diagonal end. The tone comes from metal reeds fitted in the walls of the pipes, inside the hardwood windchest through which the player blows. There is a single finger hole in each pipe which the player covers to sound the note. The *khene* and sticky rice are considered the two things which identify the Lao from other groups in South East Asia. The instrument is used to accompany the singers of the *lam*, or the *mohlam*, and each *khene* will be tuned to a particular singer's voice. The *khene* is also used to play Lao classical music, modern songs and simple Western melodies. In this work Kham-Ouane Ratanavong describes how to hold and play the *khene* and gives simple tunes which can be played.

505 **Laos.**
Terry E. Miller. In: *The new Grove dictionary of music and musicians*. Edited by Stanley Sadie. London: Macmillan, 1980, vol. 10, p. 460-67. bibliog.
A succinct but clear survey of Lao music presented under the headings, vocal music, theatrical traditions, instruments, and other peoples. There are musical and photographic illustrations to the text, and there are references in the text to other articles. The complementary dictionary, *The new Grove dictionary of musical instruments*, edited by Stanley Sadie (London: Macmillan, 1984), contains articles on particular Lao musical instruments such as the khaen (or *khene*) and the *sumpotan*.

506 **Traditional music of the Lao: kaen playing and mawlum singing in northeast Thailand.**
Terry E. Miller. Westport, Connecticut: Greenwood Press, 1985. 333p. bibliog. (Contributions in Intercultural and Comparative Studies, no. 13).
Miller's study is based on the ethnic Lao who live in the north-east region of Thailand, and this must be borne in mind since some of the directions in which music and performance have developed are developments in Thailand. It is, nonetheless, comprehensive and thorough in its approach and coverage. There is relevant and valuable work on the *khene*, its manufacture and scope. His work on *mohlam* (*mawlum*) singing techniques should be read in conjunction with Compton (q.v.).

507 **Music.**
Prince Souvanna Phouma. In: *Kingdom of Laos: the land of the million elephants and of the white parasol*. Compiled by René de Berval. Saigon, Vietnam: France Asie, 1959, p. 87-93.
A sketch of the contemporary features of Lao music, including a description of the instruments used, types of music and the way in which the instruments are used. It is illustrated by musical notation of four pieces of music.

Recordings

508   **Laos musique du Nord.** (Laos, music from the North.)
Directed by Jacques Brunet.   Paris: Galloway Records, 1973. 1 disc,
33 rpm. (Musique du Monde, no. 12 [GB600 531B]).

This record offers music from the former Kingdom of Luang Prabang. Side 1 includes
music of the court, a *phi-phat* orchestra, a *khene* solo and a love song sung in an
alternating duet. Side 2 comprises music from the ethnic minorities, a Phuan song, two
Khmu songs and Hmong funeral music. This record has been reissued by Playa Sound
(PS.33502) (Musiques de l'Asie Traditionelle, vol. 2). An anthology of Hmong vocal
and instrumental music is available as *Musique des Hmongs du Laos* (Music of the
Hmong of Laos) recorded by Eric Mareschal in 1974-75 (AMP.8.2911).

509   **Laos musique pour le khène/lam saravane.** (Laos music for the khene/
lam saravane.)
Recordings by Jacques Brunet.   Paris: Ocora, 1978. 2 stereo discs,
33rpm. (Musiques Traditionelles Vivantes. 1 Musiques de Traditions
Orales [MU218Y; 558537/8]).

Disc 1 of this recording is music for the *khene* performed by Nouthong Phim-
vilayphone. He plays eight pieces in various styles and on varying size of instrument.
Disc 2 is devoted to a performance of *lam saravane*, a style of *lam* (or performed song)
which has become popular beyond its own region due to the radio. The performers
here are Soubane Vongath and Sengphet Souryavongxay; Soubane a celebrated Lao
singer, now a refugee in Thailand, takes the prominent part in this performance. An
English version of the sleeve notes is given on an insert. This has been reissued on
compact disc by Ocora (C.559.058) with only side A of the *khene* music. Another
recording of *khene* music is *Laos: l'art du khene* (Laos: the art of the khene) recorded
by Jacques Brunet (Paris: Galloway, 1973. 1 disc, 33 rpm. [Musique du Monde, no. 26
(GB.600.545]). This features the three artists Phomma Syvath, Phet Sananikhone and
Thao Salilat.

510   **Traditional music of southern Laos.**
Recordings, text and photographs by Jacques Brunet.   Amsterdam,
Netherlands: Philips, 1973. 1 stereo disc, 33 rpm. (UNESCO Collection
Musical Sources: Art Music of South-east Asia, no. 9-4 [Stereo
6586.012]).

This is the music of the area of Champassak in southern Laos. The eight pieces
illustrate different types of music. There are three pieces for the *khene*, two songs
accompanied by the *khene*, and three orchestral pieces ranging from court to village
orchestral groupings. An extract of a *lam sithandone* is sung, the form examined by
Carol Compton in *Courting poetry in Laos: a textual and linguistic analysis* (q.v.). This
record has been reissued on cassette by Grem, Grem (CSM.012), and is scheduled for
reissue by Auvidis.

511 **The music of Laos. La musique du Laos. Die Musik von Laos.**
Recordings and commentary by Alain Daniélou. Kassel, Germany:
Bärenreiter-Musicaphon, [196-?]. 1 mono disc, 33 rpm. 10p. sleeve
notes. (UNESCO Collection. A Musical Anthology of the Orient, no. 1
[BM30.L2001]).

A collection of eleven pieces which illustrate a range of Lao music: the *khene* played
both solo, in groups and accompanied by other instruments, vocal music, and two
examples of a classical *pi-phat* orchestra. There are some pages of introductory notes in
English, French and German, illustrated with photographs.

Calendar

512 **Le calcul du calendrier laotien.** (The calculation of the Lao calendar.)
Silvain Dupertius. *Péninsule*, no. 2 (1981), p. 24-118.
Based largely on a work in Lao that the author found in Laos, he has elaborated
certain details which were unclear and corrected certain errors in the explanations. As
he says, while the Lao calendar may seem a charming, mathematical curiosity to the
Westerner, it plays an essential role in the traditional life of the Lao, both religious and
social.

513 **Note sur un aspect particulier de l'indianisation de l'Asie du Sud-Est:**
l'introduction du calendrier au Laos, données épigraphiques. (A note on
a particular aspect of the indianization of South East Asia: the
introduction of the calendar to Laos, some epigraphic evidence.)
Pierre-Marie Gagneux. *Asie du Sud-Est et Monde Insulindien:*
Bulletin du Centre de Documentation et de Recherche (CeDRASEMI)
(South East Asia and the Island World: Bulletin of the Centre for
Documentation and Research [CeDRASEMI]), vol. 8, no. 1 (1977),
p. 77-92. bibliog.
Gagneux adduces that while the Indian calendar was officially adopted in Laos in the
fourteenth century, it had been introduced to the proto-Indochinese peoples by the
Mon and the Khmer from the sixth or seventh centuries of the Christian era. He uses
this evidence to develop his theme that the populations of the region had been directly
or indirectly influenced by Indian cultural influences before the arrival of the Lao.
Thus they were able to adapt to the Lao and the culture they imposed with little
difficulty.

514 **The Laotian calendar.**
Tiao Maha Upahat Phetsarath. In: *Kingdom of Laos: the land of the million elephants and of the white parasol.* Compiled by René de Berval. Saigon, Vietnam: France-Asie, 1959, p. 97-125.
A detailed statement of the calendrical system and the eras used in Laos. How the Laotian calendar is established and the calculations used is demonstrated. The traditional system for the measurement of time is set out; this was still in use in rural areas at the time of writing. Time is divided into segments of ninety minutes, and this method was also still used for setting the time of important ceremonies. A listing of the names of the days of the week is followed by a description of the sixty-day cycle used, based on interlocking ten- and twelve-day cycles. The system of months is lunar, with the result that there is an intercalatory month periodically. A short section on the Laotian year explains that it is slightly different from the Gregorian year.

Cookery

515 **Laotian cookery.**
Andrée-Yvonne Gouineau.   In: *Kingdom of Laos: the land of the million elephants and of the white parasol.*   Compiled by René de Berval.   Saigon, Vietnam: France Asie, 1959, p. 221-28.

A discussion of Lao foods and cooking techniques. In a second article in this volume, 'Some recipes' (p. 229-34), there are ten recipes for meat, fish and sweet dishes.

516 **Traditional recipes of Laos: being the manuscript recipe books of the late Phia Sing, from the Royal Palace at Luang Prabang.**
Edited by Alan Davidson, Jennifer Davidson.   London: Prospect Books, 1981. 318p. map. bibliog.

These 124 traditional and authentic Lao recipes were written down by Phia Sing, the royal chef and Master of Ceremonies at the Royal Palace of Luang Prabang. The editors have provided introductory material on Lao eating habits, culinary terms, equipment and ingredients; this is illustrated with attractive and clear drawings. The recipes which follow are arranged with a facsimile of Phia Sing's recipe and the English translation on facing pages. These are recipes to be used, and can be prepared by anyone with access to a Chinese grocer. The non-cook can learn much about Lao food practices and foodstuffs.

Fish and fish dishes of Laos.
See item no. 61.

News Sources and
Newspapers

**517 A guide to research materials on Thailand and Laos: an annotated guide
to recently published research materials on Thailand and Laos, with
particular emphasis on newspapers and periodicals from 1973 through
1976.**
Compiled and edited by Asia Library Services.   Auburn, New York:
Asia Library Services 1977. 124p.
This work is more concerned with Thailand than Laos, but the material on Laos
includes an article by John A. Lent, 'Newspapers of contemporary Laos' (p. 29-35); a
section of profiles of newspapers from Laos (p. 36-41); and a list of news materials
available in microform (p. 105-107). It fills in the period 1973 to 1976. The earlier
period is covered in G. R. Nunn and Do Van Anh in *Vietnamese, Cambodian, and
Laotian newspapers: an international union list* (Taipei, Taiwan: Chinese Materials and
Research Aids Service Center, 1972. 104p. [Occasional Series; no. 12]).

518 East Asia: Southeast Asia.
Joint Publications Research Service.   Arlington, Virginia: JPRS and
Foreign Broadcast Information Service, 1987- . (JPRS Report).
News items selected and translated from the press and news agencies of the region; this
is a useful way of sampling the Lao press. The reports cover political, economic,
military and sociological news, as well as editorial commentary from the Lao
newspapers. This is the latest title of the series which has changed title several times,
the most recent previous title being *Southeast Asia Report*. It is a complementary
publication to the *Summary of World Broadcasts: Far East Series* (q.v.).

519 Far Eastern Economic Review.
Hong Kong: Review Publishing Co. Ltd., 1946- . weekly.
A weekly news magazine that concentrates on economic and political matters in East,
South East and South Asia, as well as the Pacific. It acts as a valuable substitute for
newspapers from the area, and provides detailed news on business and investment for

172

the businessperson. There are quarterly indexes so that items on Laos can be easily identified.

520 **KPL Bulletin Quotidien.** (KPL Daily Bulletin.)
Vientiane: Khaosan Pathet Lao, 1975- . daily.

The daily news bulletin of the Lao news agency, the Khaosan Pathet Lao. It is the source of much of the news which other agencies and news journals use. Apart from news items, an editorial from a newspaper or journal is usually reproduced as the first item, in French translation. This supersedes the *Agence Lao Presse: Bulletin Quotidien* (Agence Lao Presse: Daily Bulletin) (Vientiane: Ministry of Information, 1951-75).

521 **Laos.**
John A. Lent.   In: *Newspapers in Asia: contemporary trends and problems*.   Edited by John A. Lent.   Hong Kong: Heinemann Asia, 1982, p. 240-51. bibliog.

Lent provides a historical survey of the press in Laos, more detailed case studies of four of the newspapers published in 1973, and concludes with a survey of developments between 1974 and 1977.

522 **Summary of World Broadcasts: Far East Series.**
Reading, England: BBC Monitoring, 1946- . daily and weekly.

A published summary of material monitored from foreign broadcasts, printed sources and press agency releases by the BBC monitoring service. The reports are normally published within a few days of the original broadcast, and so provide the most immediate access to news from countries such as Laos. The items covered are selected and focus mainly on internal political and economic matters, as well as international relations between the countries of the region. For example, in the issue for 4 August 1989, there are reports on the first national conference on banking in Laos, and on the workshop on taxation and the law on foreign investments. It can also be used retrospectively to scan what was published when a major incident developed at any time. The material is usually complementary to that found in *East Asia: Southeast Asia* (q.v.).

523 **Vientiane News: the First English Weekly in Laos.**
Vientiane: Kaye Ando Technical Services, 1971-75. weekly.

An English-language weekly newspaper which provided local news, a survey of the local Asian press, social news and cultural pages. It was owned by the influential Sananikone family. Most of the news items were translated from the Lao language daily *Sat Lao* or (Xat Lao).

Professional
Periodicals

524 **Asian Survey.**
Berkeley, California: University of California Press, 1961- . monthly.
A journal concerned with the politics and economics of Asia. There is an annual article on Laos, usually in the January issue. Other issues may contain articles on Laos from time to time. There is also material on international relations in Asia.

525 **Asie du Sud-Est et Monde Indonésien: Bulletin du Centre de Documentation et de Recherche (CeDRASEMI).** (South East Asia and the Indonesian World: Bulletin of the Centre for Documentation and Research [CeDRASEMI]).
Paris: CNRS, 1970-85. quarterly.
This bulletin was designed as a vehicle for the early publication of research findings, and as a forum for the exchange of research ideas among social scientists, particularly the younger ones whose work would not find space in the established journals. In that the French had a larger number of researchers in Laos during this period than any other external group, it provides important material on research in Laos. Apart from the texts of articles, it included brief summaries of theses presented, often not formally published, short fieldwork reports and bibliographical news. Some significant articles have been treated in detail in the bibliography, but there is further material on Laos in its pages. With volume 2, no. 3 (1971) the title changed to *Asie du Sud-Est et Monde Insulindien: Bulletin du Centre de Documentation et de Recherche (CeDRASEMI)* (South East Asia and the Island World: Bulletin of the Centre for Documentation and Research [CeDRASEMI]). With volume 11 (1980) the title changed to *ASEMI: Asie du Sud-Est et Monde Insulindien* (ASEMI: South East Asia and the Island World). In 1984 a supplement was published which offered a detailed analytical catalogue for the years 1970 to 1982 of the bulletin; it provides abstracts in English and French for the articles and subject, author and classified access points to the material.

526 **Bulletin de l'École Française d'Extrême-Orient.** (Bulletin of the French
School of the Far East.)
Hanoi; Paris: École Française d'Extrême-Orient, 1900- . annual.
A major scholarly journal published by the École Française d'Extrême-Orient, which
was founded in Hanoi in the early years of the French protectorate of Indo-China. It
publishes the research of its members and other scholars. In the early years its focus
was strongly on South East Asia, China and Japan, but this has changed to a wider
focus in more recent years. The subject coverage is strongest in the fields of history,
archaeology, literary and epigraphical studies, religion and culture. It has never
published a comprehensive index, but material up to 1975 on Laos will be found in
Lafont's *Bibliographie du Laos* (q.v.). As opportunities for research in Laos have been
restricted recently, there has been far less published on it in the most recent issues.

527 **Bulletin des 'Amis du Laos'.** (Bulletin of the 'Friends of Laos'.)
Hanoi: Taupin, 1937-40. irregular.
A wide-ranging journal which covered topics of art, music, folklore and literature, as
well as studies on routes of communication, population, agriculture and geology. The
contributors were principally French and Lao members of the administration. A large
number of photographs were included to illustrate articles.

528 **Bulletin des Amis du Royaume Lao.** (Bulletin of the Friends of the Lao
Kingdom.)
Vientiane: Amis du Royaume Lao, 1970-73.
Edited by Vo Thu Tinh, this bulletin published articles on all aspects of Lao culture,
literature, language and history. Some of the articles which were published over
several issues were later reissued as monographs. The last issue published (no. 9) was
devoted to Buddhism, entitled 'Aspects du bouddhisme lao' (Aspects of Lao
Buddhism). A tenth issue was in press, but not published. This title was continued in
the French journal *Péninsule: Études Interdisciplinaires sur l'Asie du Sud-Est
Péninsulaire* (q.v.).

529 **Cahiers de l'Asie du Sud-Est.** (Notes on South East Asia.)
Paris: Institut National des Langues et Civilisations Orientales
(INALCO), 1977- . approx biannual.
Concerned with the languages, literatures and civilizations of South East Asia, its
primary focus is on the countries of the mainland (Burma, Thailand, Cambodia,
Vietnam and Laos). In the main it reports on recent research work of the scholars and
students, and so the number of articles on Laos is not high. They include contributions
by C. Norindr on recent developments in the Lao People's Democratic Republic, and
articles on spiritual and religious matters.

530 **Index Indochinensis: an English and French Index to Revue Indochinoise, Extrême-Asie, Extrême-Asie – Revue Indochinoise and La Revue Indochinoise Juridique et Economique.**
Compiled by R. D. Hill. Hong Kong: Centre of Asian Studies, University of Hong Kong, 1983. 155p.

An index of the principal articles of these four major colonial journals. The compiler has given an English translation of the titles of the articles, as well as the original French titles. The arrangement is by broad subject divisions, with subdivisions as relevant. Some topics are further subdivided by geographical subdivisions. The coverage of Laos is not large, and there are no indexes by country to assist in the use of this work, nor is there an index to the authors of the articles.

531 **Khosana.**
Thailand/Laos/Cambodia Studies Group of the Southeast Asian Council, Association for Asian Studies. Ann Arbor, Michigan: Association for Asian Studies, 1977- . bi-annual.

A newsletter for those interested in the study of Thailand, Laos and Cambodia. Based in the United States, it has more information on research, conferences and new publications in North America, but it has correspondents based in other countries and scours other sources for news.

532 **Péninsule: Études Interdisciplinaires sur l'Asie du Sud-Est Péninsulaire.**
(Peninsula: Interdisciplinary Studies on Peninsular South East Asia.)
Paris: Cercle de Culture et de Recherches Laotiennes, 1980- . bi-annual.

Edited by Vo Thu Tinh, this is a journal of cultural, literary, linguistic and historical studies on Laos and the neighbouring areas and ethnically-related neighbouring peoples. It was launched by Vo Thu Tinh with others to continue his journal *Bulletin des Amis du Laos* (q.v.). He also published two issues of an intermediary journal in France, *Présence Indochinoise* (1978-79). Issue number 10 of *Péninsule* is an index to the three journals, presenting the contents pages for each issue and providing indexes to proper names, keywords, authors and authors of reviewed works. Some items are reprinted from other publications, and some are in English.

533 **Southeast Asia Chronicle.**
Berkeley, California: Southeast Asia Resource Center, 1971-1985. irregular.

This journal was first known as *Indochina Chronicle*. It devoted each issue to one theme, concentrating on current developments in the countries of South East Asia and US involvement there. Laos is covered both in issues devoted to Laos and in topical issues such as those on the heroin trade and war in Indo-China. Issues of particular interest are no. 61 (1978), 'Laos recovers from America's war', in which church activists report in detail from Vientiane on the economic and political problems of Laos, as well as on the problems of malaria, unexploded bombs and mines littering the fields; no. 73 (1980), 'Laos rides out the storm', is an account of economic and political developments five years after the end of the war; no. 90 (1983), 'The riddle of the "Yellow rain"', offers new evidence, but no firm conclusions, on this subject; no. 91 (1983), 'Laos a long walk forward', is an examination of recent developments in Laos and United States-Lao relations.

534 **Thai-Yunnan Project Newsletter.**
Canberra, Australia: Australian National University, Research School
of Pacific Studies, Department of Anthropology, 1988- . quarterly.
Yunnan is the area from which the Tai and others such as the Hmong and the Yao
migrated into South East Asia. The Thai-Yunnan project, based at the Australian
National University, is studying the two regions and crossing the academic divide
between South East Asian and East Asian studies. The use of 'newsletter' in the
journal's title is slightly misleading, since the contents are more substantial than it
might suggest, although it is rapidly and relatively informally published. An important
element of the newsletter in its first issues is the publication of translations of Chinese
studies of the peoples of Yunnan, many of which concern the Hmong (called Miao by
the Chinese). It is also used as a forum for academic debate and the reassessment of
earlier studies of the peoples of South East Asia by Western writers.

Annuals and Directories

535 **Asia and Pacific review.**
Saffron Walden, England: World of Information; Edison, New Jersey: Hunter Publishing, 1980- . annual.
An economic review with an entry for each country of Asia and the Pacific, including Laos. It reviews the key economic events of the year and economic policies, such as those on foreign investment. A table of key economic indicators is provided, and a country profile and business guide of useful addresses and factual information. The volumes have articles on topics of more general interest at the beginning, as well as tables of currencies and key economic indicators which provide comparative information. The title of this publication has changed; it began as *Asia and Pacific Annual Review*, in 1981 became *Asia and Pacific*, and in 1990 adopted the present title, which can, however, be cited as *World of Information Asia and Pacific Review*.

536 **Asia yearbook.**
Hong Kong: Review Publishing, 1960- . annual.
Produced by the editorial team and the correspondents of the *Far Eastern Economic Review* (q.v.), this is a valuable compilation of current information on thirty-one Asian and Pacific countries from Afghanistan to New Zealand. Each country is the subject of a separate chapter arranged under the subheadings 'Politics and social affairs', 'Foreign relations' and 'Economy and infrastructure'. There is also a 'databox' of key economic statistics and a list of government ministers. The first part of the volume deals with subjects on a regional basis, such as finance, investment, energy and commodities, and contains further specific information on the countries concerned. Each volume concludes with a news roundup highlighting the key stories in the *Far Eastern Economic Review* (q.v.) for the year.

537 **Asian security.**
Research Institute for Peace and Security, Tokyo.   London: Brassey's (UK), 1979- . annual.
An annual survey of economic, social and foreign relations' factors affecting the peace and stability of countries and regions of Asia. There is always a section on Laos. In addition the volume concludes with survey essays on arms control and refugees, and chronologies.

538 **Far East and Australasia.**
London: Europa Publications, 1968-. annual.
This annual reference work is a useful source for rapid reference, and provides helpful syntheses of statistics, as well as names and addresses in the directory section. Each country chapter has a section on geography, history and the economy written by academics studying the region. This is followed by a statistical survey of key economic indicators. The directory section covers the Constitution, the government, diplomatic representation, religion, the press and broadcasting, banking, trade and industry, transport, tourism, defence and education. For more detailed material on education one would consult Europa's other publication, *The World of learning.*

539 **Southeast Asian affairs.**
Singapore: Institute of Southeast Asian Studies, 1974- . annual.
This a review of the significant economic and political developments of the previous year in the region of South East Asia. Apart from articles on trends in the region as a whole, each year there is at least one article devoted to Laos, written by an academic specializing in the affairs of Laos. In the most recent issues there is a trend to indicate bibliographical and other sources on which the articles are based, which is valuable, especially for such a controversial country as Laos.

540 **Yearbook on international communist affairs: parties and revolutionary movements.**
Stanford, California: Hoover Institution Press, 1967- . annual.
Each year there is an essay of about eight pages on Laos, outlining political developments, policy developments and foreign relations over the previous year, as well as a digest of facts on the party and government structure. It provides a useful summary for the year of monitored broadcasts and news agency releases, where the full texts can be sought if required. In recent years the articles on Laos have been written by Arthur J. Dommen.

Manuscripts and Archives

541 **Inventaire des manuscrits des pagodes du Laos.** (Inventory of
manuscripts in the temples of Laos.)
Pierre-Bernard Lafont. *Bulletin de l'École Française d'Extrême-
Orient*, vol. 52, no. 2 (1965), p. 429-545.
The compilation of this inventory was undertaken to provide a more complete
understanding of the number and location of Lao manuscripts, and also to update the
information in Louis Finot's 'Liste générale des manuscrits laotiens' (General list of
Lao manuscripts) (*Bulletin de l'École Française d'Extrême-Orient*, vol. 17, no. 5
[1917]). Lafont covers the manuscripts in the temples of Luang Prabang, Vientiane,
and Champassak. One discovery made during this survey was that the manuscripts of
Laos had a regional rather than a national distribution, and that there were regional
variations in script. The bulk of the article is devoted to a list of the texts of the
manuscripts in alphabetical order, they are indexed according the the temples or
monasteries where they are located.

542 **Scholars' guide to Washington D.C. for Southeast Asian studies: Brunei,
Burma, Cambodia, Indonesia, Laos, Malaysia, Philippines, Singapore,
Thailand, Vietnam.**
Patrick M. Mayerchak. Washington, DC: Smithsonian Institution
Press, 1983. 411p. bibliog. (Scholars' Guide to Washington DC; no. 9).
Washington DC is an area rich in libraries, archives and resource centres for those
interested in South East Asia. This guide sets out to help researchers and the
interested public make use of relevant depositories. The material is organized under
seven types of collection, that is, libraries, archives, museums and galleries, map
collections, film collections and data banks; eight categories of organization, from
research centres and United States Government Agencies to religious organizations.
The work closes with appendices of useful information, such as bookstores and
accommodation available. Access to material on Laos is possible via the subject index.

543 **A guide to manuscripts and documents in the British Isles relating to South and South-East Asia.**
J. D. Pearson. London: Mansell, 1989-90. 2 vols.

This is a supplement to *A guide to western manuscripts and documents in the British Isles relating to South and South East Asia* by M. D. Wainwright and Noel Matthews. (Oxford: Oxford University Press, 1965. 432p.). In both the original publication and this supplement the number of references to Laos is small, but they record the existence of relevant manuscripts which deal principally with British relations with Siam, Laos and France.

544 **Laotischen Handschriften.** (Lao manuscripts.)
Klaus Wenk. Wiesbaden, Germany: Steiner, 1975. 125p. bibliog. (Verzeichnis der Orientalischen Handschriften in Deutschland, Bd. 32).

A catalogue of the Lao manuscripts held in German libraries. The majority fall into the broad category of Buddhist literature. Leaves from each of the 226 titles identified in the 185 palm-leaf manuscripts described here are reproduced in an appendix.

Bibliographies

545 Le Centre de Documentation et de Recherches sur l'Asie de Sud-Est et le Monde Insulindien: CeDRASEMI. (The Centre for Documentation and Research on South East Asia and the Island World.)
Paris: CNRS/EHSS, 1979. 195p. maps. bibliog.

A report on the work of this important centre of research on South East Asia. It is highlighted because these were some of the few researchers still working in Laos in the 1970s. The report enumerates the research projects of the permanent staff and the students studying under them, and provides bibliographical references to the books, journal articles, published reports and theses produced.

546 Southeast Asian research tools: Laos.
Charles F. Keyes. Honolulu, Hawaii: University of Hawaii, Asian Program, Southeast Asian Studies, 1979. 98p. (Southeast Asia Paper, no. 16, part 7).

A survey of reference and research tools available to the scholar, it is presented in the form of an annotated bibliography arranged both by forms of reference works, such as directories or atlases, and by subject in the social sciences and the humanities. Entries are given for both European and Lao language works. The intention of the project, of which this formed part, was to identify areas of weakness in the provision of reference tools. The work was based on the reponse to questionnaires sent out in the United States; five replies referred to Laos, and Keyes notes in his preface 'These responses are indicative of the . . . rather minimal [scholarly] attention given to Laos [by English-speaking specialists.]'.

547 **Bibliographie du Laos.** (Bibliography of Laos.)
Pierre-Bernard Lafont. Paris: École Française d'Extrême-Orient,
1964-78. 2 vols. (Publications de l'École Française d'Extrême-Orient,
vol. 50).

The most comprehensive bibliography published on Laos, it endeavours to cover all fields of knowledge. Volume one covers the period up to 1962,and volume two, 1962 to 1975. It is arranged under subject headings with an author index. Thai and Lao names are organized under surnames, rather than personal names. Anonymous works, or those for which no author can be established are filed under 'X'. in the French bibliographic tradition. It includes periodical articles as well as monographic works, and endeavours to cover Lao, Thai, Vietnamese and Russian-language publications, as well as those in Western languages. The coverage of these publications is more comprehensive in the second volume, particularly works in Lao. The Asian-language publications are integrated into the main sequence of the bibliography, with a translated form of the title, and with a reference to the relevant item number in the sequence of works arranged by language. This bibliography is essentially unannotated, but sometimes items have helpful notes or pithy comments. Undoubtedly this would be the starting point for any serious study of Laos, although one would need to check other bibliographies, particularly those for specific subjects, or for material published since 1975. A helpful addition would have been a title index.

548 **Laos: a bibliography.**
Compiled by William W. Sage, Judith A. N. Henchy. Singapore:
Institute of Southeast Asian Studies, 1986. 253p. (Library Bulletin,
no. 16).

A wide-ranging bibliography that concentrates on English-language material, while not excluding work in French, Vietnamese and Lao. The period 1975-84 is covered quite comprehensively, whereas earlier material is included selectively. The work is arranged under broad subject headings, which are further subdivided. Entries are limited to bibliographic details and shelf-marks for the Library of the Institute of Southeast Asian Studies; brief annotations are provided when necessary, Lao and Vietnamese titles are translated into English. The compilers have included a large amount of report literature and other semi-published material, and they have included material found in a number of private collections. Periodical articles and articles in collective works have been indexed. There are 2,471 entries, but this includes a number of items that have been entered under more than one subject heading.

Indexes

There follow three separate indexes: authors (personal and corporate); titles; and subjects. Thai, Lao and Vietnamese names are entered in full as is the usual practice. Cross-references are provided to aid their location. Title entries are italicized and refer either to the main titles, or to other works cited in the annotations. The numbers refer to bibliographic entries, not to pages.

Index of Authors

A

Abhay, N. *see* Nhouy Abhay
Adams, II, L. P. 133
Adams, N. S. 1, 4, 102,
Agence Lao Presse 520
Ajalbert, J. 453
Alzon, C. Hesse d' 108-09
Amnesty International 28
Anderson, G. W. 298
Andersson, N. 489
Andrus, J. R. 377
Anh, D. V. *see* Do Van Anh
Archaimbault, C. 78, 188-90, 197, 252-53, 266, 269-71, 360, 392
Ashmun, L. A. 284
Asia Library Services 517
Asia Society 92
Asian Development Bank 361, 406
Attajarusit, J. *see* Jutharat Attajarusit
Australia: Department of External Affairs 124
Australia: Joint Committee on Foreign Affairs and Defence 182
Aymard, A. 470
Aymonier, E. 29

B

Ba Shin 270
Ballard, J. S. 166

Banque Nationale du Laos 385
Banyai, R. A. 386
Barber, M. J. P. 274
Barnes, S. 183
Barney, G. L. 207
Barth, A. 191
Barton, B. 357
Batson, W. 28
Bayard, D. 79
Bechert, H. 254
Bell, D. 335
Bell, J. 362
Bellwood, P. 80
Benjamin, G. 227
Berger, C. 167
Bergot, E. 116
Bernad, M. 290
Bernard, A. 43
Bernard, F. 339
Bernatzik, H. A. 218-19
Bernet Kempers, A. J. 490
Bertrais, Y. 241
Berval, R. de 2, 11, 97, 251, 264, 272, 296, 405, 429, 436, 483, 507, 514-15
Bhruksasri, W. *see* Wanat Bhruksasri
Bilodeau, C. 426
Blanchard, M. 30, 38
Blaustein, D. 324
Blaustein, P. 324
Blazenkhov, S. 24
Bleecker, T. 335
Bodinier, G. 117
Boisselier, J. 270
Bongert, Y. 325
Booth, A. 416
Boston Publishing Co. 132

Bouapha, V. *see* Va Bouapha
Boucher de Crèvecoeur, J. *see* Crèvecoeur, J. Boucher de
Boun Oum 271
Boun Souk (pseud.) *see* Gagneux, P.-M.
Bourret, R. 62
Bradley, D. 227
Branfman, F. 141, 167, 275-76
Breakey, G. F. 291
Breazeale, K. 197
Brewster, J. 416
Brocheux, P. 109
Brown, M. 132, 301
Brown, R. M. 490-91
Brunet, J. 508-10
Bruzon, E. 44
Buis, G. 32
Buller, A. 103, 383, 395
Bunnag, J. 254
Bunyaraks Ninsananda 363
Burchett, W. 125, 142-43
Burdick, E. 471
Burkhill, I. H. 59
Burleigh, C. 3
Burling, R. 203, 221
Burns, R. D. 126
Buszynski, L. 340

C

Cable, J. 118
Cahour, M. 21
Canada: Department of

185

Berkeley. Institute of
East Asian Studies 186
Uphoff, N. 169

Vries, E. de 382

Wyatt, D. K. 99, 107,
113-14

Index of Titles

A

Index of Subjects

212

Map of Laos

This map shows the more important towns and other features.

Legend:
- — · — International boundary
- ·········· Province boundary

Scale: 0 50 100 miles

PROVINCES

1. Luang Namtha
2. Oudomsay
3. Luang Prabang
4. Phong Saly
5. Houa Phan
6. Xieng Khouang
7. Vientiane
8. Sayaboury
9. Khammouane
10. Savannakhet
11. Saravane
12. Attopeu
13. Champassak
14. Sekong
15. Borikhamsay
16. Bokeo
17. Vientiane Prefecture

187

189

Berkeley. Institute of
East Asian Studies 186
Uphoff, N. 169

Vries, E. de 382

Wyatt, D. K. 99, 107,
113-14

W

X

V

Va Bouapha 336-37
Valmiki 442
Van der Kroef, J. M. *see*
Kroef J. M. van der
Van Son 19
Vang, C. K. *see* Chia Koua
Vang
Vang, L. *see* Lue Vang
Veevers-Carter, W. 73
Vella, W. F. 106
Vidal, J. 74-77
Vidal, Y. 74
Vietnam: Service
Géographique
National 48
Viravong, S. *see* Sila
Viravong
Vo Thu Tinh 89, 443-44,
528, 532
Vongvichit, P. *see* Phoumi
Vongvichit
Voulgaropoulos, E. 291

Wainwright, M. D. 543
Wall, B. 226
Wanat Bhruksasri 262
Ward, B. E. 280
Ward, J. T. 207
Wekkin, G. D. 140
Wenk, K. 544
Westermeyer, J. 300, 338
Whayne, T. F. 298
Whitaker, D. P. 20
White, G. F. 382
Whitelock, D. 247
Wilding-White, C. F. B.
477
Willem, J.-P. 289
Wolfkill, G. 181
Women's International
Group 41
Workman, D. R. 46, 50-51
Worner, W. 383
Wulff, R. M. 384
Wurfel, D. 357
Wurm, S. A. 227
Wuysthoff, G. van 42

Xiong, L. *see* Lang Xiong
Xiong, N. L. *see* Nao Leng
Xiong
Xiong, W. J. 243

Y

Yamey, B. S. 387
Yang, G. Y. *see* Gnia Yee
Yang
Yang Dao 404
Yates, W. G. 240
Yip Yat Hoong 427
Young, K. T. 123
Yule, H. 42

Z

Zacher, M. D. 140, 352
Zago, M. 268
Zakaria Haji Ahmad 309
Zasloff, J. J. 28, 156, 301,
314, 322-24, 359

Index of Titles

A

194

203

Index of Subjects

208

Investment 383, 519, 522, 535-36
  programme for transport 406
Iron 43
  mining of ore 360
Irrigation projects 382
IVS *see* International Voluntary Services

J

Japan 526
Japanese occupation
  control of banking 386
  literary movement 446
  see also History
Japanese research 67
Jars
  megalithic remains 81, 86
Jataka tales 434, 436, 440
Jayavarman I, King *see* History
Journals and personal accounts 12, 16, 35, 37, 40, 42, 176-182, 447
  fiction 475
  see also Autobiography; Biography
Judiciary 307

K

Kammu *see* Khmu
Kampuchea *see* Cambodia
Kettledrums 490
Khene 504-06, 508-11
Khmer Empire 191, 261
Khmer Republic *see* Cambodia
Khmu (people) 222, 400
  folk tales 463-65
  language 246
  myths of origin 460
  songs 508
Kinship 203, 222, 225, 277
  terminology 242, 244
Kong Le *see* History
Kou Voravong *see* History
Kresge Art Gallery,

Michigan State University 493

L

Labour 49, 199, 335, 410-14
  corvée 369, 390, 410, 413
  planning 412
  wage labour 387, 395
Labour law 335
Laccifer 59
Lahu (people) 208
Lam as literature 229, 454-56
Lam khon savan 229
Lam saravane 509
Lam sithandone 456, 510
Lamet (people) 203, 206, 224
Land boundaries *see* Boundaries
Land law 328, 334
Land mammals 60
Land tenure 220, 282, 334, 387, 395, 402
Land use 334, 397-98, 402
Landing fields 405
Landlocked states 346, 351, 357-58, 372, 375, 407
Languages 2, 5, 13, 203, 227-49
  see also languages by name, e.g. Hmong, Lao
Lanna 265
Lao (people) 36, 40, 210
  language 15, 230, 232-40, 528-29, 532
  dictionaries 234-35, 238
  grammars 232-33, 236-37, 239-40
  scripts 248, 428, 432, 541
Lao Issara 310-12, 321
Lao Nhay movement 452
Lao Patriotic Front 319, 321, 323
Lao People's Army 309
Lao People's Revolutionary Party

(LPRP) 26, 301, 303, 313, 315-16
Lao scholarship 2
Lao Soung 210
Lao Tai 210
Lao Theung 210
Law 324-38
  aviation 330
  Buddhist 329, 333
  civil code 336
  customary 40, 338
  education 425
  international 346, 407
  labour 335
  land 328, 334
  of the sea 351
  penal code 337
  Vientiane code 13
Lead 43
Leaders 114, 302-03, 305, 310, 323, 341
Legal status of Laos 312
Legal system 9, 307
Legal tales 461
Legends *see* Myths and legends
Literacy 19, 213, 217
Literature 2, 5, 8-9, 12, 428-76, 526-9, 532
  anthologies 447-50, 458, 461, 463-66, 468-69
  biographical 447
  Buddhist 440
  classical 435, 437-38, 441, 443
  English language 471, 473, 475
  epic poetry 431, 434, 460
  French 470, 472, 474, 476
  Jataka tales 434, 436, 440
  Lam 229, 454-56
  modern 452
  Nithan 78
  oral literature 453-60
  patriotic literature 446, 448-51
  poetry 11, 429, 436, 445, 453
    see also Epic poetry; Lam; Nithan
  political 446, 459
  Ramayana story 433, 442, 444

and discovery *see*
Exploration

W

Wat Phra Keo 477, 489
Wat Sisaket 489
Water 54, 374
  drinking 292
  resources 364
  storage 382
  travel 32, 49
Waterways 49

Weapons
  chemical 184
Weather *see* Climate
Women 28, 280, 283
World War Two *see*
  History
Writing systems 248-49

X

Xieng Khouang 55
  see also History

Y

Yang, S. L. *see* Shong Lue
  Yang
Yao (people) 207-08, 210,
  222-23, 262
  language 244
  paintings 481
  Taoism 481
Yaws 295
Yellow rain 184, 289, 533
Yi 220
Yumbri (people) 219, 289
Yunnan 33

Map of Laos

This map shows the more important towns and other features.

Legend:
- — · — International boundary
- ·········· Province boundary

Scale: 0 50 100 miles

PROVINCES

1. Luang Namtha
2. Oudomsay
3. Luang Prabang
4. Phong Saly
5. Houa Phan
6. Xieng Khouang
7. Vientiane
8. Sayaboury
9. Khammouane
10. Savannakhet
11. Saravane
12. Attopeu
13. Champassak
14. Sekong
15. Borikhamsay
16. Bokeo
17. Vientiane Prefecture